5/9/66

POLITICAL THEORY

After sketching the historical
development of political ideas
Professor Field analyses and dis-
cusses some basic concepts of
modern political theory, in particular the notions of the State,
of Sovereignty and the Law.

UNIVERSITY PAPERBACKS

UP 62

G. C. FIELD

Political Theory

UNIVERSITY PAPERBACKS

METHUEN: LONDON

First published June 7, 1956 by Methuen & Co
Reprinted 1960
First published in this series 1963
Reprinted 1965
Printed in Great Britain by
Western Printing Services Ltd, Bristol
Catalogue No 02/6812/49

1.2

University Paperbacks are published by
METHUEN & CO LTD
11 New Fetter Lane, EC4

PREFACE

THIS book is based on the lectures in Political Theory which I gave for a number of years in the different universities in which I taught. Two or three friends, who heard these lectures, expressed a wish that they were available in published form. Thus encouraged, I had originally intended to publish them very much as they stood. But I speedily discovered that the lecture style, at any rate as I practised it, was not at all suitable for a book, so, though most of the substance has been retained, the lectures have been largely re-written. I am afraid it is possible that traces of the lecture style have lingered here and there, but I hope that that will not affect the clarity of the exposition. There is also a fair amount of fresh material added which was not in the lectures at all, and the book, as a whole, is considerably longer than they would have been.

I might explain that these lectures were given, with short intermissions, over a period of forty years. They were originally written out and re-written from time to time, but I never stuck rigidly to what I had written, and I do not suppose that in fact I ever gave exactly the same lectures two years running. Nevertheless a few main ideas which I conceived at a fairly early stage still seem to me to have proved themselves useful guides to an understanding of the subject. I have had the experience from time to time of being approached by a member of my audience who suggested, either approvingly or disapprovingly, that in some particular passage, under the guise of laying down general principles, I was really hitting at one side or another in some contemporary controversy. And it was as likely as not to turn out that the passage in question belonged to the older stratum of the lectures, long before that particular controversy had ever been heard of.

There is one point on which I felt considerable hesitation, and that was the inclusion of the historical sketch in the first three chapters. In the original lectures half the course was devoted to the history of political ideas, and the other half to what was described in one university syllabus as 'Analytic Politics'. It was the latter half which I was interested in turning into a book, and my first intention was to omit the historical account altogether. But on second thoughts I decided to insert a summary account, for two main reasons. In the first place, I often found it helpful to make a point about present-day ideas by reference to or comparison with ideas of an earlier age. And it seemed better to give some general account of these latter to begin with than to try to explain them on each occasion. Secondly, and more generally, it seemed desirable to produce the sort of atmosphere in which our present ideas and problems would be seen as a stage in a long historical process of continual development and not as a fixed and final order of nature. I have included as an appendix an article on Greek democracy which was published some years ago in the *Cambridge Journal*, because in modern discussions about the meaning of democracy it is hard to avoid all reference to the Greek use of the term. For the rest, I have assumed in my readers some general knowledge of history and some interest in and acquaintance with the main political issues of recent times.

If I were asked for whom this work was intended I could only reply that it was for anyone who might be interested. I hope that it may prove of some use for university students for whom the original lectures were given, but I also hope that it will not be of interest to them alone. I am not sure that I should have written it very differently if it had been intended primarily for specialists in the subject. They would doubtless find a good deal of it elementary and commonplace.

But in my experience in subjects like this a great many differences and misunderstandings between specialists arise because they are afraid of seeming simple and obvious and fail to make clear the elementary ideas which they assume as their starting-point.

I am indebted to a number of friends for helpful discussions on these subjects. I would mention especially Professor Stephan Körner, my successor in the Chair of Philosophy here, Mr W. H. Burston of the London Institute of Education, and the members of the Law Faculty in this University, particularly Mr G. A. Forrest.

Democracy, Ancient and Modern, which is printed as an appendix, originally appeared in the *Cambridge Journal,* and is reproduced here by the kind permission of the publishers, Messrs. Bowes & Bowes.

Bristol, April 1955   G. C. FIELD

My husband died suddenly and very shortly after completing this book and I would like to express my thanks to Mr A. B. Cottle of the University of Bristol for his great kindness in helping me with the proofs.

A. D. FIELD

CONTENTS

ix

CONTENTS

INTRODUCTION

As a general rule it is a mistake to attempt a precise definition of a subject before starting on the investigation of it. What the investigator can do is to give a provisional indication of the general direction in which he is going to start, while reserving to himself the right to extend, restrict, or modify his field of study as the argument seems to require. So we may suggest as a provisional account of Political Theory that it is an attempt to arrive at a comprehensive, coherent, and general account of the sorts of thing that we talk about when we are talking politics.

It hardly seems necessary, at this stage, to attempt any definition of the word 'politics'. There may be a marginal territory in which it would be possible to doubt whether it would be more properly described as political or as something else. But it is, once more, a great mistake in any subject to start by worrying about borderline cases. The fruitful procedure is to start from the obvious and undoubted cases, and then, if required, we can go on to see how far our treatment of these cases can be applied to the more doubtful ones. There is certainly a wide enough field for our purpose which no one would hesitate to call political.

As for the other terms, it is to be comprehensive in that it tries not to omit any important side of the subject, though it must be admitted that no single book could cover all the points of interest that might be raised. It is to be coherent (or systematic or connected) in that it tries to see the connection between different subjects of political talk and to avoid self-contradiction. And it is to be general in that it tries to look at particular political issues or particular political phenomena, at any one time and place, as instances of some more general principle or idea.

Perhaps, something more should be said here about the use of the term 'general', in view of some rather carping criticisms that have appeared in recent years. In some of these it seems to be suggested that political theorists have gone wrong in thinking that they could extend their general conclusions about political matters beyond the limits of a particular society or kind of society. Thus, we are told, we cannot have any general theory of the State, but only accounts of particular states, and it has been suggested that the thinkers of the past, who attempted to give such a general theory, were in reality, so far as they were talking sense at all, merely describing features of their own state or society. But this line of criticism really misses the point of the kind of generality at which the political theorist is aiming. He does not expect to get a series of abstract universal statements which will apply necessarily to any kind of society whatever. He is interested in the particular political phenomena, and unless he has considerable acquaintance with them he is not likely to theorise very well. But he approaches them with the aim of rising to a higher level of generalisation, in the light of which he can survey the more particular phenomena.

Of course, like any thinker, he would naturally start his reflections on the political ideas and institutions with which he is most familiar. He is thus always exposed to some degree of danger of coming to think of the special conditions of his own time as representing the natural order of things, and of features which are really peculiar to his own particular society as being necessary elements in any society. But that is a warning of a danger to be guarded against, not a statement of a necessary limitation on his thinking. Everybody, presumably, would recognise that we can overcome it to some extent. An Englishman can talk about representative government without assuming that it necessarily means elections by single-member constituencies to a House of Commons presided over by a Speaker with a wig on his head and a mace in front of him. We are all capable of some degree of analysis of our institutions with the aim of distinguishing the essential from the accidental, or the more essential from the less essential elements in them. And this sort of analysis is one of the main objects of political theory. It would be very arbitrary to lay down rules beforehand to the effect that we can carry it so far but no further. We cannot tell how far we can carry it till we have tried.

There is a further question of method or approach to be noted here. Political theory has generally been regarded as something of special interest to philosophers: if not, strictly speaking, a branch of philosophy it may, perhaps, be described, in the lawyers' phrase, as a quasi-philosophical subject. The special approach to political theory which I should call philosophical starts from an examination of the assumptions that we can find in the various ways in which people talk and think and act in particular political situations, assumptions which seem clearly implied though not necessarily stated in these discussions. These assumptions are of various kinds. Thus we find people habitually talking about some political fact, say the State or the Law, or some political ideal such as Liberty or Equality, in a way which suggests or implies that they think of it in a particular way, though they may not state this explicitly or even be fully conscious of it themselves Or they may habitually use a particular form of argument, without ever asking themselves how far they would regard that form of argument as valid in general.

An important part of the philosophical examination of these assumptions consists in an inquiry into the way in which the words commonly met with in political discussion are in fact habitually used. Some philosophers at the present time, it seems, would maintain that that was all a philosopher could do, and that he should properly confine himself to discovering the rules for the use of the words in question in ordinary speech without concerning himself at all with the facts which the words were supposed to represent. But however this method may work in other fields it is hard to see how it could make sense as applied to political theory. We could not attach any meaning at all to the words used without some acquaintance with their context of political facts and political practice. And if we think that we can see that the words are sometimes being used in a way incompatible with the facts that they are supposed to express, it would be highly artificial to stop short at that point and say that we ought not to carry the discussion any further. Without going into a metaphysical argument about ideas and objects, we can say that we cannot go very far in understanding political ideas without trying to see how they are related to political facts. Political theory must involve a good deal of knowledge of political practice. How much is necessary we cannot tell till we have tried.

The political theorist, then, will concern himself both with political facts and with the way in which people think about them, as evinced in the way in which they talk and write. But we can go further, and say that there is no clear distinction between the two. Political ideas are themselves political facts. After all, most, if not all, political 'facts' come down, in the end, to forms of behaviour of human beings, and thinking and talking are themselves forms of behaviour, which very often have an important influence on the rest. But further discussion of this had better be postponed until we see how this approach works out in practice.

I have already indicated some of the general facts or ideas with which the political theorist will concern himself. Institutions, such as the state or, on a smaller scale, the political party, elements within this, such as law and government, forms of government, such as democracy and the like—all these are obvious instances of the kind of thing which is constantly referred to in political discussions. And our assumptions about what sort of things these are will form the starting-point of our inquiries. But besides these, there is another set of assumptions which pervade our political thinking. And that is what we may call, in the broadest sense, moral assumptions. 'In the broadest sense', because there is to be found a tendency at times to restrict, somewhat arbitrarily, the meaning of morality to certain special cases of it, and, as a consequence of this, to try to keep the fields of moral thinking and political thinking separate from each other.

In the sense, however, in which I am using the word I should say that we are thinking morally whenever we judge that one state of things or one kind of behaviour is better than another, as long as we mean by 'better' something more than a mere matter of individual taste or of what happens to be more agreeable or profitable to us personally. We assume that, in some sense, a judgement of this kind can be true or false, and that if it is true at all, it must be valid for other people besides ourselves. And further, we assume that this is, in some way, a reason for us or for anyone else to pursue what is better rather than what is worse, even if at the moment it is not agreeable to us personally. Obviously, a great deal of political discussion would be meaningless unless we recognised that at the back of it there were assumptions of this kind. Indeed it might well be argued that, so far from morals and politics being separate fields of thought, it was in politics, more obviously than anywhere else, that specifically moral questions arose. For it is there particularly that we are concerned not with purely personal matters but with views or policies which we claim to be valid universally, or at the least far more widely than our own immediate circle. And if they thus pervade our political thinking, clearly they must be taken account of by the political theorist. Whether he needs to carry the analysis and examination of them to the same lengths and in the same direction as the moral philosopher is more doubtful. But that, again, is a question the answer to which we may wisely leave to emerge as our inquiries proceed.

Moral judgements, then, are an important element in our political thinking, and, as such, they demand, in their own right, examination by the political theorist. On the other hand, our analysis of some political ideas or phenomena can be carried for a considerable way in certain directions without bringing in moral considerations or questions of better or worse at all. And it is undoubtedly desirable that we should be clear to ourselves when and how far we are doing this, and at what point moral issues begin to arise. But we may well find that in some cases the two begin to appear inextricably mixed. Certainly when we consider the ideas expressed by such words as Democracy or Liberty, we shall find that what we mean by the words includes the idea both of a factual situation and of its being good or bad in certain ways and for certain reasons. But the two elements cannot for long be kept separate, for the reasons why we think Democracy good (or the reverse) are going to affect very considerably what it means to us: for they would largely determine the way in which we should work it out in practice, if we were in a position to do so. To analyse the idea of Democracy, then, would include the examination of the reasons why people wanted or did not want it. And if we had thoroughly examined these reasons it would require almost superhuman self-restraint to refrain from coming finally to our own conclusions about their validity. I should, indeed, be prepared to argue that in some, at any rate, of this kind of arguments we could not be said to have arrived at a full understanding of what they mean until we had decided whether or how far they could be accepted as correct. But it is not necessary to hold this in order to see that, psychologically if not logically, it is practically impossible to stop short before we have come to our own conclusions.

There is one other set of assumptions which can often be detected in discussions about politics, particularly when they are concerned with practical issues. That is, the assumptions about human nature, about how people feel and act in response to various kinds of situation. Both practical policies and general theories have in fact often been built on assumptions of this kind, and they obviously call for critical examination by the political theorist. But we cannot carry such a critical examination very far without adopting or assuming some general views about human nature for ourselves. In fact, anyone who is concerned with political theory will find himself at some point making such generalisations, even if they are only negative ones. If he is wise, however, he will state such conclusions as he reaches in terms of tendencies which will influence human behaviour in varying degrees in varying circumstances. Specific prophecies will depend on the study of the particular circumstances at particular times and places. But such study will involve an analysis of the general possibilities and the influences that may play a part.

It must be remembered that most political discussions have as their final aim to arrive at practical decisions about the policy that is to be adopted or supported. And if we are starting on an examination of the assumptions of such discussions any of the considerations that come into play in arriving at these decisions may be relevant material for our study. The pure-minded logician may feel that this would make political theory a mere hotch-potch of verbal analysis, historical information, psychological generalisations, and moral judgements. To this we could only reply that that is what politics is, and if we are to make a theory about it we cannot afford to leave any of these elements out, if we are not to distort the whole picture by false abstraction. After all, if each of these elements is to be handed over to a separate specialist, who is there left who can think about their interrelations as a whole?

Chapter I

SOME HISTORICAL PRELIMINARIES (1)

OUR main point of interest will naturally be the examination of our own political assumptions and ideas. But, as a preliminary to this, it might be as well to say something about the political ideas of other ages. There is always a temptation to think of our own ideas at the present moment as representing, so to speak, the natural order of events and the final culmination of the historical process, instead of being, as they are, merely a fleeting and transient stage in a continuous development. Some knowledge of history is a valuable corrective to this. On the one hand, by presenting us with a state of things in which ideas are taken for granted which seem strange and startling to us to-day, it helps us by contrast to become aware of what we are taking for granted ourselves and to realise that they are not self-evident truths but can be doubted or criticised. On the other, by showing us some ideas very similar to our own, appearing under very different historical conditions, it helps us to analyse our own ideas and to see which elements in them are purely the product of temporary conditions of the present day and which are of more universal application. In what follows no attempt will be made to give a comprehensive account of the history of political thought. I shall only attempt to indicate, very much in outline, some of the ideas of past ages which seem of special interest to our own, either because they contain the origins of our own ideas in them or because they are contrasted so sharply with them that they make our own stand out more clearly.

1

ANCIENT GREECE

The study of political ideas naturally begins with the ancient Greeks, because, in a real sense, they were the first people to have political ideas at all. Of course, there was plenty of thinking much earlier about practical problems, how best to conquer a neighbouring territory, for instance, or how to retain one's power over it after the conquest. But the application of critical and rational thinking to the fundamentals of politics is first found, to any measurable degree, among the Greeks. It would, however, be a great mistake to exaggerate their rationality. In practice, their behaviour was too often extremely irrational. Indeed, actual Greek politics show us many more examples of what to avoid than patterns to follow. In their thinking, too, it is possible to trace the influence of many irrational elements. But, none the less, it remains true that rational thinking on these matters appears among the Greeks to a degree quite unknown before. Their great thinkers, of course, such as Plato and Aristotle, will stand comparison with any thinkers of more recent ages. Indeed, there are elements in their thought, particularly in Plato's, which were so far ahead of their period that, though they had little influence in their own time, they have much that is apposite to ours. But the greater part of their thinking consisted in developing and making explicit the implications of the ordinary ideas of their time, and sometimes urging their contemporaries to take these ideas more seriously in practice.

If we recognise it as only a sketch-plan, subject to all sorts of qualification in detail, we might think of the new contribution of the Greeks as something on these lines. In the earlier stages of social development it would on the whole be true to say that people acted as their desires, interests, and emotions led them, except in so far as they were restrained or directed by the customary rules of their tribe or society. These rules were regarded as the supreme authority over conduct, and, among many other things which they commanded or forbade, they assigned special degrees of power and authority to particular individuals. Thus, they combined in themselves what we regard as the distinct ideas of custom, law, both constitutional and private, and morality. Further, there was a tendency to ascribe to them a more than human authority; they were, for instance, often represented as the work of a superhuman being or beings, such as a divine or semi-divine ancestor. As a consequence, they were not normally questioned or thought of as alterable at will. They were taken for granted as a permanent framework within the limits of which ordinary human activities went on.[1]

This way of looking at laws and institutions does not completely disappear till comparatively modern times and its influence is still apparent among the Greeks. But the important novelty that appears among them is that they did begin to question it and to ask for a reason and a justification for these things. They first, to any noticeable degree, began to think of their institutions in terms of means and ends, to ask what purpose they served, and to consider the possibility that they might be consciously constructed or reconstructed to suit the purposes of the human beings who lived under them. So we find them ready at times to undertake a drastic reconstruction of the whole framework of a particular society, if there was an end to be gained by it. And in their theory they turn naturally to the construction of Utopias or ideal states, sometimes put forward as practical schemes, and sometimes, as with Plato, as ideal models which are not expected to be attained in practice, but which serve as a guide and standard

---

[1] This might need some modification when we consider the work of the early legislators in Babylonia and elsewhere, such as Hammurabi. But there are two points to remember in that connection. Hammurabi's code, it appears, was not, strictly speaking, new legislation, but rather a systematisation and codification of existing traditional laws. And, secondly, it was almost entirely concerned with what we should call private law. There was no question of any constitutional provisions or any changes in the political institutions, such as we find among the Greeks. So the modifications required in the statement above would not be so very great.

by which to direct and judge our practical endeavours. The idea of a rationally planned society is thus a characteristic Greek contribution to political thinking. It would have seemed the natural procedure to a Greek who took these matters seriously to think out what he wanted and then try to organise his society accordingly. This attitude, as we have noted, sometimes led to revolutionary changes. But it was also a conservative influence, in that it assumed that, once a society was properly organised, then the natural thing to do was to keep it like that as far as possible. There was a tendency to look on change, not as the natural law of development, but as justified, if at all, as an unfortunate necessity arising from a mistake in the original plan.

When people began to ask questions about the reasons for particular laws or institutions, it was only to be expected that a few of the more adventurous minds should go on to ask what were the reasons for having laws or institutions at all. Some radically-minded critics went so far as to say that these things had no claim on our respect, except in so far as they happened to fit in with our own personal desires or ambitions. It was easy to come to think of the law as primarily something which prevented us from doing what we wanted to do, and then to go on to argue that what we wanted was natural and that these restraints were artificial, man-made contrivances with no basis in the nature of things, and no authority beyond their convenience for our own particular purposes. As was natural, this destructive criticism was at first applied not only to laws in the limited modern sense, but also to what we should call the moral law, the accepted rules of right and wrong in any society. For the two were still far from being clearly distinguished. The ordinary Greek in the classical period,[1] in spite of criticisms, still normally looked on the laws as providing a sufficient standard of right and wrong in

[1] This is the period with which we are dealing and may be taken as extending, very roughly, from about 600 B.C. to the time of Alexander and his successors.

human behaviour. 'It is by the law', says a character in one
of Euripides' plays, 'that we distinguish the righteous from
the unrighteous in our lives.' The radical critics, therefore,
argued in effect that there were no objective standards of right
and wrong. There were only our own desires, and if the rules
conflicted with these the sensible man would disobey the
rules whenever he could do so safely and to his own advantage. These destructive ideas still remained for long a heresy
confined to a few advanced thinkers, at any rate as an explicit
theory, though many men, no doubt, acted on them in
practice.

Thus was initiated a great debate which has gone on, in
various forms, throughout the ages. And the answer put
forward by the Greek philosophers, particularly Plato and
Aristotle, to the sceptical critics contains much of interest for
us at the present day. To put it very briefly and inadequately,
their answer ran on these lines. The highest, and ultimately
the most agreeable kind of life for human beings was to be
found in friendly co-operation with other human beings in an
organised society, and the laws represented an attempt to set
out the rules of behaviour, which were necessary for such a
life and such a society to be possible. This would apply both
to the written laws and to the unwritten laws or accepted
codes of conduct. But in fact it was the general assumption
of these thinkers, as it would have been for most Greeks, that
the written laws, enforceable in the courts, should as far as
possible contain in themselves what was necessary to make the
good life possible. They were thus in a very real sense natural.
For it was only to a superficial view that they appeared as
primarily a restriction on our natural desires. In reality they
represented the condition of attaining the fullest satisfaction
of our needs.

Of course, the actual laws of actual societies would often
fall short, sometimes very seriously short, of this ideal. And
individuals who recognised this sometimes felt the call to set
up their own moral standards which might take them beyond

or occasionally in opposition to the rules of their community. But that was only a second best, and the men of the highest moral ideals could not be satisfied till they had found or established a community which recognised these ideals. Further, even the most imperfect system of laws could be regarded as an attempt to arrive at a moral ideal. And that is why it has a claim on our respect and obedience.

We arrive, then, at the characteristic Greek notion of the moral end of legislation and indeed of all political activity. This must not, of course, be taken to mean that the policy of the average Greek city, still less of the individual politician, was always, or even generally, actuated by the highest moral motives. But the ordinary Greek, when he thought about it, would probably, however hazily, have been ready to accept the idea that the true end of the community, the Greek city-state in particular, was to develop a certain type of character and a certain way of behaviour in its members. 'A city teaches a man,' as Simonides of Ceos wrote in the early years of the fifth century. Further, the Greek would probably have accepted the corollary, that every institution and every measure must in the long run be judged by its effects on the kind of citizen it produced and the kind of life it enabled him to lead. This is what Aristotle means in his well-known phrase that the city exists for the sake of the good life. And it explains why he describes his analysis of the good character and the good way of life in the *Ethics* as being specially the concern of the science of politics. This, again, is what Plato means when he makes Socrates say in the *Gorgias* that the true test of a statesman is whether he leaves the citizens better men than he found them. In all this, the philosophers were only asking the ordinary Greek citizen to take seriously the aims that he himself recognised as the ideal. There were, it is true, even before the end of the classical period, isolated thinkers who denied the moral end of the city community. Its proper function, they maintained, was merely to act as a sort of policeman, to keep order and protect the citizens from violence, internal or external. But this view is of little influence until a much later period, when conditions were very different.

It is considerations such as these that provided the ethical basis for the democratic movement in Greece. No doubt this movement got most of its drive from more practical, and sometimes less creditable motives. None the less the ethical basis was there. It was held, explicitly by some and more vaguely by many others, that the 'good life' itself included participation in the public affairs of the community and a due share in political power. As Aristotle puts it, it is the virtue of a good citizen to know both how to rule and how to be ruled. It was a natural conclusion that, as the community existed for the sake of all its citizens, they must all alike be given the chance of acquiring this virtue by taking part in political activity. The differences between the Greek idea of democracy and our own have, of course, often been pointed out, and sometimes considerably exaggerated, and something more will be said about them later.[1] But, for the moment, the important point to observe is that democracy and other forms of government now begin to be regarded as things about which it is possible to argue and to give reasons why one is better than the other. This really seems to be something new in the history of ideas, even among communities which, in other respects, had reached a relatively advanced state of civilisation. So far as we know it never occurred to the Egyptians or Babylonians, for instance, to discuss whether monarchy was a better form of government than any other. It was simply taken for granted as the natural order of things.

Other ideas, familiar to us at the present time, appear first among the Greeks. To take one instance, it is among them that we find the first clear formulation of the idea of social conflict and of the struggle between the classes for economic benefits, and the first clear appreciation of the pervasive influence of this on political movements. Or to take a more purely political example, we find it generally assumed that

[1] See Appendix.

among people, like the Greeks, of a high level of civilisation
the natural and proper political arrangement was the division
of their world into a number of separate states, each absolute
master in its own dominions and each absolutely independent
of any outside control. This was not by any means attained
generally in practice. There were all sorts and degrees of
domination of one Greek state by another. But in theory it
was generally recognised as the ideal towards which every
state aspired, at any rate for itself. After the classical period
this notion begins to fade from men's minds, and it does not
reappear until the time of the Reformation.

There was a tendency in Greek thought to push this idea to
extremes, and to suggest that ideally each state should be not
only politically independent but economically and culturally
independent as well. A city, in Aristotle's phrase, should be
'self-sufficient for the good life'. Further, not only should
every citizen be able to find all the requisites of the good life
within his own city, but his own moral responsibility stopped
short at its boundaries. In practice, once more, this was never
attained and the economic and cultural influence of one city
on another was often very great. There are even indications
that some enlightened spirits, particularly in Athens, had a
certain sense of pride in their civilising mission. Thus Pericles
in his Funeral Speech proclaims Athens as 'the school of
Hellas'. But there is little or nothing in the way of serious
theoretical discussion of this.

Another thing that we miss in classical Greek political
thinking is any very marked awareness of the problem, so
prominent in nineteenth-century thought, of the relation and
possible conflict between the state and the individual. It is
significant that there is no word in Greek which really corres-
ponds to our 'state'. The word usually so translated is Polis
or city, and to express Greek ideas in modern language it
would be better to represent this by some such term as 'community'. The ordinary Greek, while well aware that in particular cases an individual might come into conflict with his

community, would find it very hard to think of himself and his city as two distinct entities, standing over against each other in some sort of essential opposition, as we often tend to think of the state. The city is more naturally thought of as a society of individuals co-operating for a common purpose than as an authority over and above the individuals. We might epitomise the difference by saying that when a modern Englishman speaks of something as being the business of the state he would generally be taken to imply that it was not his business. A Greek, on the other hand, who said that something was the business of the city would be more likely to be understood as asserting that it was his business as much as anyone else's. Besides this we should also note the absence of another subject of discussion which has been prominent in modern political thought. That is the question of the proper relation of the state to the other societies of which its citizens were members. There were smaller societies within the city-states, and at an earlier period they had sometimes in practice constituted a threat to the unity of the city. But at the time with which we are chiefly concerned it was taken for granted without question that the city was supreme.

Points of view such as these would develop much more naturally in a small city-state, which was the unit envisaged in all Greek political thinking in this period. It has sometimes been made a matter of criticism of the Greek thinkers that their thinking failed to look beyond the bounds of this small community. But, so far as this is true, it was at any rate deliberate on their part. They were well acquainted with the large country states of the time but they thought that the city-state represented a higher level of civilisation. They were convinced that the large states could never begin to be to their subjects what the city-state could be to its citizens. In this, indeed, the Greeks were undoubtedly right, and in fact the large states never attempted anything of the kind. In proportion as the city-states died out the whole Greek idea of citizenship died with it.

THE HELLENISTIC AGE

In the so-called Hellenistic age, with the conquest of the Persian empire by Alexander and the establishment of the Greco-Macedonian kingdoms into which his dominions broke up after his death, a great change comes over the Greek outlook on politics. We must, however, be on our guard against exaggerating the extent of the change. The free Greek city-state by no means ceased to exist. Indeed, some city-states, such as Rhodes, still had their greatest days before them. Even in the dominions of the kings the Greek cities which they founded were the chief organs for the dissemination of Greek civilisation. To many a Greek his city must still have remained his chief centre of interest. None the less throughout the greater part of the Greek world the city was over-shadowed by the kingdoms. And these were not any longer barbarian states which had to be resisted in the name of Greek civilisation, but were themselves the champions and dis-seminators of this civilisation. It was only to be expected, therefore, that new ways of looking at things should begin to grow up in the Greek world. It is true that the germs of these new ideas could be discovered in the earlier period. But it is only now that they began to be of real importance.

One noticeable development is a further step in the direc-tion of the separation of morality from politics. As we have seen, it had already been realised in the classical period that an individual might have to take a stand against the will of his community, for the sake of a moral ideal. Sophocles' Antigone and Plato's Socrates bear testimony to that. But such an attitude did not question the duty of a man, in all normal circumstances, to conform to the standards of his community, and if, occasionally, he felt impelled to disobey the laws or commands of his city it was with the ideal of a better law in a better city in mind. But now we begin to find the idea that the highest good for man was to be found, not in political activity or in relations to a community at all, but in something, some experience or state of mind, in his own soul alone. The Cynics and, in a modified form, the Stoics preached the ideal of self-sufficiency for each individual, the greatest possible freedom from dependence on anything the world could give, whether in the way of material goods or social relations. The Sceptics, by a different route, came to a somewhat similar idea, when they proclaimed as the aim of their sceptical philosophy the attainment of Ataraxia, not worrying, the calm unruffled mind. The Epicureans preached the pursuit of personal pleasure as the ideal for each individual. This last school expressly eschewed any participation in public affairs. Stoic philosophers, on the other hand, often played a part in the politics of the time. Indeed, some of these thinkers regarded it as a duty to do so. But the essential thing for them was not to be dependent on this, but to remain 'master of one's fate and captain of one's soul' throughout.

Alongside of this, we find the development of the idea that, if we do owe a duty to anyone else, it is not to this or that particular community but to mankind as a whole. The idea of the Cosmopolites, the citizen of the world, is characteristic of the period. And among the early Stoics we find the notion of a world state put forward as an ideal. But the Stoics' most influential contribution to political thought was, probably, the development of the idea of natural law. To the Stoic this was not at all what it had meant to some earlier thinkers, the dictates of our natural animal impulses and desires. It was, on the contrary, the eternal law of right and wrong, which was the same for everyone at all times. It was not made by man for his own convenience, but was discovered in the very structure of reality. For it was the expression of the divine Reason, which was immanent throughout the universe, and of which a share was present in all human beings. It was because reason was present in all of us that we were all capable of understanding the natural law and were all equally subject to it. It was from this point of view that the idea of the natural equality and kinship of all rational beings, with all that that implied, was developed. It is true that the notion of the wise man, the Stoic sage, who to a special degree had developed the reason in him, left the door open for some degree of leadership and authority. But the idea that, in some sense, all men are naturally equal remains one of the most distinctive contributions of the Stoics and it was essentially connected with their conception of natural law.

There is much else of interest in this period, which in many respects represents a turning point in the history of thought. Unfortunately our knowledge of it is only fragmentary. Its chief significance for future developments lies in the fact that it was in this period that the first close contact of Rome with the Greek world began, and it was by the ideas of the Hellenistic age rather than by those of the classical period that the Romans were influenced, so far as they were influenced by ideas at all. It is to Rome that we must now turn.

ROME

The Romans were not a philosophically minded people and any philosophical ideas that they had were borrowed straight from the Greeks. But they were always a legally minded people and their chief contribution to thought lay in the development of a system of law. A good deal of their law, too, came originally from Greek sources. But it was developed much more systematically and completely by the Romans, and they consistently tend to look on political affairs from a legal point of view. It is worth spending a little time to consider what looking at things from a legal point of view means.

Law as a way of looking at things has certain obvious characteristics. It is general, abstract, and definite. That is to say, in the first place, that it is essentially a system of general rules, which means that the actions of which the law takes cognisance have to be classified under general heads, as this or that kind of action. The tendency of the legal point of view is always to think of an action, not as a unique, individual thing or as part of an infinite network of relations, but as a specimen of a certain class or general species of actions. To do this it has to be abstract, that is to consider only certain aspects of the objects with which it deals and to ignore the others. In concrete reality every action differs in many respects from every other. But if we looked at actions in that way we could not classify them under general rules. In other words, law could not exist.

Similarly law always aims at being clear cut and definite. If it is to deal with an action at all it can do so only if it places it definitely in one particular category and not in another. To take the most general classification, any action must be either legal or illegal. It cannot be rather legal or partly legal or more or less legal. And to decide this it is generally necessary to classify the action under some subordinate head. It is a felony or a misdemeanour, it is or is not within the terms of a contract, or so on. It may be difficult to decide this in particular cases. But if the action comes within the purview of the law it has to be decided definitely one way or the other.

The characteristics of this point of view can be brought out by contrasting it with other possible ways of looking at actions, as for instance the consideration of them in terms of purpose and results, as means to an end. Here we do not judge the action by itself but by its relation to something else, its purpose or results. We do sometimes use general rules here as statements of the kind of action that is usually likely to bring about a certain kind of result. But they are only rough working guides to what can usually be expected to happen. We can never be sure beforehand that some unusual and unexpected circumstances will not nullify them. And they have no authority in themselves. If we are unsuccessful in bringing about a desired result because we have failed to notice some special circumstance of the case, it is of no avail to plead that we have followed the rules. Such a plea would be a fit subject of satire, like the doctor in Molière's play who offered the consolation to the bereaved relatives that the patient had died according to the rules. Further, while an action cannot be more or less legal, it can be more or less successful in the results it produces, or partly successful, or successful with the qualification that the same result could have been brought about better by another method, and so on.

The contrast between these two points of view, thinking in terms of law and thinking in terms of purpose, runs throughout the history of political thought. Of course, the distinction must not be pressed too absolutely. The two points of view can be combined in varying proportions by particular people, and philosophers have tried, with varying degrees of success, to resolve the two into a higher unity. But the broad distinction remains, and we can generally find one or the other predominating in different periods and different schools of thought, even if it is generally possible to find traces of the other at the same time. With these qualifications, it would in general be true to say that the Roman tended to look at things in terms of law, while the Greek was much more ready to consider them in terms of purpose, though there was perhaps more of the opposite point of view in his mind than in that of the Roman.

We can see symptoms of this difference in their respective attitudes towards the question of the seat or the distribution of political authority. The Greek who thought about these matters at all would be inclined to argue about them from the point of view of what distribution of political authority, or what form of government, would produce the best results for the city. The Roman would tend to begin from the question what were the established legal rights of the different claimants to authority. The Greek democrat, for instance, would defend democracy on the grounds of the benefits, moral or material, that the actual exercise of political power brought to the individual citizens, for whom the city existed. And this clearly involves the conclusion that to get these benefits the citizen must himself actually participate in political activities. He cannot appoint anyone else to do this for him, any more than he could get benefit to his health by appointing someone else to take exercise for him. The Roman lawyer also had, in a sense, a democratic theory, but it meant something quite different. He held that political power in the first place rested in the people, not because it was good for them but because, in the nature of things, it belonged to them by right. But he looked on it rather as a piece of property, which, like any other piece of property, could be transferred, wholly or with some reservations, to someone else. When this was done the new owner had an unassailable title to it, not because of any results that this might produce, but because the legal right to it had been transferred to him.

One result of this was the development of an idea of representation by the Romans which was never developed in the same way among the Greeks. It is sometimes said that the ancient world had never conceived the modern idea of representative government. And if we mean by that the idea of a governing body elected by regional constituencies that is literally true. But the Romans went much further than the Greeks in developing a legal notion of representation, in the sense of the delegation of sovereign power by the community to an elected representative or representatives. In a Greek democracy, such as Athens, there were, of course, elected officials who performed certain functions. But they were thought of much more as servants carrying out the orders of their master, the sovereign people, and with their master's eyes always upon them. But the Roman magistrates, once they were elected, had, with a few reservations, the whole of the power of the people transferred to them. They were really the rulers, as long as they were in office, and their authority was recognised by the people. This way of thinking reached its culmination under the emperors. The imperial jurists laid it down, in the much quoted phrase, that 'what the ruler has decided has the force of law'. But, they added, this is only so because the people by law have conferred all their power and authority on him. Thus the legalistic conception of popular sovereignty provides the foundation for the doctrine of the legislative omnipotence of an autocrat.

We thus have clearly formulated the idea of a supreme law-making authority. But, even so, the Romans never quite accepted the modern notion that a law is a law if it is passed in the proper form by the recognised authority quite irrespective of its moral value, of its justice or injustice. No doubt, their practice came to very much the same thing. But they still maintained the belief, derived from the Stoics, in the natural law, the eternal and universal rules of right reason, which, in some sense, claimed supreme authority, and they never separated this sharply from the civil law. The civil law claimed respect as an attempt to formulate and apply the natural law to the circumstances of a particular state. The idea never entirely died out that not only was it right to do what the law said, but also that, in some sense or degree, what was right to do, just because it was right, had the force of law.

Such an idea may be dangerous, because 'what is right to do' may easily come to mean in practice what any particular body of people at any particular moment feels to be right. And the consequences may be that a great respect for the law in theory becomes combined with a great readiness to break it in any moment of excitement. The sovereign people in Athens were not infrequently guilty of this, and Plato warns his readers against the danger.[1] But the Romans were a practical people, not much given to criticising the foundations of

---

[1] In one of his latest dialogues Plato expresses the view that a system of general rules, just because it is general, can never attain to the ideal of perfect righteousness. The perfectly wise and good man, therefore, would not act according to such a system, but would deal with each situation on its merits. But as we are none of us perfectly wise and good we cannot in practice do without the guidance and support of general rules. We shall get much nearer righteousness by making laws and sticking to them, than by attempting to act according to our feelings of the moment. See *Politicus*, 298–302.

their beliefs or pushing an argument to its logical conclusion, and they always retained a respect for the existing rules, even if they recognised that they fell short of the ideal.

None the less, the recognition of a natural law as the ideal did have an effect both on their general attitude and their practical procedure. Thus, it was recognised that in some cases the rigid application of the law might need modification, or interpretation which often amounted to modification, in the interests of equity. Under the Republic and in the earlier days of the Empire, the judicial officer was authorised to do this. But—and this is a typically Roman device—he was not supposed to do this just as he felt inclined in each particular case. He had to state beforehand, at the beginning of his year of office, the principles on which he was going to proceed. In fact, he habitually took over the statements of his predecessors, with such further modifications as experience had suggested. After this procedure was abolished there arose a series of legal commentators, who in a less formal way performed the same service, and whose commentaries could be cited in the law courts. We thus find a continual attempt to bring the civil law closer to the ideal of the natural law. But, at the same time, the natural law was itself thought of as, in principle, a system of general rules, and the attempt to apply it always implied an attempt to formulate it in terms of such a system, which could be written down and known before it was applied to any particular case.

The Roman law, as finally developed, formed a majestic system, unlike anything that had been achieved before, and destined to have a profound influence on later ages. From the point of view of political ideas, it was probably the idea of natural law which had the most pervasive effect on subsequent thought. But the whole legal point of view, which expressed itself in this great construction, attained a systematic completion which had never been attained before, but was never to be entirely forgotten again.

It has been worth while to spend so much time over the thought of the ancient world because it contained the origins of so much subsequent thought. Indeed there are comparatively few ideas of later times for which it would not be possible to find some sort of parallel in antiquity. Before going further it might be useful to attempt a summary of the most important ideas that we have found so far.

Among the Greeks we find the idea of the conscious construction of societies and institutions to suit our human purposes. Talk about a 'planned society' at the present time is likely to arouse a good deal of controversial feeling. But if we compare our attitude now to that of more primitive ages we shall have to recognise that, comparatively speaking, we are all believers in the planned society. We are more so even than we were a couple of generations ago, when we were accustomed to say that 'constitutions grow and are not made' —a remark, incidentally, which even as a statement of fact would have been very far from true of ancient Greece. At any rate, we are much less ready than our grandfathers were to accept the idea of 'progress' as some kind of force which is carrying us on in a direction that we can neither foresee nor control. And so far we approach the Hellenic point of view.

The second most important idea is that of the moral end of politics, in the sense explained above. This, again, may provide plenty of matter for controversy at the present time, though, perhaps, more on questions of interpretation and of application in practice than on the general principle itself. Following from this, we get the discussion of the value of different institutions and of different kinds of constitution. In particular we get the arguments for and against democracy, as a form of government. There will be a good deal more to be said about the relations of the Greek idea of democracy to our own.

Then, we find the idea of the division of the world into a number of separate and independent states as being the natural and proper order of things This is so familiar to us now that it needs an effort to realise that over long periods of time it was not in the least taken for granted. Nor does it always occur to us to ask the question how far it is, or ever has been attained in practice. Arising out of this we have the idea that our moral obligations are owed to a special degree, or even exclusively, to the members of our own state or society. This is a product of classical Greece, while in the Hellenistic age, particularly among the Stoics, we find the beginnings of a belief in our duty to the whole of humanity. At the present day, it must be admitted that in spite of lip-service to the latter ideal, there is much more of the classical point of view in our practice than we like to admit.

From both Greece and Rome we get the belief in the rule of law as the condition of a satisfactory society. We constantly hear their claim to superiority over the barbarian monarchies around them, based on the conviction that they live under the law, not under the arbitrary will of an individual. That is supplemented, particularly in Rome, by the idea of a definite law-making authority, which in that sense is over the law. But it is over the law, not outside it, and, while it can alter the law, it is not free, in theory at least, to act arbitrarily in disregard of the law which it has enacted.

We have also in these periods the initiation of the discussion of the relations between law and morality, which has gone on ever since. From the Greek side we get the beginnings of the idea that the law, however important it may be to obey it while it is in force, may be subordinate to the attainment of some good end or purpose. From the Romans, influenced by the later Greeks, we have the suggestion that it may be subordinate to some higher code of law, the natural law, and get some part of its authority from its relation to that. Connected with these, we get the Stoic doctrine, which was received by the Roman lawyers, of the natural equality of mankind. This has often been contrasted with the assertions that we find in classical Greek thought of the natural inequalities between men, and it has been suggested that this marks one of the great turning points of thought. But this seems to be an exaggeration. The Stoics and Romans never intended to deny the differences in ability, in temperament and the like which the earlier Greek writers were concerned to emphasise. Nor did they do anything to abolish the existing inequalities of wealth or rank or prestige, which, if anything, were intensified under Roman rule. Nor did they ever contemplate any steps to abolish slavery, though that was universally declared to be contrary to natural law. It is true that, under the Empire, we find legislation aimed at alleviating the position of the slaves, and this may properly be put down to the influence of Stoic ideas. But they had been anticipated in this by the Athenian democracy. In spite of all this, however, the idea of natural equality did mean something, however elusive, and, if its effects were not immediately obvious, they have gradually percolated down to modern times.

There are some other minor points, such as the theory of representation referred to above. But these are the main ideas of classical antiquity which are of special interest to us at the present day. In what follows we shall be covering a much larger period at a much faster pace, with a good deal of possibly arbitrary selectivity. But that will only be possible because of the extent to which the foundations of all subsequent discussion were laid in the period which we have just been considering.

Chapter II

SOME HISTORICAL PRELIMINARIES (2)

CHRISTIANITY

THE next great change that we have to record is the arrival
of Christianity, and it is not always easy to estimate just
what effect that had on political thinking. The earliest
Christians had, strictly speaking, nothing that we could call
political theory at all. They constituted a small body of the
faithful, living in constant expectation of the Second Coming
and holding themselves aloof from the world and its affairs.
Towards the rulers of the strange land in which they were
sojourners they owed implicit obedience, in everything that
did not directly touch their religion. St Paul's strong statements to this effect were often quoted in later ages, even
though the conditions under which he wrote had entirely
changed. But for himself the Christian disclaimed any
responsibility for ordering the affairs of the world. It was
not until the adoption by Constantine of Christianity as the
official religion of the Roman Empire that anything that we
could call a Christian political theory was developed.

Of course, as later ages showed, it was possible to make a
plausible case for the widest variety of political views on the
basis of Christian doctrine. But at this earlier period a great
many of the dominant ideas were taken over from the Stoic
and Roman tradition, and given a specifically Christian interpretation. Thus the state of nature, in which all men were
equal and there was no slavery or domination of one man by
another, was explained as the state of primal innocence before
the Fall, which could not be expected to apply to actual
mankind, the inheritors of Adam's burden of sin. The

dominant idea among the Fathers was that living in society was natural, in this sense. Even if there had been no Fall man would have lived in communities. But government, with all its apparatus of coercion and punishment, was a consequence of man's corrupt nature. As such, it was ordained by God, and had to be accepted with implicit obedience by sinful man. These notions take us away from the Roman lawyers' idea of the popular origin of political authority, for all power is thought of as conferred by God. And they take us still further from the classical Greek notion of political activity and participation in political power as something of value in itself and a part of the good life. Government is thought of almost entirely in terms of coercion and punishment; as an unpleasant necessity, not as a co-operative activity of the members of a community.

The abandonment of the Greek idea of a positive moral function of the secular state came more naturally because this function was thought of as primarily belonging to another body or set of authorities, the Church. It is probable that the idea of the Church as an organised body with its own organs of government was the element in Christianity which made the most difference to political thinking. For it represented something which had not been thought of before, the notion of two co-ordinate authorities over human beings, performing different functions and each supreme in its own sphere. The effects of this were manifold. Whereas, on the one hand, the tendency of Christian teaching was to exalt the authority of the civil rulers and to proclaim the duty of passive obedience even to a tyrant, on the other it put a limit to this authority by setting up alongside it the ecclesiastical authority which was supreme in matters of faith and morals even over the civil ruler. There were obvious possibilities of future conflict over the exact delimitation between the two spheres. And when these conflicts did arise they provided a fertile seed-bed for the development of many discussions on the origin and limitations of political authority. But for the time being it was assumed that the boundary between the two spheres was easily distinguishable, and no conflict of principle arose. It is when we come to the Middle Ages that we get the implications of the idea of a Christian society explicitly developed, and at the same time the latent possibilities of controversy coming out into the open.

THE MIDDLE AGES

The Middle Ages is a conventional expression for a period extending roughly from the time of Charlemagne, or the generation which followed him, up to the Reformation. And it is obvious that any generalisation made about a period of six or seven centuries must be subject to all sort of qualification. But we are not here concerned with a detailed history of the ideas of the period. We may, therefore, venture to pick out for our special purpose certain tendencies of thought which can be described as typically medieval, tendencies which are much more obvious in some parts of the period than in others, but which never entirely disappear.

Writers on the history of medieval political thought have singled out two main ideas which underlie all thinking about politics of this period. These are (1) the Unity of Christendom, and (2) the Reign of Law. Both these deserve a brief notice, because they provide a striking contrast to the common habits of thought at the present day.

(1) No one seriously doubted till the Reformation that the whole of Christendom was in some sense a single society. There might be in detail different answers to the question exactly in what sense this was so. But at the least it meant something much more than the mere unity of a common belief. It implied a definite organised society with some sort of government and administration of its own. From one point of view everybody in any position of authority in Christian Europe could be regarded as an official of the one society. But there were two people who were regarded as, in a special sense, at the head of it, the Pope and the Emperor.

Those who are not well acquainted with medieval history, when they read about the separate kingdoms, England, France, and the rest, acting independently and often in opposition to each other, may wonder how much reality there was in the theoretical idea. And they do well to ask the question, for the Middle Ages, even more than our own age, seem to have been tolerant of theories which had little or no relation to actual practice. But the answer in this case is that there was, in fact, a great deal of reality in it. It is true that the power of the Emperor, outside his own domains, never in practice amounted to more than a kind of honorary seniority, even though he could describe himself on occasions as lord of the whole world. But throughout the whole period the authority of the Pope in anything that was, or could be interpreted as, a matter of faith or morals was generally recognised. The ordinary man took it for granted that in some matters he took his orders from his king and in some from the Pope, through the Canon Law and the ecclesiastical courts. And the body of ecclesiastics, though subjects of their monarchs, were to a much greater degree under the orders of the Pope. Of course, there were numerous disputes about the exact delimitations of the powers of the different authorities. Such disputes, indeed, occupy a large part of medieval politics. But the general set-up was never seriously questioned till the time of the Reformation.

We have here a striking contrast to our modern point of view, which in this respect goes back to ancient Greece. To us the division of the world into a number of separate states seems the natural order of things, and the sovereign independence of each state is in theory generally accepted as a principle which should not be violated. In the Middle Ages it was just the opposite. Though a certain degree of independence for the individual rulers of the particular countries had to be recognised, unity remained the ideal. This was supported by various theoretical arguments. Sometimes they were theological, as when writers such as Dante argue that the human race becomes more like God the more it becomes one. Sometimes they are more political, as when it is argued that to secure justice being done there must be one supreme power to decide between the conflicting claims of particular rulers. But probably the main force of the belief came from two factors. There was, firstly, the memory of the Roman Empire and the survival of the habits of thought which that had engendered. And secondly there was the sense of a common Christianity, which made people feel that membership of the same Church was, or ought to be, a more important bond of union than living in the same country under the same monarch. As that feeling weakened, the whole system changed too.

(2) But this society was not, like the Roman Empire, a unitary society under an absolute law-making authority. It is true that at some periods the Popes and the papalist lawyers claimed that the Pope had absolute legislative power, at any rate over the body of ecclesiastics. But that was an exception, and was in any case not universally admitted. The general view was that the law was supreme. Anyone who had any authority owed it to the law, and had only as much authority as the law gave him. Even the king of a country with all his powers was under the law, which he did not make and could not alter at his will. No doubt the law was really custom, and some legal writers recognised this. But the ordinary man probably thought of it more as something which was just there, in the atmosphere, so to speak, which was not made, but had to be discovered. What looks to us like legislation in the Middle Ages was normally regarded, at any rate in theory, as a statement of what the law already is. This way of looking at things had a long history, and retained some of its influence after the Middle Ages had closed. It really represents a reversion to a more primitive habit of thought, and was doubtless an inheritance from the Germanic tribes who founded most of the states of Europe.

The law, as so conceived, gave, in theory, everyone in any

community certain rights and certain duties. The head of a
particular community, the king of a country, for instance, had
very great powers, but they were not absolute or unlimited.
Every subordinate part of the community also had certain
inherent rights, which might include an element of what we
should nowadays call political rights, though the distinction
between political and private rights was not clearly conceived
at that time. It is a consequence of this that we find political
disputes commonly taking the form of claiming or asserting
rights that the law was believed to give, and not in any sense
attempting to alter the institutions or system of government
because one kind of constitution was believed to be better
than another. If the barons rose against their king it was
because they claimed that he had gone beyond his legal
powers and was infringing the rights that they possessed. It
would hardly have occurred to them even to raise the question whether aristocracy was a better form of government
than monarchy. To revert to our earlier distinction, the whole
age in its fundamental political ideas represents the triumph
of thinking in terms of law over thinking in terms of purpose.

It would be tempting to dwell on many other features of
the thought of this period. There is the importance attached
to rank and status in society as part of the natural order of
things. There is the stress on personal loyalty as one of the
springs of action. These, and others, are ideas which retain
their influence for a considerable time after the end of their
period. It would be of particular interest to trace the beginnings of discordant tendencies of thought which were eventually to break up the medieval system of ideas altogether.
Putting aside the obviously revolutionary or heretical movements, there were the possibilities of this in some of the most
generally accepted ideas of the period. Thus we find that
almost all discussion is based on certain religious assumptions
to which the appeal always returns. 'Politics in the Middle
Ages is a branch of theology', as one historian writes. Yet

there are already signs of how easy it was to be for theology to become a branch of politics. Thus, it was always possible to argue that some state of things was good, on other grounds, and then go on to assert that it must therefore be the will of God, as God always chooses the best. Or, again, the universally held idea that all power comes from God was quite compatible with the view that it might come indirectly through an intermediary, and there were endless possibilities of argument about who that intermediary was. We get, too, a revival of the Roman idea of the popular origin of at any rate secular power, though this was not universally accepted. But it would be impossible here to try to disentangle all the complicated strands of thought that we find in the period.

THE SIXTEENTH AND SEVENTEENTH CENTURIES

Early in the sixteenth century came the Protestant Reformation, which successfully challenged some of the main assumptions of medieval thought. The result was, during the century and a half that followed, to let loose a flood of political speculation, such as had not been known since the time of the Greeks. It would be quite out of place here to attempt even a summary of all the varied influences that combined to produce this movement. But it is necessary to insist that the religious motive, though by no means the only one at work, was a very real force. There can be no doubt that large numbers of people felt that their religious aspirations were being frustrated by the existing organisation and control of the Church. But the Church was itself a vital part of the political structure of Europe, so that any attack on it was necessarily a political move. Thus, to many people in this period politics was as much a branch of theology as in the Middle Ages, and it is sometimes only possible to understand a political movement when we see the religious motives behind it. Of course, the converse is just as often, perhaps more often, true. But, however difficult it may be to disentangle the different influences at work in particular cases, we cannot afford to ignore the religious element that permeates most of the political thinking of the period.

The first result of the Reformation, both in political thought and political reality, was the break-up of the unity of Christendom. From this time forth this was never more than a pious aspiration. In its place, we get, in a comparatively short space of time, the acceptance of the modern ideal which is also the Hellenic idea, of a world naturally divided into a number of separate and independent states. The historians can trace the beginnings of this development much further back, particularly in the gradual growth of a national feeling for the particular states of Europe as they began to form themselves. But as long as unity of religious belief and membership of a common Church continued, this national feeling was always limited in its effect. When this unity was removed it could develop unchecked. This did not, of course, happen all at once, and there remained for some time in the minds of many people a conflict between their loyalty to their Church and their loyalty to their state, a conflict which led in some cases to bitter warfare. But by the middle of the seventeenth century it was already clear that the state was emerging as the successful claimant to man's obedience. This was most obvious in Protestant states. But even in Catholic countries the difference in this respect from the Middle Ages is striking.

In the intervening period, however, the relation between Church and state was the object of lively controversy. But the whole problem now takes a different form. It is no longer a question of possible conflict between different officials of one and the same society, to which everybody who could possibly be concerned belonged. Church and state now emerge definitely as separate societies, even when, as was by no means necessarily the case, the same people were members of both. And, just as it was now accepted that there were a number of separate and independent states, so it had in the end to be accepted, however reluctantly, that there was more than one

Church. As for the relation between Church and state, diffcrent views emerged. The Catholic theory was that the two societies had different functions which, over a large field, need not clash or conflict at all. But if they did, the Church is the superior society and ought to have first claim on the obedience of the members. Thus, for instance, if one Church was dominant in a particular country it could by right call on the state to put down heresy and enforce the true religion. If it was a minority it could demand toleration from the state and call on its members to resist if that was refused. Substantially the same view was held by the Calvinist and Presbyterian Churches, though they were less successful in getting it recognised in practice.

Where, however, the Reformation was carried out under the influence of other reformers, such as Luther and Zwingli, a different view arose. On this view, the Church was primarily a spiritual communion, and the essentials of true religion lay in a purely personal experience which could not really be a subject of external control or regulation at all. So far as any external control or regulation was required, even in religious matters, it fell within the province of the secular state organised under the legal authority, whether the king or the magistrates of a republic. When such a view was fully developed it meant that the form and manner of the religious life of the community, and the doctrines that could be taught, were controlled by the authorities of the state, and the ministers of religion, practically speaking, became officials of the state under its ruler or rulers.

None of these points of view contemplated the toleration of different religious views as a principle that could possibly be accepted. Indeed, to most people of the period the idea that a man had a right to be wrong in religious matters or that it did not matter what he believed would probably have seemed the wildest of paradoxes. None the less, practical statesmen in some countries, who cared more about the strength and prosperity of their state than about enforcing the true religion, were being forced by experience to advocate some degree of toleration as an unfortunate necessity. And experience also began to show that, if national patriotism was strong enough, a state could survive without uniformity of religion. From the other side we find, first in some continental countries, particularly Switzerland, and later in England, the idea put forward that, as a matter of principle, any body of Christians should be free to organise themselves for the worship of God in their own way, while the state should remain neutral between them.

We can see, thus, how religious disputes began to raise problems of political authority and to initiate arguments about them which, it was speedily seen, could be applied beyond the field of religion altogether. Does the ruler of a state have absolute power, above the law or anything else, or is it limited by the rights of other elements? Are there any circumstances on which resistance to the ruler by any of his subjects is justifiable? If resistance in the name of religious belief was justified it was very easy to go on to maintain that to enforce other rights that had been infringed was equally so. In the Middle Ages, indeed, the right of resistance on behalf of a dissident religious belief would have been universally denied, while resistance to enforce, say, the feudal rights of the baronage would have been much more generally accepted. But with the growth of strong national states it had gradually begun to be realised that the latter might endanger the unity and security of the state more than the former. Hence we get in the sixteenth and seventeenth centuries the development of theories of political absolutism, which might be compatible in practice with a certain degree of religious toleration.

There are two questions which were raised in this period which logically should be kept distinct. There is the question just mentioned, whether the recognised authority in a state should be conceived as having absolute and supreme power, unrestricted by the law or by the claims of any other person or body of persons. And there is the further question, distinct from that, in whose hands this supreme power should properly lie. By the middle of the seventeenth century Hobbes had clearly made this distinction. He argues that in any state, if it is to remain a state at all, there must be one supreme authority, with absolute and undivided power. But he maintains that, though on practical grounds he preferred a monarchy, his argument applies equally whatever the authority is, whether it is a king, a parliament, a general assembly, or anything else. But other people found it more difficult to keep the two questions distinct. In fact, of course, in most countries in Europe at this time, except Switzerland, the Venetian Republic, and later the Netherlands, the only practical candidate for supreme power was the monarch. And those who most wanted to exalt the civil power in his person could not be satisfied with a rationalistic argument of the kind presented to them by Hobbes. They needed a supernatural sanction as well. So we get, particularly in France and England, the development of the famous doctrine of the Divine Right of Kings.

This doctrine goes much beyond the general notion that all power comes from God. It holds that monarchy is the only legitimate form of government and that the order of succession by primogeniture is divinely appointed, so that there can be no question as to who is the rightful king. It holds also that the king's authority is absolute and unlimited, and that he is answerable only to God for the use he makes of it. The subject, therefore, owes the king implicit obedience and has, under no circumstance, any right of resistance. The doctrine, as a whole, hardly makes any appeal to our modern way of thinking, but there is no doubt that it met a felt need at that time. To some of its advocates its chief recommendation was that it put the civil ruler on a level with or above the ecclesiastical authority which had always claimed in a special degree to be divinely appointed. It made the succession to the throne fixed and certain, so that, so far as it was accepted, it removed one, at any rate, of the possible causes of civil strife. And it gave a religious flavour to the loyalty to the king in which the developing nationalism of the time tended to express itself.

On the other side, we find, except for a short time during our own civil war, very little attempt to claim absolute power for any other authority than the monarch. The general line of opposition to kingly absolutism was a return to the medieval idea of a division or distribution of power. But the idea now takes a different form. We no longer have the picture of the whole of Christendom as a hierarchically organised society, a *communitas communitatum*, in which each subordinate part has certain inherent powers and rights as against its superior. The picture is now much more of a unitary state, in which the division of power occurs at the top. The idea frequently appears of the normal and proper organisation of a state as consisting in a chief ruler—generally the king—who carried on the actual government of the country, and a countervailing power, a parliament or a body of subordinate magistrates, which was there, not so much to share in the work of government as to act as a check and control on the ruler if he went outside the limits of his rightful authority. As subsequent history showed, this particular balance of powers was very hard to maintain. But the general idea of such a balance survived.

The rightful limits of authority were normally conceived as being laid down, in one form or another, by the law or by a legal instrument, such as a contract or covenant. This was a legalistic age, even more, perhaps, than the Middle Ages, and the development of different notions of law is one of the most interesting features of its thought. Thus, there were still occasional attempts to maintain that the law of the land was supreme, that it was superior to any possible law-making body and limited its powers. We find at one time lawyers in England maintaining that the Common Law, as interpreted by the judges, was of superior authority to any statute made by the king in Parliament and might even declare such statutes to be void. But this view was already out of date. Legislation had by now become too much part of the normal work of government for it to be accepted. There still remained, however, the feeling that there must be somewhere some fundamental law, which could not be altered and was of superior authority to anything else.

To some extent this need was met by the well-known doctrine of the social contract. This was the theory that political authority rested on a contract, either between the ruler and his people, or between the individual people themselves, to establish an organised society and set up a government. And as authority was based on a contract, so it was limited by the terms of the contract and forfeited all claim to obedience if it broke them or went beyond them. This theory goes back to the Greeks and was known in the Middle Ages but it is in the period now under consideration that it had its greatest vogue. It was used by Hobbes, paradoxically enough, as a basis for his argument in favour of the absolute and undivided authority of the ruling power. But in every other case it appears, much more naturally, as part of the anti-absolutist argument.

This is not, however, the whole story. A contract itself is a legal idea, and seems to imply a framework of law already there which controls its terms and gives it authority. So the idea of natural law and the natural rights that it gave, which had always survived from the time of the Stoics, plays a great part in the thought of the period. It was easy to argue that the contract to set up and obey a government was made in order to secure the natural rights of those who made it, and that the positive laws made by the government could not be valid if they infringed these natural rights. As distinct from this natural law some religious sects proclaimed the supremacy of the law of God, which was found in the scriptures. The distinction between the two is significant. Of course, the natural law could also be regarded, in a sense, as divine law. But the appeal to the authority of the Bible meant that the law of God could be known only by revelation. It was part of the very idea of the natural law, on the other hand, that it could be discovered by the unaided exercise of man's natural reason. It was not, therefore, dependent on any particular religious doctrine, and thus the effect of the development of this idea, whether intended or not, was all in the direction of the secularisation of political thought and its liberation from dependence on religious beliefs. Finally, we get the view of Hobbes that there is no law behind the contract, except the natural desire for self-preservation which leads men to agree to set up civil government. Then only does law begin, for 'law proper is the word of him that by right hath command over others'. In other words, a law is a law if it is decreed by the accepted authority, and that is all there is to it. We look back here to the Roman legal doctrine that what the ruler has decided has the force of law, and forward to the modern conception of positive law which is substantially the same. But Hobbes, in this respect, was in advance of his age and it was to take some considerable time before this account was accepted.

This is, of course, very far from exhausting the contributions to political thought of this remarkable period. Something, for instance, might be said of the attempts to challenge the whole legalistic way of looking at things. A writer of the period mentions and denounces the tendency when he says 'There is not anything in the world more abused than this sentence, *Salus populi suprema lex*. For we apply it as if we ought to forsake the known laws when it may be most for the advantage of the people, when it means no such thing.'[1] But two developments in particular deserve mention for their bearing on subsequent thought. One is the growth of the idea of political democracy, which comes to a head in this country at the time of the Civil War. The other is the attack on the system of private property and the demand for common ownership and economic equality.

[1] Selden, *Table Talk*, ed. Pollock, p. 93. Of course, the idea of 'reasons of state' which justify the ruler in disregarding the law goes back at least to Macchiavelli. But then it was the interest of the prince, rather than of the people, that was most in question.

The idea of democracy was doubtless familiar to all educated men of the time from their knowledge of the ancient world. But they did not normally think of it as a form of government which could possibly be advocated for their own day. There was a general distrust and fear of the power of the ignorant rabble. Thus the constitutionalists who would limit the power of the king, and even the republicans who would abolish monarchy altogether, did not as a rule contemplate the possibility of putting power into the hands of the whole body of the people. They might argue that the king derived his power from the people, who could deprive him of it if he misused it. But for all practical purposes 'the people' were regarded as represented by their natural leaders, as for instance by a Parliament elected on a very restricted franchise, or, in some cases, by the great territorial magnates. The beginnings of democracy in practice are to be looked for, not in the political, but in the religious field. Certain doctrines of the Protestant reformers, for instance 'the priesthood of all true believers', easily developed into the belief that all members of a church were equally concerned in its government. Such a belief was to some extent put into practice, first by the Anabaptists on the Continent, and later by several dissenting religious bodies in England.

Such a view does not necessarily lead to political democracy. For if 'the true believers' are only a minority in the country they may come to feel that, though equal among themselves, they are superior to the rest and may have a mission to dominate them and lead them along the true path. We may get 'the rule of the saints', which is certainly not a democracy. Nevertheless, it was from those nurtured in this religious tradition that the demand for political democracy, in the form of manhood suffrage, came. The debates in the army at the end of the Civil War produced notable statements in defence of this, and some of the phrases used have remained in men's memories ever since. 'It is the right of every free-born man to elect, according to the rule . . . that that which concerns all should be debated by all.' 'The poorest he that is in England hath a life to live as the richest he.' The cause thus proclaimed was lost at the time. But it was not forgotten, though it did not come into its own till two centuries later.

The democrats of the Civil War did not, as a rule, make any attack on the existing system of private property. Indeed, their tendency is to regard it as a natural right, and in some of their pronouncements they expressly deny to any government the right of 'abolishing propriety, levelling men's estates, or making all things common'. But there was a parallel movement at the time, represented by Winstanley and the Diggers, which attacked the whole institution of private property and demanded common ownership for the equal benefit of all. This was advocated in part for the relief of poverty and the abolition of great inequalities of wealth, and has little of interest to contribute to ideas about government. But once more, we have to recognise it as primarily a religious movement. It can be traced back a century earlier to the Anabaptists on the Continent, many of whom advocated a community of goods. A small militant wing attempted to establish their views by force, and for a time succeeded in setting up a theocratic republic in Münster, which was eventually wiped out in blood. But the great majority eschewed all use of violence, though that did not save them from the most savage persecution at the hands of both Protestants and Catholics. In all its forms this movement was religious in its inspiration. It represented, as it were, a nostalgia for the primitive simplicity of the early Christian society when 'not one of them said that aught of the things he possessed was his own: but they had all things in common'.

It was thus a backward-looking rather than a forward-looking movement. In England, it looks back, not only to primitive Christianity, but also to an idyllic state of things which was supposed, with no warrant of history, to have existed before the Norman Conquest. It is worth noting that Winstanley talks almost entirely in terms of the economy of the period, and is mainly concerned with the land and the fruits thereof. There is little idea of any more elaborate economic development.[1] There is thus not much in common with modern Socialism, except perhaps with the school of William Morris. As a whole, the movement does not seem to have had any very wide appeal at the time, and its direct influence was small. But indirectly it did do something, along with other influences, to initiate a debate on the justification for private property. A generation later we can find Halifax asserting that property is not a natural right but merely a convenience sanctioned by long usage. Locke, of course, declared property to be a natural right, in fact the principal natural right. But the grounds on which he argued this would, if carried to their logical conclusion, have cast grave doubts on the legitimacy of the existing distribution of property and of the laws that produced it.

One word of warning in conclusion. The main aim of these chapters is to indicate certain ideas of the past which, for one reason or another, seem of special interest for political theory of this present day. And this means that they are not always or necessarily set in their true historical perspective. The historian knows that the ideas which most interest us now are by no means necessarily those which seemed most important to people at the time. We find it hard to be greatly concerned about many of the theological controversies of that age. Yet they were of prime importance to many people then, and we could not afford to leave them out of account if we wanted to understand why men acted as they did. A modern writer on the period says of the time of our Civil War, 'It is probably true that, even when the Revolution was at its height, there were ten Puritans who were interested in reforming the Church to one who cared what happened to the government of England'.[2] Even the discussions on religious

---

[1] It is true that Winstanley suggested measures for encouraging the improvement of the arts and crafts. On the other hand, he disapproved of trade and commerce altogether.

[2] G. H. Sabine, *The Works of Gerard Winstanley*, p. 3.

liberty interest us less than they did, largely because, in theory at any rate, the case has been so generally conceded. Yet at the time it probably seemed to most people of far greater importance than any question of political right. Or, to consider more secular matters, if we look at the manifestos and statements of grievances of the period we cannot fail to be struck by the amount of space that is occupied by complaints about the obscurity of the law, the cumbrousness of legal procedure, its failure to give the protection that it ought against arbitrary treatment of individuals and so on. These were the things that aroused most feeling at the time and the feeling so aroused had eventually a considerable measure of success in producing reforms. The political demands were largely a by-product of these, and it was not till much later that they aroused sufficiently strong and widespread feeling to bring about some attempt to meet them.

Chapter III

SOME HISTORICAL PRELIMINARIES (3)

W^E are now approaching the area of contemporary controversy. But before leaving our historical preliminaries,
there are still two or three movements of thought which might
be mentioned briefly, in order to make intelligible possible
allusions to them in what follows. Even less than in the
preceding chapters will any attempt be made at a systematic
treatment. Only certain points in them of special significance
will be singled out.

ROUSSEAU

The first of these is a group of ideas associated with
Rousseau, in particular those contained in his famous book on
the Social Contract. There are, of course, many other sides
of his thought, for instance those concerned with education,
which have been of influence in other directions, but these
will have to be left out of consideration here. Rousseau was
one of those thinkers, fertile in ideas but, partly because of
this fertility, confused in working them out, who have often
had the greatest influence on subsequent theories. Thus, on
the political side, he has been spoken of as the father of
democracy and also as the father of totalitarianism, as the
champion of liberty and the apologist for dictatorship. And
it is true that tendencies in all these directions can be found
in his thought.

The first point to consider is his idea of a social contract.
He takes this over from earlier thinkers, but gives it a turn of
his own, which in fact makes it something quite different from
previous notions of it. To begin with, he expressly disclaims

any idea of giving a historical account of the actual origins of society. It is purely a question of people acting *as if* there were a contract, not in the least of any actual contract ever having been made. This is not altogether new: Hobbes was already feeling in that direction a century earlier. But there is a further important difference. Hobbes claimed to give an analysis of the necessary conditions of there being a civil society at all. He argued, in effect, that if people did not act as if there were a contract, civil society would be dissolved and we should revert to a primitive condition of anarchy. Rousseau, however, in spite of occasional verbal lapses, is not concerned to maintain this. He was quite well aware that most existing societies did not, in fact, behave as he thought the idea of a contract demanded. What he was concerned with was to lay down the conditions for a *good* society, in particular a society in which the exercise of political power, which would otherwise be mere tyranny, becomes legitimate. The contract is an ideal rather than a necessary condition for society.

Connected with this is a development of the idea of the purpose of the contract, or more strictly the good results that will follow if the members of the society behave as if there were a contract. Earlier forms of the doctrine had represented the contract being made and civil society set up for a specific and limited purpose. Hobbes limited it most narrowly. For him the object of there being a society at all was simply self-preservation, and that remains the fundamental human motive throughout. Rousseau talks at first as if that were its object. But when he sums up (Book I, Ch. VIII) the advantages that the contract confers on the individual citizen he goes much further. By it, he says, 'his faculties are exercised and developed, his ideas enlarged, his feelings ennobled, his whole soul elevated to such a point . . . that from a stupid and limited animal he becomes an intelligent being and a man'. We are here very close to the Greek idea that 'the city exists for the sake of the good life'. Society is no longer thought of as an external bond which alters the conditions in which men live while leaving men the same as before. At its best it really makes men different beings from what they would be otherwise, and develops qualities in them which only existed potentially before. When we get to this point it is doubtful whether there is any advantage in continuing to talk in terms of a contract at all.

Rousseau, however, continues to use this language, and he expresses the terms of the contract as the total transfer by each individual of all his power and all his rights, not to this or that particular person or body of persons, but to the whole community of which he is a member. The particular will of each particular citizen becomes completely subordinate to the general will of the community and this general will has by right absolute and unlimited sovereignty. It is this notion of the General Will that is Rousseau's most characteristic contribution to political ideas. What he has to say about it is extremely confused and sometimes contradictory. None the less it is possible to disentangle from it several lines of thought of great interest which were to have considerable influence in the future.

The General Will is the union of the wills of all the members of the community so far as they are directed to the general good. There are occasional phrases which suggest that Rousseau thought of the community as itself an individual person with a will and a good of its own distinct from that of the particular persons in it. But that is not his settled view, which is expressed in the remark (I, vii) that the sovereign community 'being formed solely of the individuals which compose it has not nor can have any interest contrary to theirs'. The good of each of us is included in the general good, and the General Will, the desire for the general good, is something which exists in each individual. There is also a particular will in each individual which may clash with the General Will. But, though Rousseau is very far from clear about the relations between the two, it does not seem that we are to think of them as merely two co-ordinate sets of impulses. For, just as the good of the community includes the good of all the individuals in it, so the General Will in some way includes the particular wills. We might perhaps say that the particular will, taken by itself, is an abstraction, a partial and limited point of view which in the nature of things must be subordinate to the more all-embracing point of view represented by the General Will. Certainly the man who sets himself in opposition to the community is forgetting that the community is the condition of the 'good life' which is what he really wants.

It would be a mistake to try to tie Rousseau down to this particular formulation of his ideas. But it may help to explain why he insists that the General Will is also somehow the will of each individual. If the sovereign power which expresses the General Will has to compel an individual to follow it in opposition to his particular will, it is in some sense compelling him to do what he really wants to do. It is in that connection that the phrase, which seems so ominous to us nowadays, is used about the individual being 'forced to be free'. That phrase alone is, perhaps, sufficient indication of the possible developments in the direction of totalitarianism and dictatorship which might be extracted from Rousseau's thought. But to lay too much stress on this would be a gross distortion of what he actually said and believed. For the one point on which he never wavers is that the supreme sovereignty belongs to the whole people, and by this he means literally the whole body of people deliberating and voting together. They alone can express the General Will, and their authority cannot be alienated.

On the practical working out of this Rousseau is most confused and unsatisfactory. If we ask how it can be guaranteed that the individual voters will not forget the general good and think only of their particular interests, he admits that this may happen but seems to suggest that if they get together under proper conditions the particular interests may cancel each other out so that we are left with the General Will. Again, he admits that the people in their deliberations may make mistakes, however good their intentions. But he does not seem to realise the importance of this admission. In one chapter, indeed (II, vii), which he seems to forget in the rest of the work, he has recourse to the idea of a 'legislator', an idea which is very imperfectly worked out. It has been variously interpreted as suggesting a divinely inspired law-giver, a statesman proposing measures to the people, or a mere parliamentary draftsman. But whatever the 'legislator' is, it is quite clear that he does not legislate. He can draft and propose laws, but has no power to enact them. That is the prerogative of the sovereign people alone. Later (IV, ii) Rousseau says that the General Will is discovered by the counting of votes, and he has some rather indecisive remarks about the significance of majority decisions. But in spite of all qualifications and uncertainties it remains perfectly clear that, for Rousseau, even if the General Will does not infallibly emerge from a free popular vote, it can certainly not emerge in any other way.

One other point deserves a brief mention. Rousseau argues that the General Will, because it is general, can command only in general terms, that is, make laws applicable to the whole community. It cannot deal with particular persons: if it does it ceases to be general and so loses its sovereign authority and its claim to obedience. The application of the laws to particular cases is the duty of the executive power, which Rousseau calls the government as distinguished from the sovereign. This may sound, to begin with, rather like a mere quibble on the word 'general', but there is an important principle at the back of it. The government, whatever form it takes, is instituted by and is always subordinate to the sovereign. It has no authority except to apply the laws which the sovereign makes, while, on the other hand, the sovereign can only make general laws and cannot act towards individuals. We thus find Rousseau, in effect, adopting in his own way the idea of the division of powers, which was first clearly formulated by Locke and was subsequently enshrined in the American Constitution. Rousseau insists so strongly on the absolute and indivisible nature of sovereignty that the reader may miss this point at first, until he realises that sovereignty applies only to the legislative function. At any rate it is clear that Rousseau's ideal state is definitely a law-abiding state, and that arbitrary treatment of individuals is ruled out. It is thus in striking contrast alike to Hobbes' idea of the absolute ruler and to the dictatorships of our own day.

It ought to be clear, therefore, that if the ideas of *The Social Contract* are taken as a whole, Rousseau's lead is all in the direction both of democracy and the rule of law. But it is not difficult to see that, if certain elements in his argument are isolated from the rest and certain of his admissions are unduly stressed, a dictator or group of oligarchs who felt that they knew what the people 'really' wanted better than the people did themselves, might claim that they were interpreting Rousseau's teaching more logically than he did himself.

THE UTILITARIANS

Another movement of thought about which a word needs to be said is that known as Utilitarianism, which is particularly associated with the names of Bentham and the Mills. The most important part of this for our purposes, and indeed for any attempt at estimating its influence on thought and action at the time and in the future, is to be found in the principle that it laid down as a practical guide for political action. This was expressed in the famous formula of 'The Greatest Happiness of the Greatest Number', with its corollary that, in the distribution of happiness, 'everyone is to count for one and no one for more than one'. This is the proper end and aim of all public activity, and the sole test by which every measure or institution is to be judged.

In the earlier developments of the doctrine this principle is presented as a deduction from what seemed the self-evident psychological truth that every man always and necessarily pursues his own happiness (or pleasure: the two are not, as a rule, distinguished). But this supposed truth, when subjected to further analysis, seemed much less self-evident than at first appeared. Indeed, it could be reasonably argued that, when its ambiguities were cleared up, it was revealed as either a tautology or obviously false. Again, it was not difficult to show that there was a yawning logical gap between the proposition that each man necessarily pursues his own happiness and the proposition that the proper end (or even a possible end) of action is the greatest happiness of the greatest number. The attempts to bridge this gap were perfunctory and unsuccessful. Yet, in spite of all these faults, the doctrine survived and maintained its influence, because it met a demand that was being widely made. People, particularly those who wanted to alter the existing state of things, were looking for a relatively clear and intelligible criterion of the aims of political action, and if one was offered to them which seemed to meet their demands they would accept it as a working hypothesis without troubling to examine too minutely its logical foundations. Thus, as many writers have shown, the Utilitarian doctrine became one of the main inspirations of the political movements of the first half or three-quarters of the nineteenth century, and its influence is by no means exhausted even today.

From the point of view of the development of political ideas, one of the most interesting features of Utilitarianism is that, so far as it is accepted, it represents the complete establishment of the primacy of the idea of purpose over the idea of law. This, however, must not be misunderstood. It certainly does not mean that the Utilitarians underestimated the importance of law. On the contrary, it was as a principle of legislation that the doctrine was first put forward, and the reform of the law was one of the chief causes that Bentham had at heart. Nor does it mean that the Utilitarian would necessarily hold that the existing law could at any time be overridden or disregarded if the *salus populi* seemed to demand it. It could very reasonably be argued that the general happiness would be promoted much better by strict observance of the law as long as it was in force than by any attempt to correct it by executive action. What it does mean is that the law must always be regarded as an instrument subserving the purpose. The doctrine is fatal to any idea of the independent authority of the law. It is incompatible with the notion of a natural law in any strict sense, or of natural rights which belonged to people absolutely, irrespective of the results they might produce. The only rights are legal rights, and these should be given or withheld by the law simply on considerations of utility, meaning by that conduciveness to the greatest happiness.

It is easy to see that this doctrine was a powerful intellectual weapon in the campaign against abuses. Vested interests, established privileges, prescriptive rights of individuals or groups which ran counter to the general welfare, antiquated institutions which had no justification except long existence —all these things were tried by the test of utility, and if they did not meet the test they were to be swept away. It was fairly obvious in the first part of the nineteenth century that a good many institutions in this country could not meet that test, and the Utilitarians were in the van of the reform movements that, to a greater or lesser degree, affected the legal system, the Church, local government, and many other spheres of public life. There was a wide field in which the results of applying the principle of utility were obvious and unquestionable. But beyond that, when the abuses had been swept away and the question arose of the positive policies to be adopted, there was plenty of scope for differences of opinion about the application of the fundamental Utilitarian principles. It was largely a matter of historical accident that Utilitarianism, on the whole, became associated with one line of development rather than another.

Thus, it might plausibly be argued that, on the whole,

every man is the best judge of his own happiness, and therefore that the general happiness is most likely to be attained if
each man, as far as possible, is left to pursue his own happiness in his own way. The state should intervene only to forbid
certain classes of actions which are clearly detrimental to the
happiness of other people. That is what the criminal law is
for. But beyond that the state should interfere as little as possible, and the positive steps in the pursuit of happiness should
be left to the initiative of individuals. This point of view,
with many further elaborations, became on the whole dominant in the movement, and Utilitarianism became associated
particularly in the economic field with a belief in the utmost
possible limitation of state control, in Free Trade and free
enterprise generally, in freedom of contract, in all the things,
in fact, which we are accustomed to associate with the term
laisser faire.

From the other side it might be argued that most people
are not very good judges of what will produce their own happiness, particularly in the long run, that it is, indeed, a very
difficult problem which needs special skill and special study
to solve. Further, it might be argued that, if this is true even
of an individual's happiness, it is far more true when it is a
question of the general happiness. The *laisser faire* idea, it
might be said, enormously underestimates the extent to
which individuals by pursuing their own happiness may lessen
or destroy the happiness of other people. So far, therefore,
from leaving individuals free to the greatest possible extent to
act as they choose, what is wanted is a great increase in control
by the state, under the guidance of enlightened statesmen and
skilled officials, and, probably, safeguarded from abuse by
representative institutions based on a democratic suffrage.
There were certain tendencies in this direction to be noted
comparatively early in the history of the Utilitarian movement. And later in the century the Socialist movement in
Great Britain, unlike the Continent, was very largely based on
Utilitarian foundations. British Socialism, at any rate in the

past, has been predominantly humanitarian in its inspiration, and this Socialism has generally been thought of as instrumental to the promotion of happiness and the diminution of unhappiness for the individual members of the community. In that way it is thoroughly in line with Utilitarian doctrine. There is, indeed, already a distinct Socialist strain to be noted in John Stuart Mill, and later Socialists, particularly perhaps the Fabians, might very reasonably claim to be the true inheritors of the Utilitarian tradition.

It is thus evident that the fundamental principles of Utilitarianism as a guide to political action could, in practice, be developed in very varied directions. But certain basic features remain constant. The best modern writer on Utilitarianism, Élie Halévy, has singled out two characteristics of special importance as marking all forms of Utilitarian doctrine. They are, on the one hand, its individualism, and on the other its rationalism. A brief word of explanation of what is involved in this description may be desirable here.

(1) Utilitarianism is individualistic in the sense that, in every form, it asserts the proper and final end of political or, indeed, any other activity to be the attainment of some state of mind by individuals. But that does not, of course, mean that it believes this state of mind to be attainable except in a society, or that it regards the way in which the society is organised as being irrelevant to it. It has, for instance, nothing in common with the beliefs of people like the Stoics, or the religious mystics, who claim that the ideal state of mind is attainable in complete independence from one's surroundings in general and from one's social environment in particular. On the contrary, the whole impulse of Utilitarianism as a reforming movement lay in its belief that the happiness of individuals could be secured only if the structure of society were satisfactory. But the structure or organisation of society and indeed any political activities are valuable only as a means to the production of this experience of happiness in individual minds. They have no value in themselves, and if it were

empirically shown that in different circumstances different forms of organisation could produce equal amounts of happiness there could be no reason to prefer one rather than the other.

(2) It is rationalistic in the same sense as that in which the term was applied in a previous chapter to Greek thought. That is to say that it believes that is possible to have a clear conception of the end, and that it is the task of statesmanship to find out the best means to this end and then apply them. Further, it claims to be of general or universal application. The end is always the same and the essential characteristics of human nature are very much the same everywhere. Of course, as already indicated, the Utilitarian can quite well recognise that in different countries or in different circumstances the best means to the end may be different. But, on the whole, the tendency was to regard the likenesses as much more important than the differences.

These, then, are the two most essential features of Utilitarianism as a system of ideas. It remains now to consider briefly some of the movements of thought in reaction against Utilitarianism which challenged either or both of these assumptions.

THE REACTION AGAINST UTILITARIANISM

One way in which the first of these assumptions was challenged was that followed by the movements of thought which put the final and supreme end, not in any state of mind of individuals or any personal experience, but in the production of a certain state or condition of a society. This may be made an object of endeavour without much thought of the effects on the state of mind of individuals. So far as there was any thought for this it would tend in the direction of the view that the state of mind of individuals must be made to conform to the proper state of society, and if they seemed to be satisfied with any other state of society they must be made dissatisfied as soon as possible.

In certain schools of thought there was a tendency to think of the society as a sort of individual with an end or good or purpose of its own, which was something beyond the ends or goods of the individuals which composed it and of more importance than they. There are traces of this in Rousseau, though it never became a dominant element in his thought. It appears more definitely in Hegel and the thinkers that were influenced by him. Here it was bound up with certain metaphysical doctrines, the upshot of which was that society or the state was in some sense more real than the individual, and the individual attained a greater approximation to reality by sinking his individuality in the wider whole. It would probably be unfair to make Hegel responsible for all the conclusions that were drawn from his teaching: indeed his influence did not by any means always work in the same direction in all the circles in which it was felt. But there seems little doubt that in his own country it was taken as a justification of the authoritarian Prussian police state with its complete control over individuals and subordination of the individual will.

Another form of a similar tendency, though in this case rather an emotional attitude than a philosophical view, was found in the ideas of nationalism, which existed in germ long before but came most fully to self-consciousness in the nineteenth century and are still a living force. There the nation is definitely thought of, or perhaps rather felt about, as an individual being with a soul or spirit of its own, which must be kept alive at all costs. This means that the nation must be free from any control by members of another nation, that its separate national culture must be preserved and intensified, that its prestige and power must be secured, and that its interests must be asserted, if necessary at the expense of other nations. To the ardent nationalist these things are absolute goods, to which everything else must be subordinated, even, when necessary, the desires and the happiness of the individual members.

Some of the same tendencies, though in a more reasoned form, were to be found in the so-called Historical school of thought. The germs of this set of ideas are to be found in Montesquieu, they are developed, not very systematically, by Burke in this country, and reach their most complete development in the first half of the nineteenth century in the work of the Historical School of Jurisprudence, particularly associated with the same of Savigny, the German jurist. The essential characteristic of this school is the tendency to think of societies, particularly states or nations, as natural objects each with a life and growth of its own, which proceeds on its own lines and is not to be altered at will by the actions or ideas of individuals. This is the standpoint from which Burke denounces attempts at revolutionary upheavals as not only wicked but also futile. In the time of Savigny, a generation later, the point at issue between this school and the rationalism of the Utilitarians came out most clearly in controversies about the reform of the legal system in Germany and some other continental countries.

Thus, the tendency of the reformers influenced by Utilitarianism was to work out on rational principles a scheme for a complete code of laws with a view to the attainment of the end, irrespective of what was already there. In spite of differences in detail, such ideal codes would always tend to approximate to each other in every country, since they all aimed at the end set before us by our common human nature. The French code, in spite of possible imperfections in detail, was taken as a kind of model of what could be done in this direction. The historical school, on the other hand, regarded law as one expression of the general life of the nation, which developed gradually in its own way. Any changes or new developments should be guided by the study of the existing state of things and, particularly, of the way in which it had developed historically. For this would reveal the lines on which alone future developments could fruitfully proceed.

The historical school naturally tended to stress the differences between one country and another. Each had its own peculiar history and that determined its proper line of development. But another general movement of thought, in some respects similar, differed from it in this point. This was the movement, or group of movements, which in one form or another attempted to discover necessary scientific laws of the development of human societies, which would apply to all of them. Movements of this kind were largely stimulated by the biological discoveries of the nineteenth century, particularly the Darwinian theory of evolution. Human society, it was suggested, was an organism which should be subject to similar laws of growth to those of any other living organism. A good many of the arguments used were based on analogies and metaphors taken from biology, and, so far as this was so, the movement has not stood the test of time. But so far as it has tried to base its laws on actual study of human societies and not on analogies from biological organisms it is still capable of making an appeal to some minds. In any case, the general attitude both of this movement and the historical school is that it is futile to suppose that we can consciously construct, or reconstruct, society in the light of some ideal that happens to appeal to us. We have to discover the way in which societies must necessarily develop, whether we like it or not, and the only choice before us is whether we shall conform our own actions to this or whether we shall waste our efforts in a vain struggle against the necessary laws of social evolution.

It seems natural to suppose that any doctrine that declares that things must develop in a particular way, whatever we do, would not be a very effective stimulus or guide to political actions. And, in fact, most of these scientific and historical theories did in practice tend to discourage movements for reform and to favour a conservative attitude. But this was not always or necessarily the case. Historical experience has shown that some fatalistic doctrines may in certain circumstances provide a very powerful inspiration to action. This is particularly so if the results that a doctrine declares must inevitably ensue are also results which make a strong emotional appeal to the persons concerned. If people feel that in striving for an end towards which their emotions drive them they are also working with the inevitable laws of human development, they are likely to act with all the more vigour. This is the special appeal of the doctrines of Karl Marx, which in most countries became the philosophical basis of revolutionary Socialism. But with the doctrines of Marx we are already in the middle of contemporary controversies, and it is time for these historical preliminaries to come to an end.

Chapter IV

THE STATE AND SOVEREIGNTY

WE now approach the examination of the current political ideas and assumptions of our own time. It would be possible to start this from a number of different points. We could begin with an examination of one or more of our political ideals, such as liberty or equality, or we could begin with an examination of our ideas about what may be called, in the most general sense, political institutions. There is no absolute right or wrong choice in the matter. It will, however, probably turn out to be more convenient to begin with the latter. And of these institutions one which pervades all our thinking about politics is the State: indeed, in normal speech, we should hardly talk of any matter as political at all, unless in some way it concerned the State.

THE STATE

The word 'state' in anything like its present sense is comparatively modern, not more than three or four hundred years old. The word, or its equivalent in other languages such as *état* in French, existed earlier, but suggested something much nearer what we should now call 'status'. But the fact that the modern sense of the word did not then exist does not necessarily prove that the kind of thing which we now indicate by it did not exist either. It would be a matter of historical inquiry how far something indicated in an earlier age by another word, 'commonwealth' perhaps, was the same sort of thing as what we now call the state. But such an inquiry would not affect the present discussion.

It would be possible to examine a large number of instances

54

of the use of the word 'state' in current speech and writing, and we should undoubtedly find that in different contexts the word did not always seem to suggest quite the same idea. But it would soon become clear that these different suggestions of the word were all connected, and represented differences of emphasis on different aspects of the same thing rather than real differences of meaning. Some of these may come up for consideration later. But at this stage it would probably be better to start from a use of the word which everyone would recognise as natural and proper. When we speak of the world being divided up into a number of separate states or when we speak of the city-states of ancient Greece or of people belonging to or being members of this or that particular state we are thinking of the word as indicating, in the first place, a group or collection of people. Next, it is an organised group, not a casual crowd. And by that is meant, in general terms, that there is within it some person or body of persons who are regarded in some sense as speaking or acting for the whole and who make decisions which are recognised as binding on the whole. That, of course, is not a feature peculiar to the state. It is the general characteristic of any organised group, a church, a university, a trade union, a club, or any similar society. From this fact it arises quite understandably that this special person or body of persons is sometimes spoken of as the state, just as the governing body of a university is sometimes spoken of as the university. This may be convenient in certain contexts, but if it is emphasised it may lead us sometimes to speak and think of the state as something altogether distinct from the individuals in it. There is not necessarily any harm in this if we know clearly what we are doing, but, if we do not, it may and often does lead to serious confusions.

The genus of the state, then, is organised group. We have next to ask what are its differentia, the characteristics which distinguish it from other organised groups. Some people have laid stress on the point that the state is a compulsory or obligatory society, not a voluntary one which we can join or not as we choose. This is partially true and may be important in certain connections. It does not necessarily mean that there is no choice in the matter at all. A man can under certain circumstances decide to leave one state and join another, though this has not been possible at all periods of history and is more difficult now than it was a few generations ago. But he normally begins by being born into a state and is not called upon, as in the case of a voluntary society, to make the original choice whether to belong to one at all. Indeed, in all normal circumstances everybody must belong to some state. It is true that the troubles of the present age have produced a small class of unfortunate individuals known as 'stateless persons'. But that is universally recognised as an extraordinary and most undesirable phenomenon, and it is certainly not a condition freely chosen by the individuals themselves. On the other hand, the state is not the only society of this kind. The family, for instance, is also a group into which we are born without any choice on our part. It is true that in this country at the present time the element of organisation in the family is not very obvious. But in some social systems the family is a highly organised group, and the authority of the *paterfamilias* or the *conseil de famille* may be defined by law or custom. We have not yet, therefore, arrived at the essential distinguishing feature of the state.

This essential feature is to be looked for in the qualifications for membership of the group in question, and it needs only a moment's consideration to see that the primary qualification for membership of the state is territorial. Broadly speaking, the state is composed of the individuals habitually resident on a particular tract of land. There are minor exceptions to this, such as resident aliens not yet naturalised or citizens of the state living abroad. But these are all connected in one way or another with the primary territorial qualification. Further, it is part of the idea of a state that it should have, in some way or some sense, exclusive rights in its own tract of land. The decisions of the accepted ruling authority in the state are binding on all those living in its territory as long as they are there, even though they are not properly members of the state. It is a corollary of this, that, just as every individual, normally speaking, must be a member of some state, so every tract of land must be in the possession of some state. There may be rare cases in which there would be some difficulty in applying this, but that is the generally accepted rule.

So far it is pretty plain sailing, but there is a further point that is more debatable. It is often assumed, when speaking of the state, that as an organised group it has the first claim on the obedience of its members, as against any other group to which they belong, and that to be a state it must be independent of any control by any other body or authority outside it. But it is questionable whether we ought to include these points in a definition of the state. For, as we shall see later, those assumptions have been challenged by some people, who have none the less still continued to use the term 'state' as referring to the territorial organisation. They would certainly not admit that it is a contradiction in terms to say that on some points individuals ought to obey some other organisation to which they belong, their church for instance, rather than the state. Nor, though this is perhaps a little more dubious, should we cease to speak about, say, England or France as states if they agreed to accept, in certain matters, the authority of some larger body, such as the European Community or the United Nations, as overriding their own. There are certainly real problems here which are not merely questions of words. But for the time being we may postpone discussion of them, and return to the consideration of the state as a territorial society, the people living on a particular tract of land organised under a common governing body which has, if not a complete, at any rate a very special degree of authority over them.

We have been using phrases such as 'governing body' or 'supreme authority', but legal and political theorists have long developed the habit of referring to this governing body within the state as the 'sovereign'—a word which in this context has, of course, no special reference to a king or queen—and the authority or whatever it is that it has in relation to the members of the state as 'sovereignty'.

SOVEREIGNTY

It will be convenient, for reasons which I hope will appear as we go on, to start the examination of sovereignty with the so-called Austinian theory, named after John Austin, the nineteenth-century jurist and friend of Bentham and the Mills, though, properly speaking, it goes back at least to Hobbes and in some respects to the theories of the Roman lawyers. Many political theorists nowadays would tell us that the Austinian theory has been too much riddled by criticism to be worthy any longer of serious discussion. And there is some truth in that as far as pure theory goes. But the main features of Austin's doctrine have become so embedded in our everyday political assumptions that, even though we reject it in theory, we constantly find ourselves slipping back into it. It is still quite naturally assumed that it ought to be possible to find in any state one authority which is absolutely supreme and whose commands must always be obeyed, and that this authority must not be subject to control by any outside authority. The theory under discussion develops this assumption into an explicit view, and claims that it can be deduced from the very nature of things.

For a brief and clear statement of this view I propose to go, not back to Austin himself, but to a much later work, a text-book of political theory, which was at one time very popular and is, or was until very recently, still being read. This is the *Introduction to Political Science* by Stephen Leacock, better known, perhaps, for his humorous works, to which his writings on political theory provide a striking contrast. He states the case as follows:

'Somewhere within the state there will exist a certain per-

son or body of persons whose commands receive obedience.
. . . Unless there is such a body there is no state. The commands thus given are called laws. A law, then, is a command
issued by the state. Can there, then, be any limit, any legal
limit, to the sovereignty, or the legal supremacy of the state?
Obviously not, for such a limit would imply a contradiction
in terms.' As 'law' *means* simply a command of the sovereign
authority, obviously a legal limit, or limit imposed by law,
can only mean one imposed by the sovereign on itself. And if
the limit is imposed by the sovereign there is no way of preventing the sovereign removing it if it sees fit. 'The lawgiving power of the lawgiving body is therefore of necessity
unlimited.'

In a way this might seem like a tautology, in which the
conclusion follows merely because we have chosen to define
our terms in such a way that it necessarily must follow. But,
of course, in all such matters it is assumed that the definition
is not purely arbitrary, but that it applies to a distinguishable
class of objects which really exist and to which the name is
applied in ordinary speech. There really are states as so
defined. It seems as if an obvious instance could be found in
Great Britain. For there it has been a fundamental doctrine
of constitutional lawyers for the last two or three centuries
that the British Parliament is legislatively omnipotent. That
is to say that absolutely anything that it enacts in proper form
is a law and entitled to the respect due to a law, there is no
limit, short of physical impossibility, to what it can enact and
there is no other authority to which appeal can legally be
made against its enactments.

This seems clear enough for this country. But it looks more
complicated when we consider the case of states with a written
constitution, particularly federal states. For there the general
rule is that what is ordinarily regarded as the highest legislative authority, for instance Congress in the United States, is
far from omnipotent, its powers, however great, being strictly
defined and limited by the terms of the Constitution. Leacock,

as a professor in a Canadian university, writing largely for American and Canadian readers, was naturally interested in this, and he has his answer ready.

'If what has been said above is correct,' he writes, 'it follows, by definition, that the creation of a federal state annihilates the sovereignty of the component states—not limits or divides it, but annihilates it. *For sovereignty either is or is not.*[1] But in the new state sovereignty does not lie in the central government: it lies in the body, wherever and whatever it may be, which has the power to amend the constitution.' In the United States, for instance, the constitution can be amended by a vote of a two-thirds majority of Congress, ratified by three-quarters of the States. It is true that such a body is not in permanent session. 'But it is clear that theoretically at any rate it exists, and can be looked upon as having legal supremacy as complete as that of the British Parliament.'

This, then, is the legal theory of sovereignty. It is admitted that there are certain organised communities to which it would not apply, communities, for instance, in the early stages of social development, in which custom reigns supreme. The customs of such communities assign different degrees of authority to different sets of individuals, but their authority is strictly limited by custom. There is no person or persons recognised as having power to change or override the customs, no authority above the law. But, it is argued, such societies are, just for that reason, not properly called states, nor are their customs properly called laws, though they might often use that term themselves. There has been a tendency to think of such societies as representing the early stages of what would eventually develop into states in the modern sense.

The points raised in these last paragraphs will come up for

---

[1] My italics. This sentence is omitted in the later editions of the book. In order to get the most definite statement of the view I have quoted from the first edition. In the later editions the views expressed are substantially the same, but qualified in certain respects. I am, of course, concerned here not with tracing the development of Leacock's thought, but solely with finding a good statement of a particular theory.

consideration later. For the moment we must concern ourselves with a modification or addition that those who adopted this general theory felt obliged to make. Even in the case of bodies, such as the British Parliament, whose legal omnipotence seemed clear, it was obvious that in practice there would be fairly definite limits to what they could do. We could imagine all sorts of extravagant commands that they might perfectly legally issue which would have no chance at all of getting obeyed. It is irrelevant to argue that in practice they would not be at all likely to do that: the question of principle would remain. In fact, however, there have been occasional cases in which governments have passed laws which were never observed at all, though naturally they would do their utmost to avoid putting themselves in such a position. The suggestion was therefore made that we should make a distinction between legal sovereignty and political, or, as I should prefer to say, real or actual sovereignty. The latter is limited, the former unlimited. On occasions, they might not even lie in the same hands. For instance, laws might be passed by a legal sovereign, which was in fact under the control of an extra-legal power, such as a powerful military leader who took the actual decisions and forced them by fear of violence on the recognised law-making body. This may be an exceptional and undesirable state of things, which would be unlikely to be permanent. But there is no doubt that it could happen.

There seem, then, to be some grounds for this distinction. And it may be convenient to begin by postponing the examination of legal sovereignty and considering what constitutes political or actual sovereignty.

POLITICAL SOVEREIGNTY

Where and how does the sovereign or accepted government get its power and authority? The question has often been put in that form in the past, and is on occasions still so put. And we can still sometimes hear it further elucidated by asking whether sovereignty rests on or is conferred by consent or by force. This further question has often been put as if it were a real question. And it represents a stage in the process of clarifying our ideas on the subject when we come to realise that it is not a real question at all. For these two, consent and force, are not mutually exclusive alternatives between which we have to choose. They are, on the contrary, not alternatives at all.

The proposition that sovereignty rests on or is conferred by consent is, properly understood, a tautology. It follows necessarily from the definition of the sovereign as 'the person or body of persons whose commands receive obedience'. The sovereign is the person or body of persons which is obeyed, and its sovereignty consists in its being obeyed. There is nothing more in it than that, at any rate when we are speaking of the political or actual sovereign. But it is impossible to find any significant difference in meaning between obeying the sovereign and consenting to his or its rule. They are really two different sets of words for the same fact, at any rate if we take 'consent' in the normal sense which it bears in ordinary speech. Indeed, it is not strictly correct to speak of sovereignty as being *conferred* by consent, as if they were two distinct things one of which followed from the other. Sovereignty *is* consent, or, if that seems going too far, it is created or constituted by consent. At any rate, the central fact is that there is a person or body of persons in the habit of issuing orders expecting them to be obeyed and a body of people who habitually obey them. The latter is, perhaps, the more fundamental side of it, if it is legitimate to speak of one as more fundamental than the other. But they are really two inseparable sides of the one state of things which can be called sovereignty from the point of view of the ruling authority and consent from the point of view of the people. Sovereignty is, thus, a psychological fact, a state of mind of the members of a community.

To avoid possible misunderstanding, it may be as well to

point out that consent does not necessarily imply a particular act of consent taken at a particular time. I suppose something like that may occasionally be regarded as taking place when a person takes out naturalisation papers and makes a declaration to the effect that he will observe the obligations of a citizen in his new country. But what is normally meant is continued or habitual consent. Again, consent does not mean, either in this context or in ordinary speech, active approval. It means simply that we do in fact obey the orders directly applicable to us and that we refrain from resisting other actions of the governing authority. Why we do that is another question, and one which cannot be answered in simple terms. The motives from which we obey the law or the sovereign will probably vary indefinitely as between individuals, and may be very mixed in the same individual. But it is probably safe to say that the main influence on most people most of the time is simply habit. We obey because we have always or nearly always done so, and it never occurs to us not to do so. But we could probably also find at the back of the minds of a great many people a conviction, vague in some and more explicit in others, that on the whole this is a good habit to acquire, and that a society in which people obey the laws, even when they disagree with them, is more satisfactory than one in which they do not. And, of course, in particular cases this may be reinforced by active approval of a particular government or a particular measure. But there will still remain a certain number of cases in which the commands of the sovereign are obeyed mainly or solely from fear of punishment. And this implies that the sovereign has the power to inflict punishment if the law is broken. That is what we mean by enforcing the law.

It is important to emphasise this meaning of force, particularly when we talk of force as the basis of sovereignty. The point may seem trivial and obvious, but in fact it is often ignored and important consequences follow from it. When we talk of a government enforcing its orders or of people being forced to do this or that or of political power resting on force we do not, in the great majority of cases, mean this quite literally. Literally, I am forced to go out of a room if I am pushed out and I am forced to refrain from any action if I am physically restrained, shut up in prison, for instance. But in the great majority of cases force in that literal sense is not, and indeed could not, be applied. What we generally mean when we talk of force being used to secure obedience is that people are left physically free to act as they choose but that certain unpleasant consequences, that is punishment, are prepared for them if they act in one way rather than another.

This distinction emphasises further the absurdity of the question, Does sovereignty rest on force or consent? Translated into precise language that is equivalent to asking, Do we obey the sovereign because we are afraid of being punished or because we obey? And that is obviously not a genuine question because the two are not alternatives at all. Consent is not a motive or a reason for obeying: it is just the fact of obedience. Force, on the other hand, provides one possible motive, among others, for consent, that is for obeying. It is certainly a very real question what part force, that is the ability to inflict punishment, plays in securing obedience, but it is not a question which can be answered in simple terms applicable to all societies. We should probably be safe in saying that it would rarely, if ever, be true to say that sovereignty rested on force, if by that were meant on force alone. For that would mean that no one ever obeyed the sovereign except from fear of punishment, which is certainly not the case in our own experience and indeed, as far as one could see, could not be the case. On the other hand, if we meant that the ability to apply force was one of the essential conditions for getting habitually obeyed, that is for being sovereign, there would be much more to be said for it. Even if we cannot lay down absolute and universal rules about this, it is possible to make some general suggestions about what force could and could not do.

FORCE AND SOVEREIGNTY

On the one side, we can see that there must be, in the nature of things, limitations to the power of force.

As we have seen, the use of force, in most cases, means producing unpleasant consequences for people who do not obey. And if they are prepared to face the most unpleasant consequences rather than do certain things, the ruler cannot get them done. Further than this there is a limit to the practical possibility of producing these unpleasant consequences. To take the extreme case, a single ruler, even if normally fully recognised as sovereign, could not imprison all his subjects if they unanimously refused to obey him. And obviously, in practice there will come a point a great deal short of that when the number of potential recalcitrants will be too great for force to be effectively applied to them. We can, perhaps, again go further and say that, if the proportion of the population who obey the law only through fear of force gets too big for force to be applied to it the law will cease to be obeyed, as soon as people become aware of the situation.

Again, we must remember what applying force involves and what sort of machinery is required. In most societies, particularly of the kind with which we are familiar, the sovereign, such as a monarch or a parliament, can do little or nothing in the way of applying force for itself. It needs a body of individuals, for instance the police or the armed forces, who will do the actual work for it. Such a body must be prepared to act in obedience to the sovereign. But, as most of the power of applying force is concentrated in its hands, it can hardly be supposed to act itself merely from fear of force. There is a well-known quotation from Hume, who argues that power necessarily, at some point, rests on 'opinion'. 'The soldan of Egypt or the emperor of Rome might drive his harmless subjects, like brute beasts, against their sentiments and inclinations. But he must, at least, have led his mamelukes or praetorian bands, like men, by their opinions.' Of course,

Hume in this passage talks much too much as if the obedience of the armed forces were entirely a matter of reasoned conviction, instead of depending as it does so largely on training and habit. But, allowing for this, the point is a real one. We might, however, in the light of what has been said previously, feel doubtful whether 'the mamelukes or praetorian bands' could permanently succeed in driving the whole of the rest of the population 'against their sentiments and inclinations'. But at any rate the general point is clear that, even for the successful application of force, other motives besides the fear of force must be present somewhere.

We can emphasise this from another point of view by considering the possibility that in some circumstances obedience might be secured where there could be no question of the application of force at all. There is a vivid description by Robert Louis Stevenson, which is said to be in substance historically accurate, of the life of a Highland chief in hiding after the '45 rebellion. 'Though he was thus sequestered and . . . stripped by the late Act of Parliament of legal powers, he still exercised a patriarchal justice in his clan. Disputes were brought to him in his hiding hole to be decided; and the men of his country, who would have snapped their fingers at the Court of Session, laid aside revenge and paid down money at the bare word of this forfeited and hunted outlaw.' Doubtless other instances of the same sort of thing could be found, but this will be enough to illustrate the point.

On the other side it would be a great mistake to underestimate the importance of force. In all normal conditions it is essential to sovereignty that there should be available a body of people able and willing to apply force at the command of the sovereign. In modern times the control over the armed forces has become generally accepted as one of the essential marks of sovereign power. And there are obvious reasons for that.

For one thing, there will always be a certain number of people, varying in different countries at different times, who obey the law only from fear of punishment. A few, of course, will not be induced to keep the law even by this fear: every state has its proportion of habitual criminals. But as long as this is kept within narrow limits it does not seriously affect the normal working of the state, and it is reasonably certain that the ability to inflict punishment is an important influence on keeping it within these limits and preventing a number of potential criminals becoming actual criminals. Further, the possibility of the application of force may make a difference even to those who in the main obey the law from other motives. Thus, a man who obeys mainly from force of habit, if he sees other people breaking the law with impunity, may eventually begin to wonder why he should continue to follow this habit, if there is anything to be gained by not doing so. Or a man may have a reasoned conviction that a law-abiding society is desirable, and prefer to keep the law as long as other people do. But there may come a point when he will feel that if other people successfully defy the law, he might as well, as a choice of evils, begin to do so himself whenever it is to his advantage. In these, and other ways, the habit of disobedience is infectious and, if unchecked by force, is likely to spread. All this may seem so elementary and obvious that it is hardly worth saying. Probably few people would deny it as it is here stated, though there are enthusiasts who seem to question whether punishment has any effect in preventing wrong-doing at all. But there is always a danger that those who deny that force is the main basis of sovereignty may fall into a way of talking as if the influence of force were wholly negligible.

Finally we have to remember the destructive power of force. It may be true that a stable rule could not be established on a basis of force alone without a good deal of support from other motives. But a relatively small body of people, who were prepared to use force, could paralyse the work of a government, even of one which enjoyed a wide measure of support, unless there were forces available to defend it. It would be no use for a government to rely on the willing consent of the great majority, if a small body of armed fanatics were willing to go to any lengths to overthrow it. So even a government whose rule is freely accepted by the great mass of the population must have force at its disposal to prevent other hostile forces, internal or external, from making the conduct of government impossible. Similar considerations apply to the armed forces themselves, when they exist as a recognised and organised body distinct from the rest of the population. They can, if they choose to act, make the exercise of authority by any government impossible. But they could hardly establish an effective government without a good measure of support from outside their ranks. 'You can do anything with bayonets except sit on them', as someone once observed. The general upshot, however, is clear. It is one essential condition, among others, of effective sovereignty, that there should be some body capable of applying force and that this body should be ready to obey the commands of the sovereign.

I do not know if it is necessary to warn readers against supposing that, because the armed forces can, in some sense and to some degree, make and unmake governments, they in some sense constitute the real sovereign. They could only be said to do that in any sense if they actually came to decisions and issued commands as a body. This may happen in some countries at some times, but is not very frequent. Normally, of course, they themselves are acting in obedience to orders. Similar considerations would apply to another possible fallacy. I have seen arguments in writings on political theory to the effect that, if the people confer sovereignty by obeying, they must in some sense be themselves the 'real' or 'ultimate' sovereign. This is a fallacy that arises from the habit of thinking in terms of purely legal conceptions which do not apply here. It involves thinking, as the Roman lawyers did, of sovereignty as a piece of property, and arguing that because the people confer it on the sovereign it must have originally belonged to them. But if we think in terms of what actually happens we can see that sovereignty consists merely in getting obeyed, and does not exist at all till the habit of obedience begins. It would be absurd to talk as if the people who do the obeying were 'really' or 'ultimately' issuing the orders themselves. It would only make sense to talk of the people as being sovereign as they actually, as a body, took decisions and issued commands, which happened in the ancient Greek democracies but very rarely anywhere else.

This then, in simple, schematic form is the picture of the situation with regard to real or political sovereignty. It ignores the complications in detail which arise in the actual working-out of this. Some of these will come up for consideration later. But the question immediately before us concerns the nature of legal sovereignty, and the value of the distinction between that and political sovereignty. And it is to that that we must turn next.

NOTE: *Laws and Commands*. The expert in verbal niceties will doubtless notice that I have spoken indiscriminately of 'laws' or 'commands' as issuing from the sovereign. I have not distinguished them because they are both names of things which are obeyed, or disobeyed, by the people to whom they apply, and it was that aspect with which I was chiefly concerned. But I am aware that the way of speaking may be challenged from more than one quarter.

Mr Weldon, for instance, in his book, *The Vocabulary of Politics*, denies that laws are commands at all. The reasons he gives for this denial, so far as he gives any, are hard to follow and I do not see how it can be maintained. It would be interesting to know at what point Mr Weldon would draw the line between a command and a law. If a schoolmaster told a pupil to bring his notebook into the next lecture that would obviously be a command. If he told all the pupils in the class to do so it would still be a command. But if he told them always to do it to every lecture he would be laying down a rule, which is a rudimentary form of law. I think, however, it would still be quite natural to speak of it as a command.

Possibly, the difference is supposed to come in when the rule is laid down for all succeeding generations of pupils, on the ground that a command must be addressed to specific individuals. But I do not think that is a really significant difference. For one thing, it would seem to have the curious consequence that a law or a rule was a command when it was first promulgated but ceased to be so afterwards. In any case, as each successive generation became aware of the rule it would come to them as a command, as something emanating from some authority which they had to obey. They might not naturally speak of it as a command, because 'command' is not, as a matter of fact, a word that we very frequently use. But they could certainly quite naturally speak of it as an order, a word which is frequently used of standing regulations, and we should be getting into impossible subtleties if we started to distinguish between a command and an order. It is, however, difficult to pursue the matter further, as I am far from clear what Mr Weldon's reasons for this view are.

On the other hand, Leacock speaks as if all commands of the sovereign were laws, and this also seems an exaggerated view. It is true that in most modern states the legislative authority is regarded as supreme and that it normally issues its orders in terms of general rules or laws. There may be very good reasons why that should be adopted as the regular practice. Rousseau, it will be remembered, claimed that the sovereign could legitimately legislate only in general terms and that it lost its claim to authority if it dealt with individual cases. But there is no reason in the nature of things why this restriction should operate. There is nothing in the least impossible about the accepted sovereign authority issuing some of its decisions in the form of general rules or laws and others as instructions in particular cases, and both being equally accepted by the people. One could, perhaps, imagine a small community with a single ruler where hardly anything in the nature of legislation was attempted, but where the ruler's orders in particular cases were implicitly obeyed.

But, short of that, there have been actual cases where the sovereign body, which was normally occupied in the making of general laws, has made decisions in particular cases which were accepted as having just the same authority. Acts of Attainder and Acts of Indemnity for individuals have been passed by our own Parliament. Up to 1857 the only way to get a divorce was by a private Act of Parliament for each particular case, and there are still occasional private acts dealing with particular individuals. These can hardly be called laws in the usually accepted sense but they have just the same authority. The conclusion is that the terms 'commands' or 'orders' are proper general terms for the decisions of the sovereign body, that they include laws in the strict sense as their chief element, but that they are not exclusively confined to that.

Chapter V

THE LAW AND LEGAL SOVEREIGNTY

I T is now time to return to the earlier distinction between political and legal sovereignty and to examine afresh what value, if any, it has. We have seen that political sovereignty is conferred, or rather constituted, by consent, the readiness of people to obey. If, then, the distinction has any significance, it would seem that we ought to be able to find something else that confers or constitutes legal sovereignty. For if the two do not differ in this respect, it is hard to see where we could look for any point of importance in which they do differ. What is it, then, that makes the legal sovereign sovereign?

We cannot, of course, say that it is the law, though that is the answer that the actual words used would naturally suggest. No doubt, it would have been a perfectly good answer at some periods, for instance in the Middle Ages. But in a state of society in which the sovereign is regarded as being the supreme maker of laws and the law as being whatever the sovereign lays down, it would obviously be absurd to say that the sovereign gets its authority to make laws from laws which it itself has made. Yet what else can be meant by talking about the legal sovereign? It looks as if we might be getting into a circle, and saying both that the law makes the sovereign and the sovereign makes the law.

As a matter of fact the antithesis contained in the last sentence can be put into the form of a perfectly intelligible question, at any rate if, for a moment, we drop the term 'sovereign' and make use of some more non-committal phrase such as 'ruler' or 'governing authority'. It is quite reasonable to ask whether the ruler makes the law or the law makes the ruler.

and the answer will vary according to the particular society of which the question is asked. In one society the general habit of mind among the people will be to think of their obedience as being owing primarily to a person or body of persons and secondarily to the laws, which they respect because they are made by this person or body of persons. In another, the ultimate loyalty will be to a set of rules and the authority of any body of people will be respected because it is given to them by this set of rules. The set of rules, however, need not necessarily be thought of, as it is in early societies, as the whole body of customary law. It may be some sort of fundamental law or instrument of government, which gives authority to various persons or bodies to make laws within the limits of the fundamental law. In that sense, this is by no means necessarily the mark of an early stage of society. At the present time, for instance, an example of it might be found in the Constitution of the United States, which has been described, without much straining of words, as the real sovereign of the country. It would certainly involve a much greater straining of words to describe, as Leacock did, the elaborate combination of authorities which can amend the constitution as being the real sovereign, for it could not, in practice, possibly function as such. When it does act, it would be much nearer the facts to think of its action as a sign or recognition that the people as a whole are prepared to recognise a modification of the fundamental rules.

This, however, is a digression, and our real concern here is with states, such as our own country, in which a person or body of persons is thought of as the supreme object of obedience. It is here that the difficulties in the notion of legal sovereignty arise. What, if anything, can be meant, for instance, by saying that the sovereignty of Parliament is legally unlimited but practically limited by what the people will, in fact, obey? There is clearly something more here than merely a question of verbal definition. And what I think is at the back of people's minds in speaking of the sovereignty as legally unlimited is that its limitations cannot be expressed in terms of law or general rules. We cannot define beforehand in clear-cut general terms the precise circumstances in which the people would refuse obedience to a particular law. If we could, we should be well on the way to establishing a constitution limiting the powers of the sovereign. But as it is, as long as we are speaking in terms of law, we say that there are no legal limits, meaning by that no limits which can be formulated in legal terms. Legal sovereignty, therefore, is not a different sort of sovereignty. It is rather an abstraction from the actual sovereignty constituted by habitual obedience, which is the concrete fact.

An illustration of this can be found in the extreme case when a sovereign is overthrown, with a greater or lesser degree of violence, and another one is established in its place. This is a process which cannot be described in legal terms, except negatively as illegal. It represents a forcible break in the continuity of our settled habits of obedience. But after the break we sooner or later develop afresh the habit of obedience to a different authority, and its commands in their turn become recognised as laws. The intermediate process cannot be described in terms of law, but its result, after a decent interval, is accepted and the new sovereign is recognised as the legal sovereign and the source of law. The lawyers, so to speak, close their eyes to the brief intervening period and open them again when the habits of obedience have been re-established. They certainly do not attempt to say that no ruling authority set up by the illegal use of force can ever be regarded as the legal sovereign, or that no real law has been made in any country since its first revolution. If they did, it would mean that there were at the present time very few, if any, valid laws in any country in the world, as nearly every existing sovereign body has been established by a revolutionary process at some stage in the history of the country over which it rules.

The result of all this is, once more, that legal sovereignty is not a separate thing which can be conferred or constituted in a different way from other kinds of sovereignty. Sovereignty in any sense is constituted by consent, the development of the habit of obedience, and by that alone. But we begin to talk about legal sovereignty only when this habit has been definitely established. So legal sovereignty is not really 'conferred' or even 'constituted' at all. It is a way of speaking which comes into use only when the 'conferring' or 'constituting' has already been done and there is no longer any occasion to raise questions about it.

A further problem arises when we consider the possible case of a law being passed by the legal sovereign or the recognised legislative authority and then being disregarded by the people universally or so widely that it ceases to be of any effect. The lawyer could only say that it was a law, just as much as any other law, and remained so till it was formally repealed. But that is not altogether satisfactory if we are trying to think in terms of actual human behaviour. For in our ordinary idea of a law, we think of it, not merely as a form of words written down somewhere, but as something which will be to some extent observed, and if necessary enforced. That is to say, we are interested in it as a possible influence on human conduct, and from that point of view a law that was never observed and never enforced would be for all practical purposes the same as if it had never been passed or, having been passed, had been subsequently repealed.

It would be difficult to find in the experience of this country an instance of a law that was duly enacted in proper form, but never observed or enforced. But something very like that situation can be found at certain times in certain places. Writing a number of years ago, James Bryce described how in some of the western states of America at that time there was a continuous flow of social reform legislation which in practice might never be put into force at all. 'Such acts often fail to be enforced, sometimes because it is the business of nobody in particular, sometimes because they are practically unenforceable, so that, as an American philosopher has observed, "Western statute books are a record rather of aspiration than of achievement".'[1] In our own country we are more familiar with laws which have meant something at one time but have long fallen into desuetude. From time to time the legislature reviews such laws and repeals a number of them, and anyone who reads the list of ancient statutes repealed will stand amazed at the number of offences that he might have been committing up till then. The lawyer, *qua* lawyer, cannot admit that a law can cease to be of any force by becoming obsolete. But if an attempt were ever made to revive and enforce such a law he would probably manage to find a way round it. Thus there was up to 1926 an unrepealed law forbidding the entry of Jesuits into this country. But when, some fifty years ago, a private individual attempted to put into force this law his application was refused, first by the magistrate and then by a High Court judge, on the ground that action in such a matter should properly be initiated by the government. And, of course, no government would in fact ever take such a step. This was in effect a recognition that this statute, though it might still be called a law, could not be put in force, and was therefore a different sort of thing from the actually operative laws which we are normally thinking of when we use the term.

All this suggests that law is made by consent just as much as sovereignty, and that there is little value in the distinction between legal and political sovereignty, except in the very limited sense explained above. There remains for consideration the possible case mentioned earlier of a person or body of persons recognised as the supreme source of law but in fact acting under the control of some other authority. Such a situation has occurred from time to time in history. We may recall Gibbon's description of the early Roman emperors, who 'concealed their irresistible strength and humbly professed themselves the accountable ministers of the Senate,

[1] James Bryce, *Modern Democracies*, vol. II, p. 85.

whose supreme decrees they dictated and obeyed'. Here it might seem there would be a distinction to be made between the legal and the real sovereign. But it is not, in practice, very important. What it means is that the people are in the habit of obeying the real sovereign, the emperor, for instance, but expect him to go through the form of passing his decrees through another body, such as the Senate. In this extreme form, such a state of things is not likely to be permanent: in Rome it eventually gave place to the doctrine of the legislative omnipotence of the emperor described in an earlier chapter. Alternatively it may survive as a mere formality, a piece of ceremonial, like the Royal Assent to Acts of Parliament in this country.

On the other hand, we must remember that the sovereign authority, be it an absolute monarch, an absolute parliament, a general assembly or anything else, is practically always affected by a variety of influences, besides its own unaided deliberations, in arriving at the decisions which are accepted as binding on the people. If, for instance, we consider any piece of legislation passing through our own Parliament and ask who in fact was responsible for the Bill with all its clauses taking just this form rather than that, we shall probably find a complicated tangle of influences at work, which all contributed something to the final decision. It would be absurd to talk as if Parliament legislated in a vacuum, entirely cut off from all possible influences from outside. Some of these may be undesirable: the term 'pressure groups' has been coined to indicate the kind of influences of which the particular speaker disapproves. But a great many are quite unobjectionable and indeed inevitable. At any rate, we might well think, if we considered the matter purely from the side of taking decisions and issuing orders, that it was very difficult to decide who the real sovereign was.

On the other hand, when we look at it from the side of consent or obedience, it is much simpler, which is a good reason for beginning at this end. We may find it very difficult to disentangle all the influences which have contributed to produce a piece of legislation. But we know quite well at what stage we begin to feel that our obedience to it is called for. And that is when all the influences have converged on the focal point of actual passage through Parliament. Then, and not till then, does our consent or habit of obedience come into action. So, whatever forces may affect the decisions of Parliament, it remains perfectly reasonable and intelligible to say that Parliament is the real sovereign in this country.

We may conclude, then, that there is not at bottom any significant distinction between different sorts of sovereignty. If we talk about it intelligibly at all we have to concentrate on the central fact that the sovereign is constituted by being obeyed, and by nothing else. Perhaps this seems a trivial and obvious proposition, but it is of great importance to keep a firm grasp on it. It is said not infrequently that the fundamental fact in politics is power. Indeed, a whole book on political theory was written a number of years ago working out the consequences of this assumption. But in reality the assumption is incorrect. Power, important as it is, is a derivative fact. The fundamental fact in politics, so far as one can talk of such a thing, is obedience, and it is from that that power comes. The primary question to ask about any political situation is not Who can crush whom? but Who will obey whom? In ordinary peaceful conditions in a country such as ours the answer is normally so obvious that we do not realise the fundamental importance of the question. But in times of crisis or of revolutionary change or disturbance we can see that this is the key to what happens or is going to happen.

In the light of these considerations, the old controversies that have come down to us from past centuries, about whether sovereignty is limited or unlimited, divisible or indivisible, take on a much simpler form. 'Is sovereignty limited or unlimited?' means in practice 'Will the people obey absolutely anything that the sovereign orders?' There have been occasionally in the course of history some extraordinary cases of apparently unlimited readiness to obey. But in the great majority of communities with which we are acquainted there are and always have been very definite limits. If we tried to make it a matter of verbal definition and say that we would call it sovereignty only if it was absolutely unlimited, we should have to say that there were few, if any, actual cases of sovereignty to be found, except perhaps in the medieval sect of the Assassins and in Paraguay under the tyranny of Francisco Lopez.

Similarly, the question whether sovereignty is divisible or indivisible is reducible to the question whether people can possibly develop the habit of distributing their obedience, of obeying one authority in some matters and another in others. And experience amply proves that that can be done, and has been done at various periods. It may be inconvenient or undesirable in certain ways, but there is nothing impossible about it. Of course, it is open for anyone to say that he will not call it sovereignty unless it is undivided. But as far as the essential fact of obedience goes, there is no reason for thus limiting the use of the term. And those in the past who have argued for the necessary indivisibility of sovereignty have claimed to be doing much more than recommending a particular use of words. When Hobbes, for instance, writes, 'There is a sixth doctrine plainly and directly against the essence of a Commonwealth; and it is this, *That the Sovereign Power may be divided.* For what is it to divide the power of a Commonwealth but to dissolve it?', he is certainly not merely offering a definition. He is claiming to give a necessary law of what will in fact happen. And, taken as a necessary law, the proposition is plainly false, though if it were put forward as a statement of a possible, though not inevitable, tendency that would be likely to show itself under certain conditions, there would be much more to be said for it. But a great deal of Hobbes' argument really comes down to the claim that we must either obey in everything or we shall not obey at all. And this is clearly absurd.

The general conclusion is that much less can be deduced from the general nature of sovereignty than has in the past been supposed. We cannot tell from the fact of obedience who is going to be obeyed, how far they will be obeyed, or who ought to be obeyed. The first two questions are matters of fact which would have to be answered by a consideration of the circumstances of each particular case. The last is a question of the policy that we are going to pursue, and the one thing that we can say with reasonable certainty is that it is important that it should be answered. That is to say, for a state, or any organised society, to function at all it is necessary for the people in it to make up their minds whom they are going to obey and to turn this decision into a habit which is broken only with difficulty and in exceptional conditions.

SOVEREIGNTY AND INTERNATIONAL RELATIONS

The foregoing analysis has been concerned primarily with the position of the sovereign within the state in relation to its other members. But it can also have some application to questions of the relations of the sovereign within a state to powers outside it, particularly the sovereigns of other states. On the strict Austinian theory the absolute supremacy of the sovereign within the state had as a corollary its complete independence of any outside power. It followed from this that everyone is either sovereign or subject: there is no half-way house. 'Sovereignty either is or is not', as Leacock put it.

But already before the end of the nineteenth century situations were arising in which the sharp disjunction between absolute sovereignty and absolute subjection hardly seemed to apply, and it was found necessary to coin phrases indicating some sort of intermediate relation. Terms like 'protectorate', 'suzerainty', 'sphere of influence', and the like came into use. After the First World War, the League of Nations was established, and certain countries received 'mandates' from the League for the administration of territories ceded by Germany. Constitutional lawyers trained to think in Austinian terminology sometimes found it difficult to handle these new ideas. At the time of the Versailles Congress Robert Lansing, the American Secretary of State, issued a memorandum critical of the idea of mandates which is full of interest. 'Where does the sovereignty over these territories reside?' he asked, and went on to say, 'Sovereignty is inherent in the very conception of government. It cannot be destroyed, though it may be absorbed by another sovereignty either by compulsion or cession.' He then asked to whom the sovereignty over the colonial possessions renounced by Germany would pass. 'If the reply is, The League of Nations, the question is, Does the League possess the attributes of an independent state so that it can function as an owner of territory? If so what is it? A world state?', and so on.[1] It is doubtless true that, on the whole, the mandate system has tended to become less and less of a reality. That, indeed, was the intention in some cases, as communities under a mandate developed into independent states. But this was a matter of practical convenience, and did nothing to prove that there was anything impossible or self-contradictory about the idea, which in some cases for some time worked quite effectively.

In any case, none of these ideas forms any theoretical difficulty if the previous analysis of the notion of sovereignty is correct. The phrases which have been quoted above—'protectorate', 'mandate', and the like—simply represent rough attempts to classify the different degrees of obedience which can be expected by different authorities in the various particular cases. As there are infinite grades of this, there will always be the possibility of dispute about where the line is to be drawn in particular cases. Before the South African War, for instance, there was a great deal of debate over the question of what precisely was implied by the relation of 'suzerainty' in which Great Britain stood or claimed to stand to the Transvaal Republic. But there is no theoretical diffi-

[1] R. Lansing, *The Peace Negotiations: a Personal Narrative*, pp. 151, 152.

culty, as long as we recognise that obedience is a thing of which there can be more or less, and that it can be distributed in varying degrees between different authorities. As we know, in certain periods of history this has been taken for granted as the natural order of things.

In modern times, particularly when national feeling is strong, there tends to be an intense emotional reaction against such ideas. This expresses itself in a demand for absolute sovereign independence for the nation or group concerned, and a feeling that the slightest restriction on this means absolute subjection to an outside power. There is an emotional rather than a rational acceptance of the Austinian idea that sovereignty either is or is not, and that there is no intermediate stage possible between absolute sovereign and absolute subject. But this is clearly not true, and in fact all sorts of intermediate stages are possible. We might even go further and ask whether the absolute independence spoken of is not a limiting case which rarely occurs in practice.

Absolute independence would presumably mean that the government of a state could guide its policy with no thought except for its own views, interests, and desires. In fact, however, most, if not all, states find at some point that their policy, sometimes even their internal policy, will affect other states. And when this happens they are bound to consider and be influenced by the possible reactions of these other states. Of course, there are great variations in the extent to which states have to be prepared to give up doing what they would otherwise choose to do because of the fear of the unpleasant consequences, in the form of economic or possibly even military reactions on the part of other states. But there are few states in a position to disregard these altogether, and often they have to regulate their policy a good deal by these considerations, particularly when it is a question of a small state in relation to a large and powerful neighbour. Indeed, one could quite well imagine the case of two states, one called independent and the other called a protectorate or something similar, where in fact the former was considerably more under the control of another power than the latter.

It is, perhaps, as well to make it clear that the fact that independence is a matter of degree must not be taken as implying that differences of degree are unimportant. On the contrary, as there will be occasion to insist in many subsequent connections, a difference of degree may be of supreme importance. The phrase, 'It's *only* a difference of degree' is nearly always a sign of political illiteracy. None the less, it is important to bear in mind that the passage from one state of things to another is a continuous process with infinite gradations, not a sudden leap across a clearly defined boundary.

All these considerations throw some light on the possibility of establishing some kind of super-national body, a United Nations Organisation or a European Community, which on some points would be accepted as capable of exercising authority superior to that of the particular states. We certainly could not argue that it would be *a priori* impossible, that such an authority would either have to annihilate completely the sovereignty hitherto exercised by individual states or else would have no real power at all. It would in fact have power just in so far as people got into the habit of obeying it. The governments of the particular states would in the long run take their tone from the people. If enough people, from any motive, got a firm hold of the idea that on certain matters they would obey the super-national authority rather than their particular state then the government of the state would follow suit. But if the great mass of the people still retained the habit of thinking of their state government as the primary object of their obedience the super-national authority could not be effective. The governments might agree to limit their sovereignty, but unless or until their people began to transfer their habit of obedience, in some degree, to the new authority, the state governments would still remain the real power and the limitations on their sovereignty would be likely to be disregarded whenever it was convenient.

In the meantime, there remains one form of super-national authority in the shape of international law. It used to be argued by adherents of the Austinian theory that international law was not true law at all because it was not laid down by a sovereign body, and because there was no specific body of persons charged with its enforcement. It would no longer be true to argue, as used to be argued, that there was no authorised judicial body to interpret it, as we have the International Court of Justice at The Hague. As for the other points, it only needs to be said that international law is a body of customary rules, like medieval law, which is law just in so far as it is recognised as such. The fact that there is no defined body of people to enforce it does not mean that it is not enforced. It is enforced by other states, by international opinion, by reprisals, and, in the last resort, by war. No doubt this is very uncertain and irregular, there is a good deal of private enterprise about it, it is particularly difficult to enforce against very powerful states and so on. But that is not so very different from the position of the law of the land in certain states at certain periods, in England in the fifteenth century or in some of the western states of America in the early pioneering days. Indeed there are countries at the present time in which law enforcement is weak and uncertain. If law is made by being recognised as such, the habit of recognition may take some time to grow to its full stature. But it is proper to speak of law even while it is, to some degree, still in the making.

Chapter VI

FORMS OF GOVERNMENT—DEMOCRACY

FROM the consideration of the general conditions for the establishment of a sovereign power or ruling authority it is a natural transition to the consideration of the sovereign body itself and the forms that it can take. The different forms of government have been classified at various times in various different ways, some of which may be convenient in some contexts and others in others. In view of our own interests at the present time, it does not, perhaps, need any apology for starting with the consideration of the form of government known as Democracy and of other forms of government regarded as rivals or alternatives to this.

In quite recent years considerable controversy has arisen about the proper use of the word 'democracy', and it has been applied to different forms of government which have little or nothing in common with each other. So much confusion has been engendered by these controversies that some people in despair have felt inclined to declare that the word is rapidly ceasing to have any precise meaning, and it has even been suggested that its use had better be abandoned altogether. But there is no reason to adopt such an extremely defeatist attitude. It ought to be possible to arrive at a reasonably clear notion of how we are going to use the term, without committing ourselves to dogmatic assertions about the 'right use' or the 'real meaning' of democracy. At least we can try to lay down conditions for the most convenient use, meaning by that the use which will be most successful in conveying a clear meaning from one person to another and in minimising possible confusions and misunderstandings.

One obvious condition is that the use should be as uniform as possible. No doubt, there will always be the possibility of differences of opinion in detail, particularly at the margins of the extension of the term. But there can be no possible advantage in using the same term to indicate entirely different forms of government. Another desirable condition is that the use should be as stable as possible. That does not mean that it cannot be modified in course of time, extended, perhaps, in some directions and retracted in others. But any changes in the meaning or use of the term should have a recognisable continuity with the previous usage. There is nothing to be said for making deliberately a sharp change in the use of any term. As a matter of fact, the use of the term 'democracy' has shown a continuous development, always retaining a recognisable core of identity, from the ancient Greeks, who first invented it, down to the thinkers and writers of the nineteenth century, and their successors of the present day. It is this traditional use of the term which I propose to examine.

As we are here concerned with forms of government no excuse is needed for considering democracy in the first place as one of these forms. That is, indeed, the primary and central meaning which it has always borne. Of course, in popular speech it has often been given various extensions beyond this. In the late war, a young soldier who could not get the kind of cigarettes he wanted in a shop was heard to complain, 'I thought this was a war for democracy'. And more sophisticated forms of the same tendency have been observed. Serious thinkers, also, have sometimes been inclined to extend the use of the term, and to suggest that we should include under it certain states or attitudes of mind which were or ought to be associated with the form of government, or certain social conditions which were regarded as necessary for the form of government to work successfully. There is obviously something in this, and more will have to be said on the point later. But these suggested extensions are all associated with or consequent on the central meaning. And it is with this that we have to begin.

It is often convenient in dealing with matters of this kind to begin with some crude and simple distinction, and to come on to the necessary refinements and modifications afterwards. And we may take as a basis the simple and familiar distinctions between different forms of government made by the ancient Greeks, who first invented the terms that we still use and first initiated discussions about their meaning.

To the ordinary Greek it seemed clear that there were three main types of government. There was autocracy or monarchy, government by a single ruler, who might or might not be called a king. There was oligarchy, government by a few specified people, which might sometimes be called aristocracy, if it was intended to claim that the few were also the best. And, finally, there was democracy, government by the whole people or the great majority of them. Serious thinkers, such as Plato, Aristotle, or Polybius, did not rest content with this simple classification, and attempted to introduce various refinements, to add intermediate forms and to make sub-divisions based on some other principle than the mere question of numbers. But they started from the threefold classification and did not question its validity as far as it went. It has descended to our own time, and the words in which it is expressed have become part of our ordinary language. An examination of their possible meanings and applications would, then, form a convenient starting-point.

What meaning can we attach to 'government by the people' or by a selected few or a single ruler? And the first question to ask is what we mean by 'government'. The simplest and most comprehensive formula would seem to be that government consists in taking a series of decisions which are accepted as binding on the community. These decisions, it may be noted in passing, may be taken at many different levels of generality. To take an instance from our own time, there may be a general decision to extend the social services. Following on that, there may be a more particular decision to establish a comprehensive Health Service. As part of that, it may be decided that hospitals shall be divided into teaching and non-teaching hospitals. And finally there may be a decision that a particular hospital shall be ranked as a teaching hospital or the reverse. But all these decisions are part of the work of government, in the general sense in which it is used here. This illustration is, of course, put in terms of a modern state such as our own. But the essential features of it could be exemplified from any state at any time, and it helps to show the complications that arise in trying to give a precise meaning to the notion of government.

If, then, government means taking decisions, it would appear that differences between different forms of government would resolve themselves into differences in the people who take the decisions. From that point of view, then, what are we to say about the old distinction, from which we started, between government by the one, by the few, and by the many? If we consider all the complications involved in this matter of taking decisions we shall see that it would be extremely difficult to imagine a state in which *all* the decisions were taken either by a single autocrat or by the whole body of citizens. It might be more possible to picture a state in which they were all taken by the same restricted group, but if we try to do this we shall probably see that it would be a highly unusual set of conditions to make such a state possible. All this applies even when it is a question of the definite persons or bodies which actually take the final decisions. But if we extend our inquiry to consider all the people who might have some influence or share in giving the decision the form that it finally takes, it becomes more obvious still. And we can conclude that in no normal state are the decisions which make up the work of government ever exclusively the work of either a single autocrat, or of the whole body of people or of a selected few. On the other hand, if we carry our examination further we may find reason to believe that in most, if not all states the decisions taken are to some degree the work of all three of these elements or influences. In terms of the simple Greek definition every state is a mixture, in varying degrees, of monarchy, oligarchy, and democracy.

The necessity for an element of oligarchy is the most obvious. It is clear that a despotic ruler, however absolute his powers were by law or custom, could not possibly attend to all the matters of government himself or deal with all the points where decisions were necessary. Nor, of course, could he personally see that his decisions were carried out. He would be bound to have a large number of ministers and officials and would have to leave many decisions to them. Further, for the decisions that he did make to be put into effect, he would depend on these officers and their readiness to carry them out. It would be possible to find plenty of instances of the commands of a despot being frustrated by the obstruction, open or surreptitious, of his officials. This is the easier the more they form a defined and recognised class or profession, which to some degree develops the habit of working together and forming an official point of view. There is the special case of this when it is a question of the forces of coercion, 'the mamelukes and praetorian bands', to which reference was made earlier. Finally, it must be borne in mind that in forming his own opinions and in arriving at his decisions the despot would be dependent on information provided by other people, and his decisions might be largely determined by the information he received and the form in which it was presented to him. Thus, at the time that Louis XIV was proclaiming, 'L'état c'est moi' a foreign observer at his court wrote, 'In fact he judges public affairs and interests not so much by his own lights as by those that are given to him', so that 'he is easily led to embrace the advice that is given him and the measures that are suggested to him'.[1]

[1] E. Spanheim, *Relation de la Cour de France*, quoted from J. Lough, *Introduction to Seventeenth-century France*, p. 137.

The same applies to attempts at government by the whole people. Even in the small city-states, Greek or Italian, where the active participation of the whole people in the decisions of government was achieved to a degree that would have been impossible under other conditions, there had to be a number of boards and officials who exercised some authority. It is true that the Greek democracies were very jealous of their power and restricted it to the utmost, and they were certainly never allowed to become an official class. That was doubtless one of the reasons for the relative inefficiency of Greek governments and for the fact that so many decisions they took could not be successfully carried out. At the same time, there was a tendency for the rise of another sort of oligarchy, a class of professional politicians, party leaders and orators, who were often in fact the persons who took the decisions and had learned the technique of 'putting them across' to the whole people.

These, then, are some of the most obvious considerations which make it inevitable that there will always be some limited group of people in any society who have a special degree of influence over the decisions of government. It is not surprising that some writer once declared that every government that the world had ever seen was an oligarchy.

This, in a sense, is true, but it is not the whole truth. For, in a more elusive way, there is also an element of democracy in every government, hard though it may be to detect in some cases. This arises from the fundamental fact, which was discussed at some length earlier, that for government to be carried on at all it is necessary to secure the obedience of the great bulk of the people, and that, in all normal communities, there are limits to the extent to which that can be done. There comes a point at which even the most absolute despot or the most efficient oligarchy can be restrained by the unwillingness of the people to obey. This does not necessarily mean active resistance or even organised passive resistance; it may be simply the dead weight of unwillingness and non-co-operation. Such a situation may not often be seen in practice, because most governments would take care not to arouse it. But the possibility is there, and this means that the mass of the people do exercise, if only negatively, some influence, however small, on the decisions of government. This applies even if there is no machinery by which the people can express their opinion. Indeed, there may be extreme circumstances in which such machinery exists but has little or no effective influence, while on the other hand a popular dictator might often feel it necessary to take measures which he would not otherwise have taken because of the necessity for maintaining or increasing his popularity. But, as a general rule, the establishment of machinery for the expression of the opinions of the people marks a definite stage in the advance of the democratic element. In any case some degree, however small, of this element must be present.

Is there an equal necessity for an element of monarchy? Is there always some one person in the state who has a special degree of responsibility for and influence over the decisions of government? Judging by the experience of modern times one would be inclined to say that there was, if not an absolute necessity, at least a strong tendency in this direction, which would seem to point to a high degree of convenience in it. We find in every state, and in almost every organisation, some one chief person, whose precise degree of authority may vary greatly, but who always has some degree more than any other single individual. It is, perhaps, unnecessary to argue at length the obvious conveniences of this. But it is interesting to note that the ancient world, where so many ideas arose that are familiar to the present age or even in advance of it, never conceived of this as an obvious principle of government. Plato seems to think that the only reason for giving one man exceptional power would be that he was superior in wisdom and virtue to the rest. And in most of the republics of Greece or Italy the tendency was to make the chief magistracies 'collegiate', that is to say that they were held by two or more officers, like the consuls at Rome, with equal and co-ordinate power. But the experience of these communities rather tends to re-enforce the modern point of view. For they often found it necessary, in times of crisis, to invest one man with exceptional powers. And there is no doubt that the collegiate system made for inefficiency of government, and very often tended to be replaced in the course of time by the rule of a single person, like the emperor at Rome. We cannot, however, say that the element of monarchy in government is quite so essential as the others.

We see, then, that it is possible to attach a meaning to the simple old distinction that the Greeks made, as long as we take it as indicating different elements which can appear to a greater or lesser degree in any government rather than sharply divided classes into one or other of which every government can be placed. Even so, there remain, of course, a great number of further problems and complications that arise. In particular, the ever-present element of oligarchy can take a great variety of different forms, according to the kind of oligarchy and the principle on which it is selected. Something will be said about this later. But for the moment we are concerned with the general conclusions to be drawn from this analysis, with particular reference to democracy.

Democracy, like the other forms of government, is, on this account, a matter of degree, and the possible variations of degree are almost infinite. This is so not only as between one state and another, but also as between the different stages of development in the same state. This is, of course, obvious when we look back on the past history of the state in question. But even when we are considering the present conditions there it is important to remember that these are not static, and that we have to consider not only the degree of democracy actually attained but also the direction in which the state in question seems to be tending, and the factors which seem to be leading it towards an increase or a diminution of the democratic element in it. It is clear, then, that it is impossible to draw a hard and fast line between democratic and undemocratic states or to lay down a precise criterion for putting states on one side of this line or the other. But, so long as we remember this, there is no harm in continuing to speak of some states as democratic and some as undemocratic, meaning by that that in one lot the democratic element is strong and in the other it is reduced to the minimum.

There is a certain parallel here to the way in which we talk about the climate. We talk of one region as hot and another as cold without suggesting that there is an exact point on the thermometer at which it becomes one or the other, nor do we refuse to call it cold because it has not reached absolute zero. This homely illustration may also serve to enforce the point made earlier about the entire falsity of the assumption which appears so often in ordinary conversation that a difference of degree is somehow unimportant. Obviously, if we were faced with the prospect of being forced to live in the polar regions or at the Equator we should think that it mattered a great deal, and should not be comforted by people who told us that after all 'it is only a difference of degree'.[1] In politics, and in questions of conduct generally, the difference of degree is very often what makes the difference between good and bad, and a difference of degree may be worth fighting and dying for if anything ever is. At any rate it must be clear that in saying that democracy is a matter of degree we are not saying anything to minimise its value or importance.

We are now in a position to offer a formal definition of democracy. A state is democratic, not '*if*', but *in so far as* the great mass of the population can exercise an effective influence on the decisions that make up the work of government. I use the relatively wide term 'influence', because it is important not to confine it to the situation where the people as a whole are called upon actually to take the decisions themselves by some form of popular vote. That is, as it were, the limiting case, but there are many circumstances in which

[1] No pun on the word 'degree' is intended.

popular opinion, so far as it is formed, can exercise a considerable influence on the decisions of government without an actual vote being necessary. There may even, as was suggested earlier, be occasions on which this influence can be exercised in countries where there is no provision for any kind of popular vote at all. But that can never, except in rare circumstances, amount to very much. What is important is to recognise that the fact that the people can vote on some matters may exercise a considerable influence in other matters which are not the subjects of a popular vote. An obvious instance can be found in parliamentary governments such as our own. Here the only direct popular vote is for the election of members of the legislature every few years. But that clearly has a great effect on the other decisions that are taken. The policy of the government is always, to a greater or lesser degree, influenced by the thought of the next General Election.

Similar considerations arise if we raise the question whether we approve of or believe in democracy. That is a perfectly intelligible question and it is possible to give a perfectly intelligible answer to it, though not necessarily in terms of precise and clear-cut distinctions. To say that I believe in democracy does not mean that I believe that all the other elements in government should be abolished and that nothing should be done except by direct popular vote. That would be impossible and no one would seriously suggest that it was desirable. What it can mean is that I believe that the democratic element in the state is something of great value, which should be developed and maintained and take a prominent position among the influences which determine the decisions of government. There is a great difference between that and the point of view which would regard the democratic element as simply a necessary evil which should be reduced to the minimum possible. That is the distinction between the democrat and the anti-democrat, and its importance is not diminished by the fact that there may be a variety of intermediate views in between the two.

So far our discussion has been at a high level of generality, and its implications need developing and its outlines filling in before we can get a satisfactory picture of what democracy can mean. There are various ways in which this could be done. There is the historical approach, which would try to give an account of the way in which democracy has grown or declined in the past. There is also the approach by way of a detailed examination of the actual working of governments that we should call democratic at the present time. Some illustrations from both these fields of investigation will doubtless be called for in the course of the argument. But the political theorist is primarily interested in examining democracy as an idea working in people's minds. And he will probably find, after he has reached the formal definition, that the most profitable line of approach is to consider the kind of reasons why people are in favour of or against democracy, in the sense described above. That will certainly have an important effect on the form that democracy, or an alternative kind of government, takes in practice.

It would obviously be out of the question to give an exhaustive list of all the possible motives that might lead individuals to prefer one form of government rather than another. All sorts of emotional factors, personal or family interests, loyalties and traditions, may come into play, in varying degrees and in different combinations. When such motives become widespread they may often lead to a mass movement against one form of government and in favour of another. Thus, general discontent at social and economic conditions may take the form of a political movement against, for instance, an oligarchy which is supposed to be pursuing its own interests at the expense of the mass of the people. This may take the form of a demand for democratic government, as with the Chartists in England. But it is just as likely to result in the rise of a popular dictatorship, like many of the 'tyrannies' in ancient Greece. On the other hand, in some cases popular resentment at incompetence, real or supposed, in handling current problems may give rise to a reaction against democratic government. There can be little doubt that some modern dictatorships have owed their rise, in part at any rate, to this cause.

These things vary indefinitely according to the circumstances of the particular time and the particular place, and do not lend themselves to general conclusions, except in a very vague form. This is particularly so when we are dealing with the kind of motives that might act on different individuals to incline them to prefer one kind of government to another. And there is the further question about the conditions in which the motives leading to preference for one form of government rather than another are likely to be effective in practice. What factors, for instance, make for successful revolution and what for preservation of the established form of government? Attempts have been made to extract historical laws for these kinds of process, but without much success. Sometimes the supposed laws are formulated in such vague and general terms that they can be made to fit any facts, while the more precise they are the more often they turn out to be wrong. What may be possible is to distinguish and set out the more important general tendencies or influences which seem most frequently to act on human minds. These tendencies will vary in strength, and which of them are likely to be dominant among particular sets of people at particular times can only be decided, if at all, by a detailed examination of the circumstances in each particular case. But that is not the task with which we are concerned here.

We are getting into the realm of political theory when we find these emotions and desires developing into or becoming associated with a set of principles or system of beliefs, which makes them definite and explicit and relatively stable. Thus, in the debates in the army during our Civil War, we find the opponents of democracy, such as Ireton, arguing against a democratic franchise on the ground that it might produce a threat to the security of private property. This attitude might

be interpreted simply in terms of personal greed for possessions. No doubt even as a personal matter such an interpretation would be over-crude. But the important point to
recognise is that the view could not have been held so strongly
or put forward so confidently if it had not been part of a
general set of beliefs which recognised the right of private
property, as part of the system of rights secured by the rule
of law, whether the law of the land or the Law of Nature or the
Law of God. This was the common assumption of the age
for all except a tiny minority. The advocates of democracy
did not, in general, question these assumptions, but confined
themselves to arguing that a wider extension of the franchise
would not, in fact, endanger private property.

There have been endless discussions about the relations
between the emotional elements and the reasoned beliefs that
are associated with them, and it is probable that no one will
be able to trace all their possible interactions. Indeed, there
is not nearly such a sharp distinction between the two as
sometimes seems to be supposed. But, in any case, it is possible to discuss political beliefs as beliefs, and to consider the
arguments that have been or could be put forward for or
against them. And that may well turn out to be a profitable
approach to the question of democracy. In that hope, I propose to state and examine what seem to be the most serious
arguments for and against democracy, and to see what conclusions, if any, emerge from this examination. It would not
be possible or profitable here to consider all the arguments
that have ever been advanced on one side or the other, particularly those which have a purely historical interest and
make no appeal to the present day. Thus, for instance, I
shall not discuss the arguments against democracy based on
the doctrine of the Divine Right of Kings, even though that
doctrine is said still to linger on among the Carlists of Navarre.
Indeed, any argument, on either side, based on the assertion
of absolute and unconditional rights, which belong to people
by divine or natural law irrespective of their consequences or

their relations to anything else, would be out of tune with our modern habit of thought, and in any case would be difficult to apply to something which was a matter of more or less, as is the case with democracy. There are quite enough arguments, which could be regarded as reasonable by our modern standards, to be examined without going into those which are based on assumptions that no one would now accept.

Most of the reasoned arguments that have been used in modern times can be traced back to their origins in ancient Greece. Of course, the Greeks saw things in much simpler terms than we do, but the essential core of the argument remains very much the same, in spite of all the complications and qualifications that modern writers have introduced. The case for democracy cannot be found stated at great length in the extant Greek literature, but enough remains for us to detect the main lines of argument which would be apposite to the present day. In modern times there has been a great spate of writings in defence of democracy, so great, indeed, that there may be a danger of getting lost among them. They often show considerable differences in their way of putting the case, partly, no doubt, determined by the different audiences for which they are writing and the different opponents that they are trying to answer. But these need not disguise from us the great extent of ground which they have in common. In particular the classical statements of the case by the writers of the Victorian age, such as John Stuart Mill, still retain their value today.

The same period saw the appearance of a number of systematic attacks on the idea of democracy. In this country the names of James Fitzjames Stephen, of Maine, and of Lecky suggest themselves as examples of reasoned criticism, whereas other writers, notably Carlyle, represent the emotional and prophetic strain. Here again it is noteworthy how much of the substance of the reasoned criticisms can be traced back to ancient Greece. Fundamentally they are in the main variations on a theme composed by Plato. Plato, of course, was criticising a much more extreme form of democracy than anything that is familiar in modern times, and no doubt some of his incidental criticisms would hardly apply now. But we must not exaggerate the importance of this. Obviously in any modern state far fewer decisions are left to the whole body of people than in ancient Athens. But Plato's fundamental objections are directed against any decisions in public affairs being left to them at all.

In quite recent times a new complication has been introduced. It is difficult, nowadays, to find instances of arguments avowedly directed against democracy. Instead, those who advocate in theory or support in practice systems of government which would, in any other age, have been described as undemocratic prefer to describe themselves as supporters of what they call 'real democracy'. Thus Hitler described the dictatorship which he advocated as 'the German democracy, which is a true democracy',[1] and similar ways of speaking can be found among the supporters of other authoritarian regimes. The claim of a dictatorship to be democratic sometimes amounts to no more than the claim that it is pursuing the true interests of the people, which it sees more clearly than they do themselves. But the possibility of a dictatorship behaving like that has long been familiar to people. Phrases such as 'benevolent despotism' were coined to describe a situation of that kind, long before it occurred to anyone to suggest that because a despotism was benevolent it thereby became a democracy. At any rate any ordinary citizen can realise the difference between having decisions made for him by people supposedly wiser and better than he is, and being called upon to take some share in making them himself. To use language which obscures that distinction can only make for confusion. I may add in parenthesis that no doubt many people on many points would prefer to have decisions made for them. But that is not necessarily democratic.

Other advocates of dictatorship or authoritarian govern-

[1] *Mein Kampf* (English translation), p. 88.

ment seem to go further and to claim that the dictator can be, in some almost mystical way, so *en rapport* with the spirit of the people that he can express what they really want without going to the trouble of consulting them. Thus, Mussolini wrote, 'Nevertheless it [Fascism] is the purest form of democracy, if the nation is conceived, as it should be, qualitatively and not quantitatively, as the most powerful idea (most powerful because most moral, most coherent, most true) which acts within the nation as the conscience and the will of a few, even of One, which ideal tends to become active within the conscience and the will of all'.[1] Such ideas, in general, seem to go back to the notion of the General Will or real will which is one side of Rousseau's contribution to political thought. But it is very difficult to find a precise formulation of this claim and still more difficult to suggest a test of its validity. It sometimes seems to come down to little more than the assertion that people will be happier under a benevolent dictatorship than under any other form of government. That is a factual statement, which may or may not be true. But if it is, it is an argument against democracy.

There is another confusion which seems to arise at times, though rather in popular writing and speaking than in serious theoretical discussion. That is the assumption that if democracy is good it must be the complete and absolute good, and nothing that can be described as undemocratic can possibly have anything to be said for it. Indeed, one can detect occasionally a tendency to convert a simple proposition and to argue as if the fact that what was democratic was good meant that anything that was good must be democratic. But if we remember what democracy means in actual fact, and particularly the extent to which differences of degree must come in, we shall see that this way of speaking is quite misleading. At any rate, it is important to recognise that serious and reasonable arguments can be put forward in criticism of democracy,

[1] *The Encyclopaedia of Fascism* (1932), quoted from M. Oakeshott, *The Social and Political Doctrines of Contemporary Europe.*

and that, even if we do not in the main accept them, we can
see that they have a certain degree of validity in certain directions. We are not obliged to accept them or reject them completely and absolutely. I propose now to attempt briefly to
state the case that can be reasonably made against democracy,
and then to consider the kind of answer that the democrat
might give and to suggest the conclusions that follow from
this. Once more we must remember that arguments against
democracy mean, strictly speaking, arguments for the view
that the democratic element in government is, on the whole,
an undesirable influence which should be reduced to the minimum possible. As we shall see, certain conclusions about how
that is to be done will seem to follow naturally from the statement of the reasons why it should be done.

Chapter VII

THE CASE AGAINST DEMOCRACY

THE rational argument against democracy, first stated by Plato and elaborated by many subsequent writers, would run something on these lines:

It is generally recognised that efficiency in any kind of work depends on the principle of the division of labour. Mankind would never have risen above the most primitive level of subsistence if every man had tried to do everything for himself. Broadly speaking the condition of any work of any difficulty or importance being well done is that it should be left to the special people who can concentrate on it while leaving other people to do other work for them. There may be trifling exceptions here and there, but that is the general picture. This was obvious even in Plato's time, but nowadays we have carried it to a far higher degree and thereby attained an efficiency in production of which he never dreamed. This applies, of course, not only to the production of material goods but equally to special services, particularly those which demand a high degree of professional knowledge and training, such as the work of the doctor, the lawyer, or the teacher.

The reasons for this are clear. For one thing, people differ in abilities and temperament, and it clearly makes for efficiency if everyone has the work for which he is naturally suited. The importance of this must not be exaggerated: we certainly cannot say that everyone is naturally suited for one kind of work and one only. But we can at least say that the most difficult and important kinds of work need people of the highest degree of intelligence and of the necessary temperamental qualities. Secondly, for most work of any difficulty special training and the acquisition of specialised knowledge is necessary. And perhaps most important of all is the need for special attention and the concentration of interest and energy on the work. Very few important jobs can be carried on efficiently if they are taken up at casual intervals and then dropped again. In many cases, the work itself does not admit of this. Things go on and have to be dealt with: they will not wait for our convenience. Also, of course, the full-time attention is the most important factor in giving the knowledge and experience which is necessary for efficiency. One can think of possible, if somewhat far-fetched, exceptions to all this. But generally speaking the broad principle stands that special ability, special training, and special attention are the conditions of effectiveness in any work of importance.

Now is there any reason why the same principle should not apply to the work of government? It would be hard to maintain that this work is either so easy that anyone could make the right decisions or so unimportant that it does not matter what decisions are made. How, then, can we justify leaving any of these difficult and important decisions to be taken by a vote of the whole people, in which everyone, intelligent or stupid, well-informed or ignorant, public-spirited or selfish, counts exactly the same? We should not think of deciding other difficult questions in that way, and it seems irrational to say that the most important questions, that is to say the questions that affect the greatest number of people, should be so decided. Surely, the only reasonable way of getting the right decisions would be to select people of high intelligence and character with an appropriate education and training who would be able to devote their full time and energy to the study of the questions to be decided, and then leave to them the complete responsibility for deciding one way or the other.

That, in a very summary form, is the case against democracy as we find it in Plato and the modern writers who have followed his line of thought. In our own day we do not often find the argument so frankly stated. But there is a good deal of feeling which tends in that direction in practice. Enthusiastic reformers and efficient administrators alike, however much they may profess a belief in democracy in principle, are always apt to be impatient of the uncertainties of democratic procedure in practice and to find an excuse in each particular case for side-stepping it if they can. Many of them in their hearts would probably sympathise with the remark attributed, very likely apocryphally, to Woodrow Wilson, 'If this thing is to be democratically managed, I must have complete control'.

Thus, shortly after the war a correspondent of a British newspaper was in an Eastern European country, observing an election which was supposed to be free, but in fact was very much the reverse. He reported hearing an official of the dominant party say that they could not be expected to run the risk of having their carefully prepared plans for the good of the whole country upset by a lot of ignorant peasants. In a milder form something of the same spirit can be observed at times in this country. In the later years of the last war there was a campaign, particularly associated with the name of Harold Laski, to induce the Coalition Government to introduce large measures of Socialism at once. It was essential that it should be done at once, and not postponed till after a post-war General Election, because 'it is impossible to foresee what the trend of public opinion, measured in votes, will be at the end of the war'.[1] The electorate, in fact, are not to be given a chance to vote on these sweeping changes because they might possibly vote against them.

What sort of alternative government, then, does this argument point to? Plato, who initiated it, thought the conclusion plain, that the whole power in the state should be in the hands of a limited number of people of outstanding intelligence and character, specially trained for the work, and above all ready to devote themselves whole-heartedly to it. This was essen-

[1] *New Statesman*, 5 May 1942.

tial, not only because the work itself demanded their full attention, but even more because of the necessity that they should have no other interest which might possibly conflict with the supreme claim of their work for the whole community. In the well-known scheme, in the *Republic*, this is carried to lengths that no one would seriously contemplate nowadays. His ideal rulers were to have no private property at all, but were to live an austere life in communal barracks, receiving their bare keep from the rest of the community. They were not even allowed to have a private family life of their own. Some of his regulations may seem to us far-fetched and even fantastic, and in all probability he never supposed himself that it would be practically possible to put them into force as they stood. But we can see the kind of dangers that he was trying to guard against—desire for personal gain, nepotism, family rivalries, and the like—and we might find an attempt to guard against similar temptations even in the present day in the rules of monastic orders, which in some respects, though not of course in all, resemble Plato's Guardians. The rare cases in which a religious order has actually exercised government, as the Jesuits did in Paraguay, provide the nearest historical parallel to the rule of the Guardians.

The argument, then, points to some kind of oligarchy or aristocracy as the ideal form of government. But it certainly does nothing to support the claims of some other forms of aristocracy which have existed in the past. For instance, special political power for wealth or for noble birth would be condemned by it quite as decisively as democracy. The only qualifications for political power are special ability, special training and the readiness to make the work of government on behalf of the whole community the sole interest. But the possession of wealth in itself is no proof at all of the possession of these qualifications. Plato saw this clearly and asked whether, if we were going to make a voyage, we should prefer to entrust the navigation of the ship to the richest man on board or to the most skilful and well-trained navigator. Indeed, wealth may be a positive disadvantage in a ruler. For it is hard to have great possessions without caring about them and there is always the danger that this might distract the ruler's attention from the care for the good of the community. Of course, small possessions may be equally distracting, and Plato thought that the ideal ruler should have no possessions at all. He should know, and accept the position, that whatever he did could not affect his personal wealth.

There is possibly a little more to be said for the rule of a hereditary aristocracy. For there seems to be evidence that some of the qualities required in a ruler, or at any rate the potentiality of them, are often transmitted from parents to children by heredity. And certainly valuable attitudes of mind, the tradition of public service and the like, are largely acquired through the influence of the family. It might even be the case, as Plato thought, that, once the ideal aristocracy had been established, its ranks in the future would in fact be largely filled by the children of the previous generation of rulers. That might be so, but that would be no warrant for laying it down as a rule. For the inheritance of intelligence and other qualities is by no means certain or invariable, and the rulers would have to be selected for these qualities whether or not their parents had them. It would be fatal to any such scheme to give anyone the right to power merely because his parents had it. That would be so even if the ideal aristocracy had been established. But, of course, no actual hereditary aristocracy has ever approached within measurable distance of the ideal.

It is worth mentioning these points because the arguments against democracy have, in the past, often been used to support the claims of one or the other of these forms of oligarchy, whereas in fact they lend little or no support to them at all. Further, it is important to remember that democracy in the past has often been advocated as the only practicable alternative to one of the undesirable kinds of oligarchy. As such, it could be supported with perfect consistency even by those who did not regard it as the ideal form of government, though they might hope that in time it could be replaced by something nearer to their ideal.

We must now consider a little more in detail the kind of qualifications that the argument requires in those to whom supreme power is to be entrusted. It is, of course, the assumption of the whole argument that they should be people who were prepared to make the well-being of the whole community their supreme aim. But good intentions are not enough, and the previous discussion has stressed the need for special ability, special training, and special knowledge. This might possibly suggest to some people the picture of a community in which everything was controlled by different groups of specialists, health matters by medical men, military affairs by soldiers, agricultural questions by scientific agriculturalists, and the like. No doubt, the various groups of specialists themselves might often hanker after such a state of things, and might feel, particularly if their specialisms involved some scientific knowledge, that they could make a wonderful success of their jobs if they were only free from the interference of ignorant politicians. But the non-specialist would view such a prospect with a considerable degree of suspicion. And he would be quite right to do so, for the whole idea is based on a failure to recognise certain essential distinctions.

It is, of course, perfectly true that there are a number of different activities, like those mentioned and many others, which are of importance for the life of the community. It is true, also, that there is always some particular skill or knowledge involved in each of them, which the specialist possesses. Each of these activities contributes something to the good of the community, but no one of them is the sole and sufficient condition of its being attained. Further, they cannot be carried on in isolation, because they affect each other, sometimes by co-operation and sometimes by rivalry and competition. It seems essential, therefore, to have some co-ordinating authority which can decide the proper place of each specialism

in the life of the community. To be able to do that demands
very special qualities but not the qualities of the specialist. It
demands, to put it roughly, the ability to think in terms of the
good of the whole community, to survey all the different
specialisms and their relations to each other, and to evaluate
the particular contribution of each. This is the ability which
is necessary for the ideal ruler. He must, of course, also be
in a position to make use of the specialists' knowledge, which
means he must have it always available. But, at the same
time, he will never forget that it is the natural tendency of
every specialist, even if he is perfectly free of self-interest, to
exaggerate the importance of his own specialism, which is
why he needs some authority over him. A modern writer has
epigrammatically summed up the proper position for the
specialist as 'always on tap and never on top'.

This distinction has had perforce to be recognised to some
extent in practice, but it has not always been explicitly laid
down as part of the theory of government. A generation ago
Bernard Bosanquet, in emphasising the difference between
the two kinds of skill or knowledge, tried to popularise the
use of the terms 'specialist' and 'expert' to indicate respectively the person possessing the specialised knowledge of the
kind previously described and the person who has the ability
to make use of the knowledge of the various specialists. He
was not very successful in this, and at the present time the
two terms are generally used indiscriminately. There are in
fact no single words in English as ordinarily spoken which
exactly express the distinction. For the earliest clear statement of it we go back, once more, to Plato. In a later dialogue,
the *Politicus*, he is concerned with distinguishing the art of
skill appropriate to the ruler from the various special arts
which he may have to make use of. Thus, the general or the
military specialist knows how to conduct a war once it has been
started. But that special knowledge does not give him the
capacity to decide whether a war ought to be started or not.
That decision can be entrusted only to the possessor of the

highest knowledge, the art of the statesman. This requires a clear understanding of what the good of the whole community consists in, and what the various special arts can contribute to it. Only the statesman can decide when and how far these special skills are to be put in practice, 'weaving them together', in Plato's phrase, into the pattern of the perfect state. This is obviously a task of great difficulty which requires exceptional qualities and a high degree of concentration on it to be carried out successfully.

Before leaving this point, it is perhaps worth emphasing that this distinction between the 'specialist' and the 'expert', to use Bosanquet's phraseology, is a relative distinction which runs through the different levels of many forms of activity. If we take the army as an instance we shall find in it the specialists in tank warfare or in the use of artillery, with a chain of command above them reaching up to the highest military authority, for instance the Chief of the Imperial General Staff. Within the army, he is the 'expert' and those under him are the 'specialists', but in relation to the government he is the 'specialist'. It is only when we get to the supreme authority that we reach the pure 'expert', the expert in government.

To return to the main argument, those who have adopted this point of view in theory, or tried to act on it in practice, have developed various ideas about the ways in which such an aristocracy might be selected and how it might achieve power. Plato in his *Republic* draws a picture of what the ideal aristocracy would be like once it had been established, but has little or nothing to say about the practical means to its establishment. Indeed, it is doubtful whether he thought it could ever be attained in its completeness. As far as we can judge from his actual practice, he seems to have hoped that it would be possible to produce by education, such as was given in his Academy, a select body of people who would have something like the qualities of his ideal rulers. He was opposed to any idea of establishing their rule by force. But he appears to have hoped that when it was generally realised what sort of people they were, the mass of the population would be ready to leave the difficult and troublesome work of government to them. In fact, he had a much greater degree of success in this aim than is generally realised.

In our own country in the early years of the present century somewhat similar ideas could be detected, for instance among some of the intellectuals of the Socialist movement. H. G. Wells, who in one at least of his books was avowedly following on the lines suggested by Plato, was constantly concerned with the problem of how to discover and develop an ideal aristocracy which could eventually attain power. In successive works he looked for it in different directions, though he seems to have remained unsatisfied till the end. After the First World War there were those, besides the professed revolutionaries such as the Communists, who toyed with the idea of forming a secret *élite* who would be in a position to seize power, if necessary by force, if an occasion offered itself. This was the plan of one influential member of the Labour Party, as described by a close acquaintance. 'The Labour Party was to win an election on a programme . . . comprising whatever assortment of pledges would, in a given area, get its candidate in. This was the public platform: a sufficient number of picked and reliable persons among the candidates were to be secretly bound to quite another—the revolutionary seizure of power.'[1] But, of course, such ideas had no chance of survival in the actual atmosphere of the Labour Party.

It was quite different in other countries, Russia, Italy, or Germany for instance, where a revolutionary party actually succeeded in seizing power. It is significant that in these movements, particularly in Communism, the only one which developed a coherent theory, the stress was laid on the party as an *élite*, to be kept select by periodical purges, peaceable or violent. In every case, the party forms in effect an oli-

[1] See Mary Agnes Hamilton, *Remembering My Good Friends*, p. 118.

garchy or aristocracy in whose hands all real power rests. These parties have at times been compared to Plato's ideal rulers, occasionally by way of commendation, but more often as grounds for condemnation both of Plato and the parties. In fact, the parallels are not very close. The most plausible one is with the Communist Party in Russia, indignantly though they would repudiate it. The Communist Party resembles Plato's Guardians in that it is a select body of rulers, based on a philosophical theory which they are all supposed to master. They are also supposed to exercise a certain degree of personal self-denial, though not, it appears, to the extent which was imposed on them in the earlier stages. Within the party itself there is a hierarchical organisation, and all effective power seems to be concentrated in a few people at the top. We have very little inside information of the means by which members rise to the topmost heights. But what we have does not suggest that they are means of which Plato would have approved. Indeed, the whole method of attaining and keeping power practised by the Communist Party would hardly have appealed to him.

There is another and much less spectacular direction in which those who look forward to the gradual reduction of the democratic element in government might turn. And that is to the professional Civil Service. Here we have an institution in many respects parallel to Plato's Guardians. Its members are selected by an intellectual test, and gradually rise in authority according to their ability and experience and knowledge of the work. They are trained in traditions of integrity and public service, and there are well-recognised restrictions on any private activities which might tempt them to neglect or act contrary to their public duties, though they could hardly be expected to exercise the degree of self-denial that Plato advocated. They are full-time administrators, and, though in theory they are not empowered to take any of the major decisions of government, in practice their influence makes itself felt in all of them. Here, perhaps, as some people may hope and others may fear, we should look for the possibilities of a new ruling aristocracy.

The experience of our own country, which can be paralleled to a greater or lesser degree from many others, affords a good illustration of the development in the position of the civil servant. A hundred years ago, when suggestions for the reform of the system of recruitment were first mooted, the critics of the new proposals dwelt upon the relatively humble functions that the Civil Service had to perform. 'The officers of the Civil Service', one critic wrote, 'cannot in ordinary cases aspire to become statesmen, and to carry out systems of policy. Their humble but useful duty is, by becoming depositaries of departmental traditions, . . . to keep the current business in its due course', with more to a similar effect. Another critic thought that a system of competitive examination would select people of much too good a quality for the Civil Service as it then was. Indeed he doubted whether any man of real intellectual power would 'submit himself to an arduous examination in order to win a post so ill-paid, so obscure and so subordinate'. Ninety years later, an official document from the Civil Service Commission declared that the civil servant is 'concerned with the formulation of policy, with the co-ordination and improvement of government machinery and with the general administration and control of Departments. The ideal candidate would possess intellectual ability of a high order . . . be adaptable, far-sighted and persevering, and have enough strength of character and leadership to hold his own, take decisions and exercise responsibility. He would have enough practical imagination to enable him to devise, in broad outline, workable plans for dealing with an unprecedented situation', and so on.[1] There is not much more that one could say about the ideal ruler.

We are not yet at the stage where the civil servants could be accepted as the real rulers of the country. But the ten-

---

[1] I have taken these quotations from Professor K. C. Wheare's lecture on *The Civil Service in the Constitution*.

dency in that direction at the present day arises from the increasing difficulty and complexity not only of government but of all organised life and activity. Those who would try to avoid it by reducing the activities of government would be, from the point of view of the democrat, not solving the problem but abandoning any attempt at its solution. For they would be handing over the decisions in many matters which affect us all to even less responsible people, for instance to the managerial class which increasingly exercises the real power in matters of business and finance. Everywhere the 'iron law' of oligarchy holds, that the more difficult and complicated things become the more those who are on the spot all the time and devote their whole attention to the work will exercise effective control over the decisions taken.

This, then, is another direction in which the critics of democracy might well look for their alternative government. It would be a state in which the real power would be in the hands of the higher ranks of the Civil Service, reinforced, perhaps, by a few independent experts and a few impressive figureheads. There would be no need for any sensational attempts at seizing power by force. The whole apparatus of voting and election of representatives might continue in form. But as the mass of people gradually came to realise their limitations, it would become more and more of a pure formality. The situation, in fact, might come to approximate to that in some large limited companies, where the shareholders, who are the nominal owners, in fact take no part in the government of the concern at all. Everything is left to the directors, nominally elected by the shareholders but in fact co-opted by each other.

But these are all speculations about future possibilities, though no one could say that their realisation was inconceivable. The main argument stands, irrespective of these, that government is such a difficult and important job that it should be entrusted only to those properly equipped for it who are prepared to give their whole attention to the task.

The complications of modern life have emphasised the necessity of this, and perhaps made its realisation more possible. But, in principle, the argument applies to any community above the most primitive level, to any community, in fact, where there is anything that we could call government. In no case is there anything to be said for leaving important decisions to all the citizens indiscriminately. Some degree of this may be unavoidable in certain conditions. But the wise man, if he is really anxious that the decisions taken should be the right ones, will bend all his efforts to reducing the amount of it to the minimum possible.

Chapter VIII

THE DEMOCRAT'S ANSWER

How would the believer in democracy answer such an argument? He would have to begin by recognising what a great amount of truth there is in it. No doubt he could suggest certain modifications in the presentation of the case. But though these might soften its hard edges they would hardly touch its central core. Thus, it would no doubt be true to say that we cannot always present political problems in the form of clear-cut questions to which a right or wrong answer can be given. On the other hand, we shall probably find, if we make a resolute effort of analysis, that we can do much more in that way than appears possible at first sight, and the will and capacity to make such an effort is just the sort of quality that we shall hope to find in our ideal rulers. But, it may be argued, that might apply when it was a question of discovering the best means to an agreed end, but it is different when it is a matter of the choice between possible ends. This raises the question of the distinction between means and ends in politics, about which there will be more to be said later. For the moment it suffices to point out that the distinction, though useful up to a point, is not nearly so sharp and clear-cut as is sometimes supposed, and in fact it is a rare limiting case when a political dispute can really be presented as a difference about ultimate ends.

On this question of ultimate ends there is, at this stage, only this to be said. Suppose we assume that there is a real right and wrong about the possible ends that a country can aim at, it is obviously very important that the right ones should be chosen. The anti-democrat would argue that to discover these is a task that demands a very high degree of moral and intellectual enlightenment and a single-minded concentration on it that few people would be able or willing to achieve. This is the basis of Plato's famous assertion that rulers ought to be philosophers. It seems an odd claim to us nowadays when we tend to think of philosophy as a special subject in an academic curriculum. But what he means by it is that those in power should have a clear-sighted vision of the true end of society, and guide their policy with that in view. This is a perfectly intelligible position, quite apart from the peculiar metaphysical doctrines with which he associated it. Even from a purely practical point of view, it might well be argued, the man who sees clearly what he is aiming at is more likely to be effective than the man who has no idea, or a confusion of different ideas, about his ultimate aims. Incidentally, it is worth noting that Plato never supposed that philosophical insight into ultimate ends was by itself sufficient qualification for the ruler. He needed practical experience, in addition, and ample provision is made for this in the scheme of training in the *Republic*. But the practical knowledge cannot be effectively used except in the light of a clear conception of the end.

Be that as it may, a good many people would undoubtedly say that all this talk of ultimate ends is too remote from actual practice to have much relevance. They might say that ultimate ends can be conceived only in such general terms that they can give us no guide, or at any rate no positive guide to what we ought to do. They might suggest, further, that the only practicable aim is to try to give people what they want, and to find out what this is some arrangement for consulting them, in other words some democratic machinery, is necessary. In reply to this, the anti-democrat would probably express considerable doubts whether most people really know what they want. At most they may have a series of more or less vague pictures of states of things which appeal to their imagination, at different times, though these may be quite incompatible with each other and have little or no relation to actual facts or practical possibilities. In fact, 'knowing what you want' is a comparatively rare state of mind which needs a good deal of effort and considerable powers of insight to attain. This is so to some extent even in people's private lives and activities. But it is obviously a great deal more so when it comes to public matters which affect the whole or a great part of the community. Here, again, the enlightened few are much more likely to give people what they want than a popular vote. This is not, of course, the last word to be said on the matter. But so far the anti-democrat would probably not feel seriously shaken in his position.

He would probably also have to admit another qualification of his original argument. When it is a question of the decisions to be taken in any particular situation it is not, except in rare cases, a matter of one set of decisions being absolutely right and all the other possible decisions being absolutely wrong. There may be occasions when alternative methods of meeting the situation may turn out in the long run equally satisfactory. More often, probably, there will be one way which is, on the whole, the best, but other possible alternatives which may be quite good second—or third—bests. We may speak of the best solution as the right one, but if we go on to speak of the others as wrong we cannot mean by that that they are necessarily absolutely disastrous. Still, it would be argued, it is obviously desirable that the best solution should be chosen, and, though the expert rulers will not be infallible, they are far more likely to discover this than would be the mass of people in a popular vote. Further—and this is a point on which the anti-democrat would probably lay particular stress—if there are alternative policies, any one of which might achieve a measure of success, the only chance for this would be that the policy chosen should be pursued consistently and persistently. A second-best policy that was carried out with determination and continuity would be much more likely to be successful than a first-rate policy carried out half-heartedly and spasmodically. And for this one could depend far more upon a government of a small number of expert rulers, secure in their position and free to make their own decisions, than on any government which was dependent in any degree on the shifting winds of popular feeling.

We have not, then, yet come to grips with the main defence line of the anti-democrats. But this preliminary reconnaissance will perhaps be found to reveal to the democrat certain possible openings for the attack on his opponent's position. Before going on to that, however, it is well to remind ourselves that the two sides in this dispute are not occupying exactly the same kind of ground. The anti-democrat is whole-heartedly opposed to any intrusion of the popular element in the decisions of government, and thinks it desirable and practicable to reduce the possibility of this to such minute proportions as to be practically negligible. The democrat, on the other hand, need not regard the expert element in government as something evil. He may accept it as necessary and indeed desirable. Even the Greek democracies, who were much more suspicious of it than any modern state could afford to be, had to accept in practice a greater degree of it than they would admit in theory. What the modern democrat is concerned to argue is, on the one hand, that the expert element, valuable though it may be, should not be entrusted with absolute and unchecked control over the decisions of government. And, on the other hand, he maintains that the presence of the democratic or popular element in government gives something of positive value, which the anti-democrat fails to see.

Approaching the question along these lines, the democrats might begin by stressing the extreme improbability of the ideal aristocracy ever being attained in practice. Some might concede that, if it could be attained, the rule of such an aristocracy would be the best form of government. But, they would say, the possibilities of getting such an aristocracy are so remote and the risk of any conceivable kind of aristocracy becoming in practice very far from ideal are so great that democracy, with all its weaknesses, would be safer.

Thus it would be suggested that any select body of people, however carefully chosen and trained, if they were freed from all control, as the argument requires that they should be, would be bound in time to become a special class with interests of their own, which they would be likely to pursue, if necessary, at the expense of the rest of the community. This does not necessarily mean economic interests, particularly in the form of direct financial rewards. If such interests did come in, it would be more likely to take the form of the demand for various conveniences and amenities, first priority in housing or the provision of motor-cars, for instance, which could be plausibly represented as necessary for efficiency in their work. We know from experience how much that may mean. But a more serious and more subtle temptation would be the love of power for its own sake. Experience suggests that this can attack those who live the most ascetic and self-denying lives as far as material conditions go. It is very easy for them to think of the maintenance of their own power and position as so essential that in the end they come to think of it as more important than the use they make of it. They may become more concerned about the organisation of the forces, such as the secret police, which can be used to suppress any possible discontent than about anything else. There are other ways in which the same tendency can show itself. In general we might say that the more firmly convinced they are that they represent the 'real will' of the people in the abstract the more likely they are to come to think of actual people as potential malcontents against whom they must always be on the defensive.

Even if it did not go as far as this, it would be almost inevitable that an aristocracy of this type, however well-meaning, would tend to become more and more aloof from the mass of the population and incapable of understanding them and entering into their feelings. It would become less and less capable of interpreting the real wishes of the people and giving them what would really satisfy them. Even if it was claimed that the ultimate object of government was not only to give people what they want but also to produce a certain kind of character and a certain pattern of life, it would still be true that that could hardly be effectively done by rulers who were too remote from the rest of the people.

These, and other similar considerations, represent the kinds of argument that could be put forward for the view that uncontrolled power would inevitably corrupt even the most carefully selected and trained aristocracy. They are undoubtedly of considerable weight and must be borne in mind in any consideration of the subject. But the believer in democracy would, I think, hardly find them completely satisfactory, taken by themselves. It is difficult to be finally convinced by any argument of the type that such-and-such a thing would be desirable, but would not work in practice. There are few things on which people have been so often wrong as these generalisations about impracticability. Probably most reforms that have ever been carried out have been declared to be impracticable at first. That does not, of course, mean that any and every suggestion for reform is practicable. But it does mean that we should be cautious about accepting too easily statements of impracticability if we believe the reform suggested is really desirable. Further, it must be remembered that when we ask whether a reform will work or not, we do not ask for an assurance that it will work absolutely ideally with no difficulties and no defects. No institution does that. The only relevant question is whether it will work well enough to be better than the possible alternatives. Altogether, the democrat will not feel that his case is satisfactorily established until he has found reasons for believing that, even if the ideal aristocracy could be made to work as well as was humanly possible, it would still not be desirable.

In looking for such reasons, he would probably begin by taking advantage of the loophole offered by the previous concession that there was not generally one and only one right decision possible in any given situation, but that various alternative courses of action might work well enough to avoid disaster. Not that that by itself will take him very far. But it does at least give him, so to speak, a certain amount of room to manœuvre, in that he may claim that a distribution of power which does not necessarily ensure that the absolutely best policy is adopted may still be desirable if it secures other advantages. And he would look for these possible advantages by trying to go back to ultimate ends and asking what the final test is by which any institution and any measure is, in the long run, to be judged.

Let us take as a working hypothesis the Greek idea that the final test is to be looked for in the kind of people and the pattern of behaviour that are likely to be produced by this course or that. We need not try to construct a complete picture of our ideal pattern and then to deduce what we ought to do from that. All that is necessary is to consider any course of action that is proposed and to see, if we can, what effect that is likely to have on the general characters, lives, and behaviour of the people concerned. No doubt we shall find that many particular measures have little or no effect one way or the other, except perhaps very indirectly. But permanent institutions necessarily have some effect on our pattern of life, and from that point of view the way in which decisions are reached, that is to say the general political organisation, may be just as important as the decisions themselves. And as democracy and its alternatives are primarily different ways of reaching decisions, we may consider their general effects over and above the particular decisions that they are likely to reach.

We might begin by considering the sort of character that the absolute rule of a selected few would tend to produce. As far as the effect on the rulers themselves is concerned something has already been said about the subtle influences that might possibly pervert them. But it is more important to consider the effect of such a régime on the rest of the citizens, the great majority. And we must think here, not so much of the possible perversions which may creep in contrary to the intentions of the advocates of such a régime, but rather of the characteristics or attitudes of mind which are necessary or highly desirable in order that the régime should work efficiently. If it does not work efficiently there is, of course, no justification for it at all.

Obviously the first characteristic required from the mass of the people will be the habit of absolute and implicit obedience and respect for authority. They must have no will of their own and it would be dangerous even for them to have opinions which might conflict with those of their rulers. The whole case for excluding the mass of the citizens from the decisions of government rests on the assumption that they are very unlikely to arrive at correct conclusions about them. Of course, it would be a good thing for them to think about doing their own jobs well. But any attempt for them to think for themselves or develop critical views about public questions or the general interests of the community would necessarily have to be discouraged. Certainly such a constitution would give them no encouragement or incentive to do this, as their thinking could not express itself in any practical decisions. It looks as if the great virtue of an ordinary citizen in such a state would lie in minding his own business and not having any ideas outside it. Certainly that would make for a safe and comfortable life for the man himself.

In some non-democratic states apathy and indifference to public affairs on the part of the ordinary citizen might suit the rulers very well. On the other hand, so far as they wished to pursue an active policy, either internally or externally, they would require something more than that. For it would be very desirable at times for them to be able to arouse active feelings of loyalty and even enthusiasm for the government and its measures. The obvious technique for doing that would be, in the first place, to establish a rigid control over all sources of information and all expressions of opinion. And beyond that it would be necessary to organise an elaborate apparatus of propaganda appealing to the emotions. The people, as a whole, would be conditioned to respond readily to such appeals and to accept without question the information and opinions handed out to them. It would, of course, be essential that any elements in the population which showed a tendency to scepticism or criticism of such information and opinions should be promptly eliminated, lest their dangerous thoughts should prove infectious. It may be noted, incidentally, that, if people are to be prevented from thinking for themselves and thereby possibly coming to unorthodox opinions about political affairs, it will probably prove necessary to control their thinking on a variety of other subjects as well. For instance, states which have, to a greater or lesser degree, worked on these lines have generally exercised a fairly rigid control over the kind of history that is taught or written and have sometimes even extended it to some branches of science.

The tendency to develop these characteristics or attitudes of mind is not to be thought of merely as a possible danger against which governments by expert rulers would have to guard themselves. It is rather a necessary development which follows logically from the fundamental case against democracy. And part, at any rate, of the fundamental case for democracy would be based on the belief that these characteristics are not desirable, but that certain other characteristics, opposed to these, should be developed not only in a select few but in everyone as far as possible. The democrat will not necessarily hold that the qualities he regards as desirable can be developed in everyone up to an ideal level. But he believes that it is better to have more of them rather than less, and even a little than none at all. He will maintain, further, that the establishment of a considerable degree of democracy and of the machinery for democratic government is an important influence in producing the qualities he values. He does not

necessarily suppose that these qualities will follow immediately and automatically from the establishment of democratic institutions. But he is convinced that there is little or
no chance of their developing without such institutions.

If we ask what the qualities are which the democrat particularly values, we can look for the answer in the first place
by contrast with the qualities which a non-democratic government must necessarily develop in the mass of the people. The
democrat does not, for instance, like apathy and indifference
to public affairs on the one hand, nor does he like credulousness and suggestibility on the other. He would like everyone
to feel some degree of interest in and responsibility for the
interests of the whole community, but he does not want this
to be merely emotional, blind loyalty, or patriotism. Of
course he does not want to eradicate such emotions, but he
wants them to be combined with and tempered by active
critical thinking. He thinks it a good thing for people to be
ready to discuss and use their own minds about things that
concern the community even if they do not do it as well as
he might like. And he sees little prospect of getting them to
do it at all unless they have some chance at some point of
having a share in the decisions of the state.

There are two qualities in particular which the democrat
regards as virtues and which the undemocratic state must
necessarily try to suppress. One is independence, the insistence on the right to think for oneself and form one's own
opinions. The other, which is not always found with this, is
the recognition of the same right for other people. That is
tolerance, the respect for the right of other people to have and
express their own opinions. This is as far as possible from
mere apathy or 'indifferentism'. It rests on a positive respect
for other personalities, and often requires a good deal of self-
discipline, and control over our natural impulses to resent
other people having different opinions from our own. The
democrat believes that the combination of these two, independence and tolerance, is an essential part of a satisfactory

relation between individuals which is, in its turn, a test of a satisfactory organisation of society.

On this view, then, the ultimate justification for democracy is as a means to producing certain states or attitudes of mind in the citizens, independence of mind, respect and tolerance for others, interest in public affairs, willingness to think about them and discuss them, and a sense of responsibility for the whole community. There may be other incidental advantages, positive or negative, but these by themselves constitute an ample basis for the democrat's belief.

This fits in quite well with a view that has been expressed by some writers to the effect that the object of democracy is to create a public opinion. That does not, of course, mean that it aims at securing complete agreement on every question, though no doubt when genuine agreement does become widespread that is to be welcomed. The most it necessarily demands is agreement to differ, which implies, not only accepting the fact of differences of opinion, but also agreement on the way in which these differences are to be settled in practice. But the important point is that public opinion should become really public and really opinion. It should be public in the sense that it should be widespread and based on a concern for the whole community, and it should be opinion in the sense that it should consist of conclusions reached as a result of thought and discussion, not unthinking acceptance of formulae handed down from above. This has much in common with the ideas that Rousseau seems to have had in his mind when developing his theory of the General Will.

But the fallacy of Rousseau, and of some modern writers who speak of government by public opinion, lies in talking about the General Will or public opinion as something that is already there, and only waiting for the proper machinery to be developed to express itself. In reality, the terms stand for something which, to begin with, is only a potentiality but which has to be gradually developed all the time and is never

realised in its completeness. We want to make our will as
general and our opinion as public as possible, but cannot
expect to reach the ideal limit. No doubt, however, in so far
as something approximating to a genuine public opinion is
formed, the democrat will want it to have its way. That is
not because he believes that it will necessarily represent the
wisest decision, but because he thinks it desirable that people
should form the habit of making up their minds and accepting the responsibility for the results. Election slogans are
necessarily very imperfect expressions of political ideas, but
the phrase coined by William Jennings Bryan in 1896, 'The
people have a right to make their own mistakes', comes much
nearer to expressing the essence of democracy than Lincoln's
hackneyed formula of 'government of the people, by the
people, for the people'.

  This, then, in bare outline, is the kind of case that could
be put up for democracy as against even the most perfect
form of non-democratic government. As a safeguard against
the possible evils of imperfect forms of such a government its
value is obvious. The next point to consider is what conditions are necessary or desirable for the most complete realisation possible of the democratic ideal in practice. It is, perhaps, hardly necessary to say that the first essential condition
is the establishment of democratic machinery and institutions. By that is meant provision for giving at some point
the whole or the great part of the body of citizens the legal
right to give a decision on important political questions. This
involves, in the first place, the right to vote. But it also involves certain consequential provisions necessary to make that
right a reality. An obvious instance of that would be the provision of adequate polling places. We may recall that in the
ancient world such elements of democracy as there were in
the Roman Republic were made entirely meaningless, when
Roman citizenship was extended far beyond the bounds of
the city, by the fact that the citizens could only cast a vote in

Rome itself. But this, and similar points, are matters of detail into which it is unnecessary to go further here.

The important point to recognise, however, is that the mere establishment of democratic machinery by itself is not enough. There must also be the will to use it. There would be no value in establishing universal suffrage, for instance, if no one ever troubled to cast a vote. On the other hand, it would be a great mistake to underestimate the importance of machinery and institutions. The will to use them would be of no effect unless they were there to be used. Indeed, the existence of the institutions will often itself provide the stimulus to use them, a stimulus which may sometimes produce its effects only slowly and gradually.

None the less, the democrat will recognise that there may be certain conditions in certain societies which would make it in practice impossible for democratic institutions to be used even if established. It might be possible that in such conditions the immediate establishment of such institutions would do positive harm to the ultimate ends of democracy. In those conditions even a convinced democrat might quite reasonably wish to delay the setting up of democratic institutions until the conditions had been improved. But this argument requires to be used with the greatest caution. It is the natural weapon of those whose belief in democracy is more a matter of public profession than of inward conviction. Our old friends, the efficient administrator and the ardent revolutionary or reformer, would once more be likely to combine in putting it forward. In general, the statement sometimes heard that people should not be given democratic institutions till they were fit to use them is, taken literally, absurd. It is rather like saying that we must not go into the water till we know how to swim. The case for democracy rests on the belief that the qualities that the democrat values cannot be developed except by the use of democratic institutions, and it is only by practice that people can learn how to use them. It may be added that, in some cases, the establishment of these institutions might provide the most effective stimulus for the removal of the unfavourable conditions. It was not a mere coincidence that, in this country, the step towards democracy taken by the second Reform Bill was speedily followed by the first establishment of a national system of education. Robert Lowe's well-known remark 'We must now educate our masters', which he made after the passage of the Reform Bill, was an indication of this.

At any rate it is clear that there are a number of possible conditions which might help or hinder the development of democracy. They are not, of course, all on the same level. Some may make so much difference that they could be described as practically essential (or fatal) to democracy. Others might make it much easier or more difficult but not to a degree that could not be counteracted. Others, again, might make only a small degree of difference. In what follows an attempt will be made to indicate some of the most obviously relevant conditions. In each case the question to ask is: How far does this or that condition make it easier or more difficult for a public opinion to be formed among the mass of the citizens and, when, or in so far as, it is formed, to have an effective influence on the decisions of government?

Chapter IX

THE CONDITIONS FOR DEMOCRACY

WHAT conditions, over and above the legal establishment of democratic institutions, are favourable or necessary for the working of such institutions and for the attainment of the results at which they aim? Some of the more obvious will suggest themselves at once. In setting them out, I shall present them in the form of ideal conditions for the perfect working of democracy. But, of course, no conditions ever are ideal and no form of government ever works perfectly. It is sufficient to say that the nearer we come to satisfying these conditions the better will democracy work. Further, we must distinguish between the pre-conditions (if any) which must be fulfilled before democracy can begin to work at all, and the conditions which can only gradually be fulfilled in the actual working. This is particularly so with regard to the moral conditions, the states or attitudes of mind which seem required. Some of these may be just those states of mind which can be developed to any great extent only by the actual practice of working democratic institutions. Yet it may be possible that some small degree of them must be present before the institutions can begin to work at all.

(1) An obvious instance of this can be found in our first requisite, a general interest in public affairs. This clearly is something that can be developed to any degree only if the opportunity for effective participation in politics is present. Even when it is we should never expect to find a community in which every single individual took an active interest in political questions. The democrat would be reasonably satisfied if a considerable majority did so, and he would probably think it better than nothing if it was only a minority, as long

as that minority was distributed throughout the different sections of the community and not confined exclusively to one class or group.

On the other hand, it is not easy to see how a democratic constitution could start working at all unless there was some degree of this interest to begin with. If we could imagine a community which had never heard of democratic institutions and showed not the slightest interest in them, it would probably be futile for an external power to try to impose such institutions on it, without at least a prolonged period of education and effort to stimulate the necessary degree of interest in them. In our own country, as in many others, the line of development has been for a minority, which alone possessed political rights at first, to extend these by a series of steps to the whole body of citizens. As this happened the interest in politics was extended also.

In some cases this was supplemented by organised agitation of the unprivileged citizens for the grant of political rights. Such agitation, in certain circumstances, could itself provide the first lessons in the use of democratic methods and produce the beginnings of the results that could be hoped for from the establishment of democratic institutions. At the time of the first Reform Bill in this country Francis Place commented from his own observation on the civilising effects that the agitation for reform had on some of the wilder industrial districts in the north of England. He notes that 'in spite of the demoralising influence of many of our laws . . . it has impressed the morals and manners and elevated the character of the working-man'. He mentions the great improvement in public order and, among other things, the fact that 'in every place as reform has advanced drunkenness has retreated'. And he goes on to ask, 'Why, except for the fact before stated that people have an object the pursuit of which gives them importance in their own eyes, elevates them in their own opinion', and so on.[1] Such a result could only be

[1] Quoted from Graham Wallas, *Life of Francis Place*, p. 145.

expected when agitation of this kind was possible, as, except for sporadic acts of repression on the part of the authorities, it was at that period. If total repression were attempted, the result would probably be either that the aspirations of the unprivileged were crushed out altogether or that they took the form of conspiracy and violence. And that would tend to produce quite a different set of characteristics among those concerned, which would be much less favourable to the future working of democracy.

On this general question of interest in public affairs, one slight qualification has been suggested, which is worth a moment's consideration. It was once said that the English make a success of their political system because they don't take their politics too seriously. We need not discuss how far the first part of this dictum is accurate. But the epigram as a whole, while, like most epigrams, hardly defensible if taken literally, points the way to a side of the truth which may easily be ignored. In a sense, it is impossible to take politics too seriously. But that does not mean that we must not take anything else seriously: there are plenty of things of importance in life besides politics, things, moreover, into which politics do not, or need not, enter. If this applies to politics in general, it applies even more to particular political issues, many of which may easily be taken too seriously. The tendency to feel that all is lost if a particular measure does or does not get through, or, more frequently, if a particular political party does or does not get into power, is one that may easily be carried to a point at which it becomes a threat to the spirit of democracy. No doubt active politicians may often come to feel like that, though those who rise to the top generally attain a wider view. But that makes it all the more important that they should be balanced by a sufficient number of people in the country who, while keenly interested in politics, retain enough sense of proportion to see them in their place in all the wide variety of human activities.

(2) Another condition which seems at first sight necessary

or highly desirable for the working of democracy is a minimum standard of education, amounting at least to literacy, throughout the population. It has at times been suggested that a literacy test for the vote ought to be applied. The democrat would not necessarily find anything very objectionable in that, provided always that opportunities for education were open, or were in process of being made open, to everyone. On the other hand, it is interesting to note that in some countries where complete self-government has recently been attained, the franchise has been extended to wide sections of the population which were completely illiterate. How that will work remains to be seen. But even in these cases it would seem that this was regarded as a provisional state of things, while awaiting the results of a general extension of educational facilities.

(3) Our third condition is, perhaps, the most essential of all. Indeed, it might almost be called part of democracy rather than a condition of its working successfully. That is free expression of opinion and free discussion. We cannot absolutely identify this with democracy, as under certain conditions it has been found under governments which could hardly be described as democratic. In eighteenth-century Prussia, for instance, under the autocratic rule of Frederick the Great, a considerable degree of freedom of discussion and criticism was allowed and even encouraged. Frederick is reported to have said, 'My people and I have an agreement: they are to say what they like and I am to do what I like'. But such a state of things is inherently transient and seems bound to develop either in one direction or another.

It must also be recognised that, as a matter of history, things that we regard as among the essentials of democracy— free speech, settlement of political questions by discussion, and the like—have generally, in the first place, been put forward as demands only by a minority of the population. Parliamentary government, which is the usual form in which this demand has been met, has nearly always begun on the

basis of a restricted franchise, and there have been periods in
some countries in which the mass of the people seem to have
preferred an autocratic government. But there can be little
doubt that the establishment and maintenance of these habits
of constitutional procedure, even if only among a minority,
have been of inestimable value as a basis for the subsequent
development of democracy, which means, in effect, extending
these habits from the minority to the whole people. This is
obviously a much easier thing than trying to inculcate them
into the whole population at once.

But, with all qualifications, the connection between freedom of discussion and democracy is essential for the fulfil-
ment of the aims of the latter. The twin virtues of independence and tolerance necessarily express themselves in the
habit of free discussion and can be developed only in such an
atmosphere. Nothing that we can call public opinion, in the
sense described above, can develop if all information and
expression of opinion can come from only one source. And
there can be no question of the opinion of the people having
an effective influence on the decisions of government, because
that opinion, in so far as it can be called an opinion at all,
will, within very wide limits, be just what the government in
power chooses to make it. But the point seems too obvious
to need further discussion.

A question that does need discussion is whether there are
any limits to the freedom of speech which must be the general
rule under a democratic government. In modern times, the
question has often been put in the form of asking whether a
democracy is bound to extend toleration to political groups
which do not believe in democracy, in our sense, and would
certainly not tolerate other views than their own if they got
into power. Are we bound to allow democratic liberties to be
used to undermine and destroy democracy? Some people,
for instance, have held that if the German government had
been a little less tolerant in practice they could have sup-
pressed Hitler's movement at a comparatively early stage,

before it had gained too much popular support. If this had been done it might have prevented the final destruction of all elements of democracy in Germany.

It is, of course, not in question that a democratic government, like any other government, would use force against an attempt to overthrow it by violence. And that would naturally be extended to direct incitement to such an attempt and to direct preparations for it as, for instance, by the collection or distribution of arms. At the other extreme, reasoned criticism by individuals of democracy as a form of government would surely have to be tolerated by any democratic government worthy of the name. Even the Athenian demos, which was always intensely suspicious of anything that had even the slightest suggestion of favouring an oligarchic revolution, never, so far as we know, put Plato in peril for writing the *Republic*. The problem in the main arises when it is a matter of an organised party or group of people who, there is every reason to suppose, would be prepared to seize power by force when occasion arose, and in the meantime devote themselves by propaganda and other kinds of indirect action to undermining the foundations of an existing democratic government.

It would be hard to say that there is anything illogical or inconsistent in a democrat advocating the suppression of such a movement. The tolerance that is a condition of democracy is a mutual tolerance, not a one-sided one, and those who do not accept it as a condition of their own action have no claim to benefit from its acceptance by others. There is something analogous here to the position of a country which is working for the peaceful settlement of international disputes and is always ready for its own part to submit its claims to arbitration. There is nothing inconsistent here in its preparing to defend itself by arms against another power which tries to get what it wants by force. But none the less the democrat will regard this line of argument with considerable suspicion. Though logically impeccable it may be psychologically disastrous. For there is plenty of experience to show that the habit of repression, once started, may very easily grow and extend far beyond any legitimate bounds. It is not very difficult to find far-fetched and remote possibilities of a threat to democracy in all kinds of different views and to use this as an excuse for repressing any view that one dislikes, so that eventually freedom of opinion may be destroyed in the name of freedom of opinion. In ancient Greece the cry of 'Democracy in danger' was one of the most potent weapons in the hands of would-be dictators. In the ages of religious persecution some militants could argue that force should be used, not only against heretics, but against men of orthodox views who were not sufficiently energetic in the suppression of heresy, and the militant democrat might easily be tempted to argue in the same way. In any case, democracy cannot be permanently founded on a basis of repression, and the democrat will run a great many risks rather than have recourse to it. None the less, it remains true that there may be rare and exceptional occasions when the temporary suppression, at a critical moment, of a particular set of opinions, even if they fall short of an open advocacy of immediate violence, may preserve a democracy which might otherwise be overthrown. But, just because such occasions are rare and exceptional, it is impossible to lay down clear-cut rules beforehand to decide when they arise.

The question of possible restrictions on freedom of speech arises again when it is a question of the dissemination of false information and the making of false charges against individuals. Obviously the use of deliberate falsehoods in political discussion is no service to democracy, but very much the reverse. And if we could discover an infallible lie-detector there would be everything to be said for the suppression of such methods of controversy. But, in the world as it is, it would be necessary to proceed with caution. It is a frequent result of strong political views to believe that one's opponents are arguing dishonestly and sometimes telling downright lies. In many cases such charges are most satisfactorily dealt with by open discussion with its rebuttals and counter-rebuttals, until in the end public opinion comes down on one side or the other or somewhere between the two. But in cases where the legal issue can be clearly defined and brought before a proper judicial tribunal it is certainly desirable that the making of unfounded charges, particularly against individuals, should be penalised by law. Our own laws of libel and slander have often been criticised and very likely their operation is far from perfect. But, on the whole, there can be no reasonable doubt that their operation provides a much healthier atmosphere for democratic discussion than would a state of things in which any unscrupulous person was free to make the most baseless charges against anyone that he wished to discredit.

I have spoken so far of restrictions on freedom of discussion which might be imposed by the sovereign power in the state. But there are many possibilities of such restrictions being imposed by other agencies, restrictions which could not normally be as complete and overwhelming as those imposed by the state but which might come much closer to our daily lives. Various possibilities in this direction have been explored by different people at different times. Some socialist writers have dwelt on the 'potentially coercive relationships' inherent in the positions of employer and employed under a capitalist system, and their opponents have replied that the potentially coercive relationships would be much greater if the sole employer were the state and the managing capitalist were replaced by the managing official. Less attention has been paid to the potentialities of coercion arising from our relations with our families, our mates or professional colleagues, or our neighbours. In reality, potentially coercive relationships are omnipresent, existing, in fact, wherever one person or body of persons is in a position to make things unpleasant for another. It is a legitimate subject of discussion where the greatest danger comes from in any particular set of circumstances, and how it can best be guarded against. Obviously no particular system can remove the possibility altogether.

Certain measures against it can be taken by law, as for instance when intimidation in elections is made an offence subject to legal penalties. But the main safeguard can be found only in a developed public opinion.

(4) There is a further condition, connected with this, which it is difficult to formulate in precise terms. One way of putting it would be to say that free discussion, to produce its full value, must be real discussion in the sense that it may possibly produce some result. People's minds must be in some degree open to influence by it. Of course, no precise quantitative estimate of this is possible, but even in making a rough judgement of it, there are certain cautions to be borne in mind. Above all, we must not look for too immediate an effect. For people's minds to be open to argument does not necessarily mean that in a short space of time by a single train of reasoning, or even in a single election campaign, it ought to be possible to convert them from one opinion to another. That may occasionally happen but it is very rare, and, indeed, not necessarily to be desired. Those who expect it are almost certain to be disappointed, and are then inclined to end up by saying that other people, or at any rate their political opponents, are quite impervious to argument. But that misses what is really much the more important result of continued discussion, that is its effect on the slow and gradual modification of opinion. There is a remark by Mr Attlee in a letter to Harold Laski which is very much to the point here. 'In my time', he writes, 'I have seen a lot of useful legislation, but I count our progress much more by the extent to which what we cried in the wilderness five-and-thirty years ago has now become part of the assumptions of the ordinary man and woman.' No one can doubt that this sort of thing happens, and, though doubtless other influences come in too, it would be unreasonable to deny that the habit of open discussion has a good deal to do with it. Indeed, it is natural to suppose that if this habit is developed and generally accepted, it *must* have some effect on people's opinions sooner or later. But, of

course, that may vary in degree and some conditions may be more favourable to it than others.

Another way in which a similar point has sometimes been put is by saying that it must be possible to turn a majority into a minority. It was once said that the sole right of a minority in a democracy was to turn itself into a majority if it could. And it has also been pointed out that that involves a good deal more than might appear at first. It involves the right of free speech, the right to organise a group or party to propagate its views, and other consequential rights. All this is true as far as it goes, but seems to lay too much stress on this matter of majorities and minorities. It has sometimes been said that democracy is government by majority, but this may easily be misleading. The intention of democracy is to bring as many of the citizens as possible into the task of making or influencing the decisions of government. And when a number, large or small, of people are concerned, as equals, in making decisions, if general agreement is not reached the final decision has to be taken by the vote of a majority. But that is a practical necessity rather than part of the ideal.

There is a natural tendency to think in terms of the burning questions of the moment on which differences of opinion are so strong that a vote is the only way of settling the matter. We readily forget the much wider range of possible issues which have become, in fact, in any particular community, matters, not necessarily of absolute unanimity but at least of widespread general agreement. In smaller bodies it is a quite common experience to find that a general discussion results in the end in a decision that is accepted by everyone, or nearly everyone, as the most satisfactory possible. This is usually regarded as a desirable result. It takes much longer to arrive at in a large community. But everyone could think of views which have been at one time regarded as highly controversial and the subject of passionate debate, but in the end have become generally accepted or tacitly dropped. They have become, in fact, in Mr Attlee's words, 'part of the as-sumptions of the ordinary man and woman'. The position of the monarchy, religious toleration, the need for universal education, women's suffrage, voting by ballot are examples that suggest themselves in this country.

There is also a tendency, when we talk of 'turning a minority into a majority', to interpret it in terms of the party system as meaning that one party loses its majority and the other one gains it. But it might equally well mean that the same party retains its majority but gradually comes round, in whole or part, to the policy of its opponents. Of course, this would not satisfy ardent party members who want an imme-diate and complete conversion, and also, irrespective of policy and opinions, want their own group to be in power. There undoubtedly are advantages, for a variety of reasons, in a change from time to time in the personnel of those in office, and it is certainly essential that there should be the possibility of this. But even if the voters do not take advantage of this possibility, the essentials of democracy are preserved as long as a change of opinion and policy as a result of discussion is possible.

There are, however, countries in which political activity is to a greater or lesser degree carried on by groups divided by unalterable differences. An obvious instance would be the division, more frequent formerly than it is now, into social or national groups within a state. These are not susceptible to argument or discussion, and if one group is in a minority it will always remain a minority. That need not prevent a good deal of free discussion, which may produce an effect in time. But if the voters in electing their representative think of nothing but the particular national group to which he belongs that would certainly not be favourable to democracy. That is a special case of a wider possibility. It may happen that over a prolonged period voting is determined solely by one issue and nothing else is thought of. For instance in Ireland for more than half a century votes, apart from occasional personal disputes, were cast entirely either for Home Rule or the Union. As long as that state of things lasted any considerable degree of democracy could not develop, though the potentiality was there.

(5) A point on which a great deal of controversy has arisen is the effect of economic conditions on the development of democracy. It must be admitted that discussions on this subject often tend to produce a great deal more heat than light. It is certainly a highly complicated question and cannot be answered by any simple formula. It seems likely that some social and economic conditions will be more favourable to democracy, in the sense in which the term is used here, than others, though that does not necessarily mean that any one set of conditions is absolutely necessary or absolutely fatal. But which these conditions are and how great their influence is can be decided only by a careful analysis of the facts in each particular case. The question to ask is: How far does this or that set of conditions make it easier or more difficult for the mass of the people to form their own opinions on political questions and for the opinions so formed to have an effective influence on the decisions of government?

It would take a whole volume to deal with all the considerations that have been or could be raised in this connection. Here it is only possible to suggest some of the questions that might reasonably be asked.

(a) Is a certain standard of economic or material welfare necessary for democracy to work? This point has sometimes been raised in connection with views that assert that this or that economic system, which supposedly would raise the standard of living for the population, is an essential condition of democracy. Lenin, for instance, wrote in 1917 that under the capitalist system 'the modern wage-slaves are so crushed by want and poverty that "they cannot be bothered with politics"'. Taken as it stands this statement is too obviously in contradiction with the facts to be taken seriously. But there is very likely some truth in the implication behind it, that a certain minimum standard of material welfare is necessary before people can begin to 'be bothered with politics'. Where the line is to be drawn, it is impossible to say with any precision. On the other hand, it is certainly not true that the better off people are the more they become interested in politics. Indeed, discontent with their material conditions is one of the commonest motives which can lead them to demand or to make use of democratic institutions.

I do not know if it is necessary to explain that this does not cast the slightest doubt on the desirability of raising the general standard of living. And there is no evidence whatever that democracy is not as capable of doing this as any other form of government, and it is quite as likely as any other to make it one of its main aims. But the two are not the same. It is perfectly conceivable that a country might have a high degree of general prosperity under a despotic government, and, on the other hand, people have been prepared at times to sacrifice a certain amount of material benefit in order to be able to govern themselves.

(b) A more complicated question is the degree to which considerable disparities of wealth are a hindrance to democracy. It is probably true that, as a rule, the tendency of a democratic form of government, once established, would be to iron out these disparities, though this may not always be the case if the minimum standard is high enough. But it has been maintained that the disparities must be ironed out *before* anything that could be called democracy could begin to work. On the whole, the evidence so far available does not seem to support this view, at any rate as a universal rule. It is not now a question of how far the influence of rich men could prevent democratic institutions being established, but of how far they could prevent them from working democratically once they had been established. And the answer to that will depend on a variety of factors, on the traditions of the community, on the other institutions, and on the state of mind of the people concerned.

Taken by itself the mere possession of wealth does not necessarily give any particular degree of political power at all. To reduce it to its simplest terms, the mere fact that someone is richer, even very much richer, than I am does nothing to prevent me from thinking for myself about public questions, from expressing my opinions freely, from coming to a conclusion after discussion, and from casting a vote which will count just as much as his. We can, of course, imagine possible conditions under which the fact that some people were richer than others would give them a considerably greater degree of political power. In a country where bribery was widely prevalent, for instance, the rich man would have a much better chance of buying votes or bribing politicians or civil servants to a degree which would influence important decisions of policy. But there is nothing necessary about this, and in many countries such conditions do not exist, at any rate to an extent which could seriously affect major decisions. The danger, so far as there is any, is one that can be guarded against. The same applies to other less direct ways in which the influence of rich people might be exercised. In any case the question must be answered by examining specific and concrete conditions, not by vague and general statements about the influence of wealth.

It must be clear that the discussion here is purely concerned with the ownership of wealth, which is not necessarily the same thing as power within the various concerns from which the wealth is derived. To talk of a rich man still sometimes conjures up the picture of a man who owns and controls a large business concern and takes an active part in its management. No doubt, under some forms of industrial organisation the fact of legal ownership can give a man the opportunity of exercising active control over a particular concern, but that will not amount to much in practice unless he is prepared to give a good deal of his time and effort to it. No one can have very much power without working for it, and there are, of course, many cases of businesses in which the nominal owner or owners exercise little or no control over the actual manage-ment. On the other hand, a man may be very wealthy and derive all his wealth from investments, for instance government stock, which give him no legal control over the management of anything whatever.

(c) This leads on to the much more important question of the influence of various types of industrial organisation on democracy. Is, for instance, the tendency towards large-scale industry a favourable or unfavourable influence? Or does it make very little difference one way or another? Our answer would depend partly on what we are comparing it with. There are those who would maintain that the most favourable field for democratic government would be a community of peasant-farmers and small independent craftsmen and traders, and no doubt a strong case could be made out for such a view. That does not, however, mean that it is the only possible condition, and in any case it is not a practical alternative for most modern states. As between the large limited company with widely disseminated ownership, where the real control is in the hands of salaried directors and managers, and the medium-sized business controlled by one or a few working owners, it is hard to say which the democrat would wish to see predominate. It is possible to think of various subtle ways in which one or other would affect the working of politi-cal institutions, but it is doubtful whether the effect would be very great either way.

(d) This assumes that a substantial part of industry still remains under some form of private ownership. But there are those who would argue that this in itself is, if not fatal, at least a grave hindrance to the proper working of democratic institutions. One way of putting this point of view is to claim that we must have democracy in industry or economic democ-racy before political democracy or democracy in the govern-ment of the state can work. But these terms are used in a great variety of ways, not always clearly distinguished by those who use them. It is necessary to attempt a brief examination of their possible meanings before we can see what effect they could have on the working of political democracy.

'Economic democracy' is a particularly vague term. Sometimes it seems to mean little more than equality of wealth or income. Something has already been said about this. But it is clear that, in itself, it has no necessary connection with any form of government. Obviously, equality in this sense could exist in a society which was autocratically governed by one individual or a small group of individuals and where the people, as a whole, were never called upon to have or express an opinion on political affairs at all. It would merely make for confusion to talk about democracy here. 'Democracy in industry' is somewhat more precise. 'Industry' is a collective name for a number of organised bodies, which, like all organised bodies, have some form of government. It makes sense to ask how far there is, or can be, a considerable element of democracy in this government. But this element has been looked for in a variety of different directions. Three different forms of it, not necessarily incompatible with each other, suggest themselves at once.

(i) When the Webbs wrote their great book on *Industrial Democracy* they were thinking primarily of the work of the Trade Unions. And certainly the existence of Trade Unions does introduce an element of democracy into the government of industry. They represent, or aim at representing, the great majority of the people engaged in any industry, and they exercise a considerable degree of influence on the government of that industry. They do not, as a rule, attempt to control the day-to-day decisions in which the government of industry so largely consists. But they do attempt, often successfully, to influence or determine more general decisions on certain important matters, in the way of making rules which control the conditions of work for their members and seeing that these rules are observed. These rules, in their turn, will often be found to exercise, if only indirectly, an influence on the other decisions which the management make.

For our purposes, however, it is more important to ask how this will affect the working of democracy in the government of the state. Certain obvious advantages from that point of view suggest themselves. Trade Union activities provide a field in which many people can get an interest in and training for the working of democratic institutions which may be transferred later to the field of national politics. Again, so far as there are possibilities of political pressure being exercised by employers on the employed, the Trade Unions provide a valuable defence against this. Incidentally, this applies equally whether the 'employers' are private capitalists or state officials. It is true that the Unions can develop their own 'potentially coercive relationships'. But there are limitations on the possibility of this, and there are other influences which might counteract it. Again, there are sometimes believed to be considerable possibilities of undue pressure being exerted by big employers not on their employees as voters but on the government after it has been elected. So far as that is a real danger the existence of powerful Trade Unions provides a possible counterweight. Altogether it seems that, in a complicated modern society like our own, strong Trade Unions and professional organisations generally, though they have their own dangers, form an element distinctly favourable to democracy.

(ii) Sometimes, however, the idea of democracy in industry is carried further, and on one possible interpretation it is taken to mean the control of industry by a democratically organised state. Of course, in any case politics are largely concerned with industrial questions and in every country industry is run under general rules and conditions laid down by the state. But a good deal more than that may be implied and it may be taken to mean the ownership by the state of the whole or a great part of industry. The desirability or otherwise of this has been the subject of prolonged discussion for many generations. But a good many of the arguments used have no direct bearing on the question with which we are now concerned, namely the effect that this would be likely to have in strengthening or weakening the democratic element in government. Only one or two suggestions on this point can be attempted here.

No one, probably, would be so simple-minded as to suggest that the ownership of industry by a state, however democratic its political constitution, would necessarily mean that the people as a whole took an active part or even exercised any considerable influence on the actual running of industry. Indeed, the effect might be the very opposite. The complications of the task might have the effect of throwing more power into the hands of administrators and officials, and this, in turn, might give them an increased influence on the decisions to be taken in other matters outside the bounds of any particular industry. On the other hand, there is no reason to suppose that this would necessarily be the case, if the danger was recognised, and various possible safeguards against it have been proposed. The fact seems to be, as was suggested earlier, that the importance of ownership by itself may easily be exaggerated. And that tells both ways: for if the advantages may be exaggerated so may also the dangers. What really makes the difference is the way in which things are organised and administered, and who the people are who are in a position to make the effective decisions in each case. From that point of view it only makes for confusion to talk as if ' the state' were a single person or even a single large government office. In every case we ought to ask, whenever anyone speaks of 'the state' doing this or that, what individuals are actually concerned and take the actual decisions. At any rate, it is clear that state-owned industry may be organised in a variety of different ways, and there are numerous possibilities of division and decentralisation of effective power. The whole question calls for much closer and more detailed discussion before a conclusion could be arrived at. But the first impression seems to be that both state ownership and private ownership of industry call for appropriate precautions to fit them in to the working of a democratic state. But there is no

reason to suppose that these precautions could not be successful if there was a general will to apply them. This may seem
rather a tame conclusion and will certainly not appeal to the
enthusiasts on either side. But it is not necessarily any the
worse for that.

(iii) There is another possible system to which the term
'democracy in industry' could be reasonably applied. That
is the scheme by which the various industries were to be
organised as self-governing units democratically governed,
with every individual person in the industry having an equal
vote. This was advocated by the Guild Socialists in England,
and, in a more extreme form, by the Syndicalists on the Continent. In the usual form it contemplated an organisation in
which whole industries were taken as units, but a similar idea
could also be applied to smaller units, the 'self-governing
factory' for instance. This last has occasionally been tried in
practice, but the ideas of the Guild Socialists have remained
in the realm of pure theory. In the absence of any actual
experience it is difficult to say what the effect of such a system
would be on democracy in the government of the whole
country. One can see possibilities of either favourable or unfavourable effects, but it would be a mistake to dogmatise on
the subject. In any case, the question of its political consequences is only one of the questions that would have to be
answered before arriving at a conclusion about the general
desirability of such a system. And some element of it or
approximation to it might quite reasonably be approved of by
those who could not advocate its adoption in its complete form.

All this, of course, is only to touch the fringe of a big subject. But I will content myself, in conclusion, with recording
a personal impression that no economic system in itself is
essential or fatal to the working of political democracy if the
people as a whole really desire it.

(6) There are other conditions which might be considered
as possible helps or hindrances to the working of democracy.
One that greatly interested the Greek thinkers but has been

very largely ignored in modern times is the question of the
size of the community best suited to democracy. Most Greeks
were inclined to take it for granted that beyond a certain size
a community would cease to be a community at all in the
sense that they required. Obviously many of the natural
limitations on the optimum size for a Greek city-state no
longer apply today. Aristotle, for instance, said that a city
should not be too great for all the citizens to hear the voice of
a single herald, whereas we should only need to think in
terms of a single wireless announcer. But are we justified in
assuming that there are no limits to the size of the community
in which democracy could work successfully? How far, for
instance, could we really imagine a world-state being democratically governed? The question is worth pondering over,
along with others of the same kind.

After all this, there remains the practical necessity that, if
democracy is to work at all, it must come to terms with oligarchy. That is to say, some working arrangement must be
reached which will provide for the influence both of the expert
element and the popular element in the work of government.
Without the expert element the popular element cannot get
what it wants efficiently done, and nothing would be so frustrating to a democracy as to find that, when a real popular
opinion in favour of something had been developed, it could
not be carried out at all or could only be done so inefficiently
as to make it not worth attempting. That is just the kind of
situation which might produce a reaction against democracy
and a movement for a strong autocratic ruler. Some degree of
oligarchy must necessarily arise in any organisation of any size,
and this had better be recognised and accepted. The particular
institutions of modern democratic states can profitably be examined from that point of view, and the question asked how far
they secure the efficiency for which the expert element is necessary, and how far they help to create a genuine public opinion and
to give it an effective influence on the decisions of government.

Chapter X

THE MACHINERY OF DEMOCRACY—
REPRESENTATIVE GOVERNMENT

BEFORE going on to consider the forms of organisation or constitutional machinery which may be devised to meet these necessities of democracy two preliminary warnings should be borne in mind.

In the first place we must not talk as if everyone concerned had had a clear notion in his mind of what was needed to make democracy work and had then proceeded to construct constitutional machinery designed to meet these needs. Different states vary in the degree to which conscious purpose has been present in the construction of their machinery of government. But even when this purpose has most clearly been there in the early stages of a particular constitution, the machinery has been constantly modified, not always consciously, in the actual working in order to meet immediate practical needs. What we can say is that in a democracy there is generally present at the back of people's minds some sort of feeling both of the need for expert efficiency in government and of the need for making possible the participation of the people in the decisions of government. The former, perhaps, is more likely to be aroused in times of emergency, whereas the latter is less intense but more lasting. But the appeal to the people is also a common feature of those occasions when a strong opposition challenges the decisions of a government. In any case, the necessity of reconciling these two needs, even if it is not formulated in general terms, is a constant influence on the development of political institutions. It is therefore legitimate to examine these institutions from that point of view, and consider them as attempts to meet these needs.

Secondly, there can obviously be no question here of any detailed examination of the institutions that have arisen in modern states in the course of the attempt to make democracy work. It will only be a matter of pointing out some of the general features. But generalities by themselves do not always mean much unless they are illustrated by particular instances. And in looking for particular illustrations I propose to look in the main at the institutions of our own country. In a book written primarily for British readers that seems the natural procedure. But it does not, of course, mean that British institutions are to be regarded as the only possible ones or the best ones or the normal ones. It merely means that in looking for illustrations of the ways in which certain general ideas can be expressed in practice it is simplest to look in the first place to expressions of them with which we are most familiar. We can then see for ourselves how, in other cases, there might be divergences in detail from the particular instance that we have chosen as typical. Some of these possibilities will be pointed out in the course of the exposition.

The first general institution, then, which we find in all modern states which have any claim to be called democratic is that of Representative Government, the system by which, to put it briefly, the voters, instead of deciding political questions directly for themselves, elect a body of representatives to take the decisions for them. We take this so much for granted that we are apt to identify it with democracy. But to an ancient Greek the identification would have seemed by no means obvious. It is worth while spending a little time to consider firstly the general nature of representation, and then the forms that it can take, and the way in which it can be used to secure the aims of democracy.

The general idea of an individual or a group appointing someone else to represent him or them for certain purposes is simple and familiar and hardly seems to call for further analysis. Nor is there any special difficulty about the sort of case with which we are concerned, where the particular purpose for which the representative is chosen is to go to meetings of some central body where certain questions are discussed and decisions taken. But we have to note here the possibilities of considerable variation in the position of the representative and his relation to his appointing body. It has become customary in common speech to distinguish two main types of this, and to speak in one case of a delegate and in the other of a representative. As these terms are generally defined they stand for two extreme types which are rarely, if ever, met with in practice, though it is often possible to find approximations to one or the other. By 'delegate' is meant someone who is appointed by a body which has already made up its mind on all the questions to be dealt with, and which sends him to represent, to speak, if necessary, and to vote, for these views. He is completely bound, has no choice of his own, but has simply got to act as instructed. The representative, on the other hand, in the extreme form is chosen as the best man for the job and left absolutely free to make up his own mind on all the questions that come up for consideration. The terms seem rather unfortunately chosen, as the delegate is the man who represents the views of the electing body whereas the representative is the man to whom it delegates its powers and responsibilities. But we have become too much accustomed to them for any attempt at alteration to be worth while.

Clearly, the pure delegate is possible only under very limited conditions. The issues on which the elected body is going to vote must be known beforehand so that the electors may come to a decision on them and instruct their delegates accordingly. Something like this situation may occur at large congresses of professional or other bodies, where the branches have had the agenda beforehand and have discussed and come to a conclusion on all the items in it. In such circumstances the discussions at the congress do not affect the voting at the time, but may have an influence on opinion in the future. The most perfect example of pure delegates can be found in the members of the Electoral College in the United States, which nominally elects the President. The original intention was that they should be representatives, chosen for their wisdom and free to exercise their discretion in the choice of a President. In fact they are chosen simply to cast a vote for the candidate whom the majority of their electorate favours and have no discretion in the matter at all. The result is that they have, in reality, no useful function to perform and the institution might just as well be abolished.

The absolute representative is even rarer, at any rate when it is a question of election to a body which has any authority or power of making binding decisions. It is different, of course, when it is a matter of an advisory body or a body charged with the duty of inquiring into and reporting on some question or questions. Even in the first case there may be occasions when a representative is appointed with complete discretionary powers and without any commitments. This may work all right when it is a question of election by a small group of people with a close personal knowledge of the possible representative or representatives. But the larger the number concerned becomes and the less the possibility of personal knowledge of the candidate for election, the more: perilous becomes the risk involved in appointing anyone to a position of power without knowing how he is going to use it. At any rate, such a procedure would not be democratic. It would not be entirely oligarchic, because it would still retain the responsibility of the voters for choosing between possible candidates, but it would certainly be a movement in that direction.

The question of most interest in the present connection is the position of the elected member to a representative assembly, such as a House of Commons or a Chamber of Deputies or a Congress. To which extreme does he or should he approximate most nearly? Obviously he cannot be a pure delegate: that would be impossible for a member of a body which was elected for a period of any length and which had to deal with any question that might come up for decision during that

time. In most cases we shall find that as far as his legal position goes he is a pure representative, free to vote as he chooses
without regard to the wishes of his constituents. There is,
of course, always the fear of the next election, which may be
more or less effective according to circumstances, but as long
as the existing mandate lasts, there is no judicial process or
administrative machinery by which the electors can exercise
any control over the way in which their representative votes.
There have been at times attempts to exercise such control.
A century and a half ago Burke's constituents in Bristol
claimed the right to send instructions to their member, a
claim which he vehemently and successfully repudiated. In
recent times a few states in the United States have experi-
mented with the institution of the 'recall' by which the voters
could at any time revoke the mandate of their representative.
But that has never been widely adopted. In general, the representative is subject to no direct control, and there have been
occasions on which a representative has voted against the
known wishes of his constituents and in contradiction to the
purposes for which he was originally elected.

These, however, are exceptional cases, and in the ordinary
usages of politics there are certain conventions which regulate
the relations of a representative to his constituents, though
these often become a subject of controversy and are, in any
case, to some extent flexible. Thus, there is a general obligation on him to support the views and policies which he was
elected to support. But that does not turn him into a mere
delegate, because they are in the first place his own views, and
he is elected because he has persuaded the majority of the
electorate to agree with him. That is to say, he is not elected
and then instructed how to vote. He is elected because it is
already known how, in general, he would choose to vote himself. This knowledge, however, may vary in definiteness.
Sometimes it may be no more than a knowledge of the general
direction in which he is likely to move, for instance towards
more or less state control, towards internationalism, or to-

wards a vigorous foreign policy or appeasement, and so on. Sometimes it may be a detailed programme of measures. Sometimes, though more rarely, it may be his views on one question which dominates people's thinking at the moment, to an extent which makes the election practically a referendum on one subject, such as Home Rule in 1886 or the position of the House of Lords in 1910.

But under a parliamentary system, such as is found in the British Commonwealth and most of the countries of Western Europe, there is nearly always one question on which the electors require to be informed before all others. And that is the leader or leaders whom the candidate is going to support. We can see for ourselves at any election the extent to which our voting is determined not by a preference for one candidate in the constituency as against the other but by a preference for the Conservative or Labour leader or group of leaders as against those of the opposite party. We are really voting primarily to put a particular man or team of men into power. So prominent is this factor that people at times have compared our House of Commons to the American Electoral College. That is, of course, a great exaggeration, for the individual member may make a considerable difference to what happens. He may have an influence in Parliament, and he can certainly have an influence within his party, where he influences the decisions of the leaders and in the long run has his share in determining which individuals are to emerge as leaders. None the less the exaggeration has a certain element of truth in it.

One result of this is that, when we talk about our representatives and their relations to their constituents, we have to make it clear whether we mean the individual members for whom we vote directly or the group of leaders for whom we vote indirectly. As a general rule, the member is regarded as being bound to support the leaders of his party, more particularly if they are in office, when a vote against them might mean a change of government. Exceptions to that rule are only rarely admitted in exceptional cases. The leaders, however, would be generally recognised as having a good deal more latitude, particularly when they have to deal with fresh problems which have not been much discussed at previous elections. The electorate expects them to follow certain general lines of policy, but they are fairly free to interpret what that means in practice. Normally, they are supposed to be bound by any specific declarations of policy made at the previous election, but there have been cases where a government in power has departed from these. That is the most obvious kind of occasion on which individual members may feel justified in voting against their leaders. Thus, the majority of the Conservative Party abandoned Peel when he repealed the Corn Laws in 1846, and a strong minority of Liberals broke with Gladstone when he became converted to Home Rule for Ireland.

Other questions have been raised in this connection. From time to time the men in power may feel called upon to deal with matters which have not been dealt with, prominently or at all, in the discussions which preceded their election. If they bring in very controversial measures on these points they are often attacked by their opponents on the ground that they have no 'mandate' for these measures. But there is no generally accepted principle here. The only established convention seems to be that those who object to the measures should make protests of this kind and that those in power should take no notice of them. This seems on the whole a sensible arrangement. In any case, the government has been elected to make decisions, and, in default of explicit pledges or clearly indicated intentions, those who elected it expect it to act as it thinks best in the circumstances. On the other hand, it is no doubt true that in a democracy it is the duty, as well as the interest, of representatives to take account of popular feeling, and they should be very slow to introduce important measures which are widely disliked. But this is a general obligation and has nothing specially to do with election pledges. There is, of course, the practical difficulty for a government of deciding whether the dislike of a proposed measure is genuine and deep-rooted, or whether it is a temporary dislike, based largely on misunderstanding which will disappear when the measure is seen in actual working. The thought of the next election is generally sufficient security that a government will be careful in its judgement of this.

The situation is, of course, different in a presidential democracy, such as the United States, where what we should think of as the government is elected directly and the representative bodies are elected separately and have no responsibility for making a government. Even here some of the same problems arise, when it is a question of how far the elected houses are to co-operate with or obstruct the policies of the administration. There are also differences, though less fundamental ones, in parliamentary democracies where there are a number of different parties none of which can expect to gain a majority by itself. There the representative assembly certainly makes the government, but the electorate does not vote for this or that government. It votes for one or other of a number of different groups, each of which has a mandate to secure as much influence as it can in the eventual formation of the government. This gives the representatives as against the electorate a good deal more freedom of action than under a system such as ours, and the influence of the electors on the formation of a government, though it exists, is considerably more indirect. There are various intermediate possibilities, which it is unnecessary to explore here.

Another question which has been raised on various occasions is how far a representative is supposed to represent the special interests of his constituency and how far the interests of the whole country. The answer that is given in fact to this will vary with the circumstances of each country. Under a presidential system, where the active head of the state is directly elected by the people, there will be likely to be to some degree a tendency in the former direction. A popular

American magazine stated quite recently that the members of Congress were elected to look after the interests of their particular locality and that only the President was responsible for thinking in terms of the good of the whole country. It may be doubted whether the members of Congress themselves would accept altogether such a limited view of their functions. But there is no doubt that a much stronger tendency in this direction is recognised and accepted in the United States than would be the case here.

In this country the theory still generally accepted is that laid down by Burke when he told his Bristol constituents that he was elected a member for Bristol but, having been elected, he became one of the members for England. Ideally the member of Parliament is elected because he represents the views of the majority of his constituents about what is for the good of the whole country. On the face of it, this seems to be more in accordance with democratic ideas, since one of the aims of democracy is to habituate people to thinking in terms of the good of the whole community. But on the other hand in practice this must not be carried too far. Though representation wholly or mainly of sectional interests is contrary to the spirit of democracy a certain amount of it inevitably creeps in, and perhaps this is not altogether undesirable. For it is not really to the interests of the whole that the interests of any section should be altogether overlooked or neglected. If there is any danger of that it is just as well that there should be a member or members who can speak for these interests, either in Parliament or within the party. But it is important not to admit this as his chief function and to insist on the overriding duty of thinking of the country as a whole. And, of course, the nearer a member gets to a position of leadership the less he is expected to think of sectional interests. No one, for instance, would wish the Prime Minister to let the special interests of his own constituency influence the direction of his policy.

We are now in a position to get a picture of the machinery by which a democracy can attempt to secure the combination.

in due proportions, of expert efficiency and popular opinion in the work of government. It will be convenient, as previously suggested, to take our own constitution as our typical illustration. There would, no doubt, be many adjustments and modifications in detail to be made when we came to deal with the constitutions of other countries. But I think that the basic elements that can be found in our own constitutional machinery could be detected also in that of any modern representative democracy.

It will be desirable, in the first place, to look beyond the old-fashioned distinction between the legislative and executive functions of government. It is, no doubt, useful up to a point, but it does not take us very far and may easily be misleading. What we have, as suggested earlier, is a series of decisions of different levels of generality. Naturally decisions of a higher level of generality are normally regarded as of superior authority to those below them. But that runs right down the scale and it is largely arbitrary if we try to draw a line and say that decisions above a certain level are matters of legislation whereas below it they are matters of executive action. The distinction becomes even more misleading when we try to apply it to different bodies of persons and to describe one as the legislative and the other as the executive. It is true, of course, that we have decided to call by the name of 'laws' general rules which are regarded as having superior authority to any other general rules and that we have decided not to recognise them as laws until they have gone through the final stage of being passed by Parliament. This is a useful convention for legal purposes, but totally inadequate if it is regarded as a description of the realities of government. It tells us nothing about what we chiefly want to know, namely what persons or bodies of persons are responsible for the decisions which have to be taken before this final stage is reached. In other words, who really makes the laws?

For the purpose of understanding the working of democracy, it may be found helpful to picture the organs of government as a series of links in a chain extending from the popular element at one end to the expert element at the other. The most completely popular element is, of course, the electorate, while the most completely expert element is found in the Civil Service. In between we have, firstly, the House of Commons, which, taken as a whole, is close to the popular element, and then the Cabinet which comes nearer to the expert element. Each one of these, in its own way, can be concerned with decisions at every level of generality, from the most general declarations of policy, down through the formulation of these in the general rules that we call laws to the individual decisions in particular cases. Let us consider briefly each one of them in their turn.

About the electorate there is not much that needs saying. We most of us know what it is like to be an elector. But there are two things which need specially to be borne in mind. One is that the function of the elector is not confined to casting a vote every few years for one candidate or another. That is the ultimate sanction by which he secures some attention being paid to his needs or his views at other times. But it gives him an influence which extends much more widely. No one who surveys the political scene in this country over a number of years can doubt that so far as a public opinion is formed it often exercises a strong influence on the decisions that are actually taken, even when an election is not immediately in prospect. It is very hard to estimate the extent of this with any precision, but that there is some degree of it is certain. Sometimes the effect is positive, and sometimes negative. There are reliable reports of cases where members of a party have contemplated making a political issue out of some matter before the country, and then after receiving reports from their constituencies have thought it wiser to drop it. The other point to remember is that the opinion of the electorate is by no means exclusively concerned with general questions of policy. These may be the main factors in determining votes at elections. But at other times public opinion may become just as excited about a particular executive action as about a legislative measure, and this excitement in turn may affect the actual decisions taken.

This influence is generally exercised through the next link in the chain, the House of Commons or other elected assembly. That, indeed, is the main function of the ordinary member of Parliament. It must always be remembered that Parliament is not a body of experts elected to govern the country. If it tried to do that it would probably do it very badly. It is true that the members of Parliament constitute, as it were, a reservoir from which those who chiefly govern the country are drawn. But which among potential leaders are actually going to form the government is decided by many other influences, in particular by the votes of the electorate. It is true, also, that there may occasionally be found members with special knowledge on a particular subject or subjects, who, because of this knowledge, exercise a special degree of influence on the decisions taken on certain questions. Indeed, most members have some kind of special knowledge of their own. But it remains true that the main function of the ordinary members is to keep the government and the electorate in touch with each other. They have to interpret public opinion, as each of them sees it, to the government, and to act as a brake if the government shows signs of following a course that might be too generally unpopular, particularly if it looks like endangering their seats. And equally they have to interpret the government to the electorate. No doubt this interpretation may often take the form of a violent controversy with an opponent. But that may be quite an educative process. Here again it must be noted that Parliament, though it is spoken of in legal terms as the legislature, is very far from confining its interest to legislation or questions of general policy. It is constantly concerning itself with particular administrative actions. One special form of this is the protection of individual constituents from hardship or injustice that may arise from the way in which laws or rules are applied by administrative officials. It was with that in mind that the phrase was coined that 'question-time in the House of Commons is the cornerstone of British liberties'. But vital though this service is, it is generally accepted in this country, at any rate in theory, that it must not be allowed to pass the somewhat narrow line that separates it from jobbery and nepotism, pressure for special favours, and the like.

We then come to the Cabinet, which is so much at the centre of things that in this and in other countries it is commonly alluded to quite legitimately as 'the Government'. Its members are the people who have the greatest degree of influence on the most important decisions. Here we find the closest union of the expert and the popular elements. Cabinet Ministers, while they are in office, give their whole time and attention to it, and most of them have given a good deal of time to learning the business of politics beforehand. More than anyone else they fill the place of Plato's expert rulers, in that they are supposed, to a special degree, to think in terms of the good of the whole community. At the same time, they depend on popular support for their being in office at all, and it is equally recognised as part of their duties to try to give a lead to public opinion on the great questions of the day.

Cabinet government also embodies a recognition of the impossibility of keeping up the theoretical distinction between the legislative and executive functions of government. With a few exceptions Cabinet Ministers are individually heads of the chief government departments. As such they exercise a general supervision and control over the administrative and executive work. Collectively, on the other hand, they form, in effect, a committee of the majority party in Parliament for the purpose of preparing legislation. Almost all the important pieces of legislation that pass through Parliament are presented to it by the Government, and a good deal of the time of the Cabinet is taken up with the consideration of the Bills that are to be presented. From this point of view, it would not be far off the mark to consider the Cabinet as the First Chamber of the legislature.

Finally, we have the Civil Service, about which something has already been said when we were considering possible directions in which the anti-democrat might look for his expert rulers. Civil servants are the only people who are permanently and professionally engaged in the work of government, and as such they necessarily exercise a very great influence on the decisions to be taken at all levels. The old theory that they are simply there to apply, under the order of the Minister, the laws laid down by Parliament to particular cases is entirely inadequate to the actual situation. In fact, no law of any importance would be drawn up without previous consultation with the civil servants concerned, and they will often have a good deal of influence on the final form it assumes. No doubt their primary concern is to see that it is administratively workable. But the limits of this cannot be defined precisely, and the leading men in the Civil Service will often find themselves in a position to give advice on more general questions of policy. It might be said that their position inclines rather to that of the specialist than the expert, to use our earlier distinction. That is true up to a point in that most of them are specially concerned with the work of one particular government department. Even within the departments, however, a distinction is made between the administrators and the real specialists, for instance the scientific or technical advisers. In any case, a senior civil servant who has to assist in drawing up legislation will inevitably find himself to some degree looking outside his particular department and thinking in terms of the general interest.

This, then, is a simple schematic picture of the kind of machinery that can be developed to make democracy workable. There are, of course, many other influences that may play a part. I have said nothing, for instance, about the independent experts, writers or thinkers or researchers, who succeed in getting themselves accepted as authorities on various political questions and who exercise a considerable influence on the development of public and official opinion. The Webbs provide an obvious example of this, and there are many others. Such people are an inevitable by-product of the freedom of speech which is essential to democracy, and they play an invaluable part in a democratic society. But the general framework is, perhaps, by now sufficiently clear.

Before closing this part of the discussion, it may be desirable to say a word in explanation of what some people would regard as a serious omission. That is the absence of any reference to the judicial function and the position of those who exercise it. With us, at the present time, the necessity of a separate and independent judiciary has become deeply engrained in our ordinary habits of thought, and people at times speak of it as one of the essential elements in democracy. This, however, is a mistake. For, however desirable it may be, it has no necessary connection with democracy. Obviously an independent judiciary could be established under many different forms of government. In this country the independence of the judges was secured long before there was anything approaching democracy. On the other hand, in most of the ancient Greek democracies the sovereign people exercised a great part of the judicial functions of government, and they certainly did not keep a sharp separation between their judicial functions and their political aims and opinions. Indeed, the whole idea of the judiciary as a separate branch of government is comparatively modern, at least in theory, though it was developing in practice much earlier. Locke, who was among the first to develop the idea of the division of powers and made a clear distinction between the legislative and the executive, has nothing to say about the judiciary, which he seems to treat as a branch of the executive. Indeed it must be admitted that, looked at purely as a matter of theory, the distinction between saying what the law is in any particular case and carrying it out does not seem so fundamental that it calls for an entirely different set of people for the two functions. Even in modern times there are countries in which the sharp distinction between the two that we are accustomed to is not regarded as nearly so essential, and no obviously disastrous results seem to follow. Nowadays English lawyers have come to realise that there is a great deal more to be said for the French system of *droit administratif* than they used to think a generation or two ago.

The important thing is to secure the supremacy of the law, and that not for any reason specially connected with democracy but as a general condition of a satisfactory life for the citizens. That we should know as far as possible what our rights and obligations are, that we should be tried and punished only for defined crimes, that authority over us should be exercised according to settled rules and not purely at the discretion of individuals—these and others like them are generally recognised among us as desirable conditions of life. The absolute separation of the judiciary from the executive is one way of securing these things that we have discovered by experience. But it is only a means to an end, and there is nothing about it in itself which makes it either desirable or undesirable.

Chapter XI

THE PARTY SYSTEM

ANOTHER institution or piece of constitutional machinery which has developed in all modern representative governments is the political party. It is a curious fact that in Great Britain, where anything that could be called a party system first began, political parties are still unrecognised by the law. There is no Act of Parliament or judicial decision which mentions any political party, and parties, as such, have no legal rights and no legal obligations. This is not necessarily the case in other countries where the position and conduct of parties have often been the subject of legislation. This is particularly so in modern times, and is part of a general tendency, noticeable in this country as much as anywhere else, for parties to become more highly organised, more rigid and more all-embracing than they were in their earlier stages. So marked has this been that some people have even suggested that we ought not, properly speaking, to talk of a party system at all earlier than about a hundred years ago, or even, as has been claimed, before the beginning of the present century. There does not, however, seem much to be said for this view. People in this country had begun to talk in terms of parties as early as the later years of the seventeenth century, and the development of parties, though it has been considerable, has also been continuous. But in any case this is a matter of historical interest. We are concerned here with parties as we know them, and the more important general features that we can note in them would probably be found to apply at any time in, at least, the last seventy or eighty years, and could be found in embryo much earlier.

Let us, then, attempt a short preliminary definition of a political party. Obviously, it is a group or association of people, with some degree of organisation. Further, it is a voluntary group: people are, normally, free to choose whether to join this party or that or any party at all. Like all voluntary associations it will have an object or purpose, and the test or condition of membership will be the willingness to further the object or objects of the association. This object need not be precisely defined, particularly if the association is not legally recognised, but we shall expect to be able to discover it from the ends or purposes which the association actually pursues and which the members are expected to accept if they are to remain members. In the present context we are not, except incidentally, concerned with all the particular ends which particular parties have pursued or could pursue at different times and places. We want to see if it is possible to find a general formula for the sort of purpose that every party must pursue if it is to be a party at all.

The idea has often been put forward that the primary and essential object of a party is to further a particular policy for the country and that the test or condition of membership is agreement at any rate on the general lines of the policy that ought to be followed. No doubt there is a close connection between the political party and the policy, and indeed for certain parties at certain times this description would fit well enough. But as a general description applicable to all parties it is clearly inadequate. For it is perfectly possible for a party to exist and to hold together as one party while its members are deeply divided in opinion on some of the most fundamental political questions.

Thus in the United States since the Civil War political activity has been carried on almost exclusively by the two great parties, the Republicans and the Democrats. But at many periods it would have been difficult or impossible to find any clear-cut differences of opinion which divided them, and, what is more important, much deeper differences of opinion or attitude towards political questions could be detected within the parties themselves. It has generally been possible to distinguish in each party what might be called a liberal or progressive and a conservative wing, and, allowing for local differences, a liberal Democrat and a liberal Republican might well have far more in common with each other than either would have with an extreme conservative in his own party. As a general rule, over a long period, the procedure has been for the issue between the two wings to be fought out within the party and then, for election purposes, the whole party would line up behind the leaders who emerged victorious.

In our own country this tendency has never been developed to anything like the same extent, but distinct traces of it have been apparent from time to time. In order to avoid current controversies, we may look for an instance further back in history in the career of Lord Randolph Churchill. His general sympathies were, by the standards of that time, distinctly progressive, but he preferred to remain within the Conservative Party and, in his own phrase 'educate the party' to his point of view. His own career was a failure, but there is no doubt that he did, to some extent, have an effect on the attitude of the party. Parallels, more or less close, can be found at other periods.

This feature of the political party can be brought out by contrasting it with another kind of political organisation which springs up from time to time and may, in certain circumstances, exercise considerable influence. That is the organisation which is formed for the sole purpose of advocating or opposing a particular measure of reform. Examples in this country would be the Anti-Corn Law League, founded in 1839, the Education League which had a considerable influence in bringing about the passage of the first great Education Act of 1870, or the Tariff Reform League, which was first formed at a time when the Conservative Party was not yet completely converted to a policy of Protection. Here the sole reason for the existence of the organisation is to advocate a particular policy, and any member who changed his opinion about that policy would have nothing to do but to leave the organisation. It would be absurd to imagine a member of the Tariff Reform League, who had become converted to Free Trade, staying on in the organisation and trying to convert it to Free Trade. Yet that can happen in a political party and, indeed, in some countries may become the regular procedure.

But there is one point on which all members of a party must be agreed if they are to stay in the party and work together at all. That is in the desire to attain political power for the party. Members of a party might differ on any or even all lines of policy. But anyone who definitely did not want a particular party to attain power (except, perhaps, temporarily, as a matter of tactics) could not possibly remain a member of that party. So that our brief formal definition of a party would be that it was a voluntary association of people for the purpose of attaining political power. It might, perhaps, be as well to add 'by constitutional means'. There are to be found at times organisations which call themselves parties whose aim is to seize power by violence and suppress all other parties. But they have little in common with the parties as we know them in democracies or any kind of representative government, and it is a pity that they have come to be called by the same name. At any rate, it is not with that kind of party that we are concerned.

With regard to parties in the usual sense there still remains something more to be said about their relation to policy. For if a party has attained political power, or a share of it, it has then got to decide how to use it, that is to say it must have a policy. This means that *at some point* the members of the party will have to reach an agreement, not necessarily on what they would like, but at least on what they would be prepared to accept in the way of measures. It is possible, however, for a party to go on for a considerable time before

arriving at such an agreement, particularly if it has no immediate prospect of attaining power. As a general rule, though
there are, of course, many exceptions, differences of opinion
are   more   noticeable   in   oppositions   than   in   government
parties. Further, of course, a party is not committed for ever
to any particular line of policy. It may change it in whole
or in part while still remaining the same party. But while it
is in power it must agree in general if it is to remain there.

This, then, is a summary statement of the minimum conditions necessary for a party to be a party and to function as
such at all. But there are many further questions that suggest
themselves, and as soon as we begin to ask them we run into
all sorts of complications which in some cases make any
simple answer impossible. Why, for instance, does a person
attach himself to a particular party? Here there is a particular complication at the outset, for attachment to a party
is a thing which admits of a wide variety of degrees. A political party is rather like a comet, which has a solid nucleus at
the head and a long gaseous tail which follows it. So in a
party we find a hard core of members, candidates, party
officials, and active workers, and then a much larger number
of people who enrol themselves as members and perhaps pay
a subscription, but do little more except vote at elections, and
so on down to the much greater number still who habitually
vote for one party but never formally join it. It would be
simplest, perhaps, to consider the case of those who definitely
join the party with the intention of taking a more or less
active part in politics, and then we can, if we wish, go on to
see how far our conclusions would apply to those whose
attachment is looser and less definite.

It is possible to think of all kinds of motives which might
lead a man to attach himself to this party rather than that, but
we must remember all the time that rarely, if ever, does
anyone act from one motive alone. Thus at one extreme we
can imagine a man thinking out carefully what he would
regard as most beneficial for the country as a whole and then

deciding to attach himself to the party which seemed to him, after full consideration, to represent most nearly his views in this matter. This would be an ideal case which would probably never be realised completely in practice. None the less it would be foolish to deny that this process of rational thinking might be one among other influences which determined a particular person's decisions. We may suspect that it has played a particularly large part in some cases of people who have left one party, perhaps at some personal sacrifice, and joined another.

At the other extreme there is the possibility that a man might think out clearly which party seemed likely to give most scope for his own personal interests and ambitions and then decide to join it. This, also, is a possibility that is rarely realised in its completeness: few people are as clear-sighted or single-minded as that. But here again it may be one among other influences to affect a person's choice. It might be reasonable to suggest that it plays a part in certain other cases of change of party, particularly when a man leaves a party which seems to have little future before it in order to join one which appears to be on the up-grade. Of course, such a motive would work mostly on people with political ambitions who hoped to play an active part in politics. But in countries where the 'spoils system' was prevalent it might apply very widely.

Much more important is the influence exercised by the interests of the particular group, the trade, class, or profession to which the person making the choice belongs. The relation between 'interests' of this kind and political parties is a complicated matter and something more will be said about it later. Here we may note that the ordinary voter, particularly if he is not keenly interested in politics, will naturally be largely influenced by what he supposes to be the interests of his particular group, and, as was suggested earlier, this up to a point may not be wholly undesirable. Even here other influences come in and the competing interests of groups with overlapping membership may cut across one another. But we are chiefly concerned at the moment with the more active members of parties. Here the interests of a particular group may certainly be an influence in the choice of party. In countries where there is a number of small parties some may, indeed, be expressly formed to represent the special interests of a particular group, like the agrarian parties which at various times have played a part in the politics of European states. There is a particular complication in some of these countries in the presence of parties with a special connection with some religious body, particularly the Catholics. Here group interests may come in to some extent, for instance in matters of education. But on many matters, such as foreign policy and to some extent social questions, there is no necessary connection between the religious beliefs and the policy of the party. But where there are two, or at most three, large parties, as is the general rule in English-speaking countries, the connection cannot be so close. Here again there will be a certain tendency for people from some groups to gravitate towards one party and people from other groups to the other. But there will be found so many exceptions and the interests of so many different groups will be involved that any general equation of membership of a party with the interests of any particular group would be plainly impossible. None the less that remains one among other possible influences on the choice of party.

It is not necessary to say much about the idea which has occasionally been put forward, that there are inborn temperamental differences which incline an individual towards one party or another. No doubt there are temperamental differences between individuals which may have a considerable effect in some directions on their political thinking. But so far as it is possible to trace such effects at all they cut right across party lines, and in any case they are so overlaid with other influences that it is quite impossible to take any account of them in this connection. What is much more important is the influence of family connections. There is a popular idea that children always tend to react against the opinions of their parents. But as far as politics are concerned this seems to be verified more often in literature than in real life. If we look at the people who are active in politics in our own country we shall find in the vast majority of cases that the son enters politics on the same side as his father. And that is only natural if we consider how much of our early information and impressions about politics come from the family, particularly if it is a family in which the political interest is strong. Sometimes, also, there may be settled political traditions in a wider group. This may combine with the influence of group interests, but it may be largely independent of that. In the United States, for instance, it used to be said that people of Irish descent would traditionally incline to the Democrats and people of German descent to the Republicans. And in our own country we sometimes find, though less than formerly, that certain districts or regions have a traditional attachment to one party. In this sense, many of us may almost be said to be born into a party, and W. S. Gilbert's famous lines have a certain application though not perhaps in the exact sense which he intended.

So much for the question why individuals join a particular party in the first place. Following on that a more important question arises as to why people stay in their parties, or, to put it from the other point of view, what holds a party together. To some extent the same answers will apply here. But they are hardly sufficient in themselves. As we have seen, some sort of agreement on policy at some stage is essential, and in politics as we know them best it plays a large part. And that is just where the difficulty comes in. It might be suggested that the party starts from certain general principles or ideals which all its members share and that the practical policy will follow from these. But that is hardly a satisfactory answer. It would no doubt be possible in some cases to formulate general statements of principles or ideals to which all members of a party could subscribe, particularly if the formulation was not too definite. But there are other cases in which it would be difficult or impossible. And in any case political principles are not fixed and clear-cut laws from which the practical policy to be followed can be deduced with logical certainty in all situations. General principles when they are worked out in practice may often seem to mean very different things to different people. And in any case their application will largely depend on judgements about many other things, as for instance the factual situation at any particular time. On the other hand, we can often find people who would formulate their principles or ideals quite differently and yet might come to an agreement on the immediate practical policy to be followed. Further, new problems and new situations are always arising, which call for fresh thinking to deal with them. It is clear that it is agreement on the practical policy to be followed that is necessary for a party to hold together, and the question still remains how that is to be secured.

The answer is largely to be found in the fact that agreement is arrived at by members of an already existing organisation. And that fact has a strong influence on their thinking. When a new problem arises or an old one takes a new form, the members of a party do not go away quietly by themselves, think out the problem independently and then come back and find that they have all come to the same conclusion. They begin by thinking about it as members of a party, they discuss it primarily with other members, and they start with a strong predisposition to agree with the members of their own party and, as a general rule, to disagree with the members of opposing parties. In fact, on questions of practical policy the party forms the opinion much more than the opinion forms the party.

The full significance of this cannot be appreciated till we take into account a further factor which plays a great part. That is the general psychological tendency to the development of what, as a convenient name, we may call group loyalty.

One of the few generalisations about human nature that we can make with reasonable certainty is that all normal human beings tend to develop towards any group to which they belong, for no other reason than that they belong to it, a sentiment of loyalty. Loyalty is a complex of emotional tendencies involving in varying proportions a feeling of affection towards the group and a wish to be at one with it, a desire for its advantage, a pride in it and a wish to be able to regard it as superior to other groups, anger or resentment at any attack on it in deed or word, rivalry or hostility to other groups which are in conflict or competition with it, and other allied feelings. This does not necessarily mean that every human being in fact actually feels like this to every group to which he belongs. But he always tends to do so, that is to say that he will do so unless some positive counter-influence is strong enough to suppress or drive out the feeling. Thus he may feel so intensely for one group that there is no room left for similar feelings towards others. Or the interests of two or more groups to which he belongs may clash or conflict, and the loyalty to one may drive out the loyalty to another. Or a group may treat one of its members so badly that his love for it may turn to hate. Again, some of the groups to which he belongs may be so unimportant and play so little part in his life that the feeling remains in embryo. Yet hardly any group is so trivial that it cannot arouse these feelings in favourable circumstances. I have heard the manager of a large holiday camp say that after a very few days in the camp an intense feeling of rivalry, or even hostility, will arise between the residents in 'Balmoral' and the residents in 'Sandringham', or whatever the different buildings in which they are housed are called.

The potentiality of the development of this sentiment is present in any group. But in which groups it will develop to an extent sufficient to influence action at all seriously will depend on a variety of factors and will differ from one time and place to another. In modern times the loyalty to the national group, which we call patriotism, bulks particularly large, and is generally regarded with the highest degree of approval. But that has not always been so and is, indeed, not invariably the case nowadays. In England we have developed very strongly the idea of loyalty to an educational institution, 'the old school tie' sentiment, which is almost unknown else-where, at any rate to anything like the same degree. But when we come to the political party it is obvious that the conditions are favourable almost everywhere for the develop-ment of a high degree of this sentiment. Members of a party, particularly if they are active in politics, are necessarily always keenly aware of the group to which they belong, and in the nature of things the party group is constantly in opposition or hostility to the rival party or parties. We know that our national patriotism tends to be aroused particularly strongly in time of war. And political parties are always at war.

The point of particular interest is the relation between group loyalty and the development of opinion on political questions. Broadly speaking we can say that whenever a group is consciously formed and organised with a special connection with any set of opinions the effect on those hold-ing the opinions and forming the group is considerable. The opinions themselves get a greatly increased emotional force, they are held with stronger conviction, doubts disappear and change or modification of opinions becomes more difficult and unlikely. At the same time the feeling against those in another group which holds different opinions is intensified beyond anything that mere difference of opinion would account for. This is even more noticeable when an individual changes his opinion and leaves his group: the 'turncoat' or 'renegade' is often denounced with a bitterness that exceeds that directed against those who have always been of a dif-ferent opinion. Experienced politicians know well that form-ing or joining an organised group hardens opinion and inten-sifies differences. At the beginning of the present century the Liberal Party in this country was seriously divided in opinion on some important issues, and a good deal of ill-feeling was engendered thereby. Their shrewd leader, Campbell-Bannerman, said repeatedly that he could tolerate any differences of opinion but he could not tolerate a separate organisation being set up. More recently Earl Attlee has said much the same thing in connection with disputes within the Labour Party. In general we have to recognise that, once we attach ourselves to a party or any political organisation, it is inevitable that a considerable degree of group loyalty towards the organisation will be developed in our minds and that this will necessarily colour all our thinking on public affairs.

This feeling of loyalty to the group may, under certain conditions, come to overshadow matters of opinion altogether. In the United States in 1912 Theodore Roosevelt broke with his party because it would not accept his lead on matters of policy, and he tried to set up a new organisation. In spite of his great popular appeal he failed decisively, and an experienced observer at the time said that most Americans seemed to feel that to leave one's party merely because one disagreed with its policy was almost as discreditable as deserting one's country for a similar reason. In this country that point of view has never developed to the same extent, in spite of Disraeli's 'Damn your principles! Stick to the party'. But we can detect a tendency at times to think of the adoption of a policy as a means to the success of the party rather than the other way round. Of course, other influences may affect the formation of opinion and this fact may at times set up a tension between opinion and party loyalty which in extreme cases may produce a general break-up of party ties. But this is exceptional. In general, party loyalty is sufficient to secure at least a working agreement on policy, and it is certainly one of the most powerful influences working in that direction. More than that, it can sometimes produce a positive enthusiasm for a policy, even among individuals who have at first accepted it with many doubts and reservations.

In the light of all this, what part does the party play in the machinery of democracy, as described in the previous chapter? On the one side, it is impossible to deny that there are strong oligarchic tendencies in the party system. To begin with every party is itself an oligarchy. For in every party, as far as I know without exception, the enrolled members form only a proportion, often a very small proportion, even of those who vote for the party at an election.[1] And obviously in the affairs of the party only the actual members have any say. So the party is always a minority even when it receives the support of a majority of voters. Further, even of the members themselves only a small proportion have the opportunity or the ability or the enthusiasm to take an active part in the work of the party. It is the rule in any organised society that effective control over the decisions taken necessarily tends to fall into the hands of those who can give most time and energy to the work. From the other side this tendency is reinforced by the sentiment of group loyalty which makes members of a party ready to accept decisions even when they have had little or no share in reaching them. Further, the sentiment of loyalty often tends to look for a personification of the group in some individual or individuals, and so translates itself into loyalty to the leader or leaders of the party. This tendency varies in different cases according to the personality of the leader, the traditions of the party and various other factors. But there is always a considerable degree of it and in some cases it rises to such intensity that it becomes the main bond of union in the party. This obviously leaves a great deal of discretion to the leaders, who can be assured that whatever decisions they take, within very wide limits, they will have the devoted following of at least a large section of the party.

The main democratic corrective to all this lies, of course, in the fact that the party has to submit itself from time to time to the judgement of the electors. But the extent to which this

[1] Duverger in his *Political Parties* gives figures for the ratio of party members to voters for the party in the Socialist parties in the different countries of Europe. Nowhere does it approach a half, and in one case it falls as low as eight per cent. The average is about twenty per cent.

is effective varies with a number of factors, particularly with the way in which the party is organised. In some parties the chief, or even the decisive, influence on the policy that the party is to adopt lies with the parliamentary party, that is to say with the members who have been elected to the representative house. And among them, in turn, the predominant influence will be exercised by the leaders, for instance, the Prime Minister and the members of his Cabinet or the Leader of the Opposition and his 'shadow Cabinet'. On the other hand, there may be parties in which the effective control lies in the hands of an extra-Parliamentary body, a party caucus or group of political 'bosses', which decides policy and instructs the representatives how to vote. This may or may not include a number of the elected representatives, but the balance of power within it will be quite different from that in the parliamentary group. There are, of course, various intermediate possibilities, but these two represent the extremes and most parties tend towards one or the other.

Looking at this from the point of view of the whole country, there can be no doubt which is the more democratic. For the electors in a democracy it is of the first importance that they should know for whom they are voting, in other words that the ostensible leaders should be the real leaders. Obviously the more the control of the party policy lies in the hands of those outside the parliamentary party the less is this condition fulfilled. Besides this there are other differences in the effects of the two systems, difficult to measure precisely but none the less of great importance. The party caucus may be little but a self-elected body responsible only to itself. But at its best in parties which claim to be democratically organised it is elected by the party and feels itself responsible to the party. In practice that means that it represents the minority of party members, itself a minority of the electors who vote for it, which has the energy and enthusiasm to take an active part in the affairs of the party. This will naturally tend to consist of the most wholehearted and uncompromising supporters of the party, and the opinions that they form will naturally tend towards the extreme party line, with the least possible concessions to any doubts or qualifications of it that might occur to other people.

The elected members, on the other hand, are chosen by and responsible to the majority of voters in their constituencies, and this includes not only the active party members, the so-called 'militants', but many others as well. It includes all those who, as things stand at the moment, prefer one party on the whole but do not necessarily approve of all the tendencies in it and do not necessarily want these tendencies to be carried to the extreme. Among these will be found the people who constitute what is often called 'the floating vote', that is to say those who sit lightly to party ties and are prepared if one party goes too far in a particular direction to transfer their support to another. As a rule the party 'militants' tend to despise and ignore such people. But the parliamentary leaders are much more aware of them, and will generally regard it as part of their duty to take into account in the framing of policy both the opinions of the 'militants' and the opinions of the 'floating vote'. And from the point of view of democracy they are obviously right. For democracy means that as many people as possible should be given some degree of influence on the decisions on matters of policy. The 'floating voters' are citizens just as much as the militant party members and have just as much claim to consideration of their opinions. An incidental corollary of this is that democracy within a party is by no means the same thing as democracy in the country. Indeed the one may very well be an influence unfavourable to the other.

There is much more to be said on all this and, no doubt, many qualifications to be made in its application to particular cases. But it is time now to consider some of the undeniable advantages of the party system from the point of view of democracy.

In the first place it obviously stimulates interest in politics.

It is not the only influence in that direction, but it is probably the strongest. Critics of the system might argue that it was not the kind of interest that we want. It is too much like the kind of excitement aroused by a dog-fight or a football match in which we simply want one side to win. No doubt there often is an element of that, and if there was nothing more it might not be much worth having. But there is bound to be something more. For party warfare is necessarily carried on, to a great extent, by argument, and it is very difficult to go on using arguments for long without beginning to pay some attention to their value as arguments. Most people do need some sort of stimulus to start considering arguments. It is rare to find unselfish anxiety to discover what is best for the country, or disinterested love of truth, acting as sufficient motive for such consideration at the early stages of an individual's political development.

Connected with this is the fact that the party system secures constant discussion and argument. It always provides someone to put the opposite point of view, and, moreover, someone who cannot be ignored, as an individual critic, however able and intelligent, might well be. The government must listen to the opposition and must consider their arguments at least sufficiently to find an answer to them. There, again, it might be argued that this is not the kind of discussion we want. The effect of it is, it might be said, to make one party always ready to criticise the proposals of another just for the sake of criticising, whether they are bad or good. And the other party takes the fact that the criticisms come from their opponents as an excuse for ignoring them as merely made for party purposes, or at most for thinking, not whether there is anything in them, but what answer can be found to them.

Now, if we looked at a single discussion by itself, for instance a particular debate in Parliament, we might get the impression that there was something in this. No doubt it is considerably exaggerated, but there is certainly a tendency for the party system to produce this sort of attitude. On the other hand if we look, not at the immediate effects on a particular occasion but at the long-run effects, the story is very different. It has already been suggested that the effects of political, or indeed any kind of discussion show themselves, as a rule, not in any immediate conversions on the spot, but in the slower and more gradual formation of public opinion. People may reject arguments and criticisms on the spot because their party feeling has been aroused. But they have to think about them if only to find the answer to them. Further, they have to think of the possible effect on the opinions of those whose party ties are not so strong. And once thinking has begun it has an insidious way of undermining ill-founded opinions. The party system is a way of stimulating these discussions and ensuring that they receive attention, and it is difficult to see what better way could be found. In general it acts as a constant reminder that there are other points of view, which have to be tolerated and, in the long run, given serious consideration.

There is another point, though not specially connected with democracy, on which the existence of political parties may have an effect which on the whole is beneficial. That is through their relation to particular sectional interests. It is no doubt often the case that a particular party will have some degree of connection with some particular interest or interests, though one must beware of taking too seriously the assertions of opposing parties to that effect. Certainly people who represent some particular interest will often incline to one party rather than another. But the party itself is a body with an interest of its own, which is never, or hardly ever, exactly the same as the interests of other groups or sections. A man may be concerned with the interests of his particular trade and think that one party is more likely to favour them than another. But if he becomes an active member of a party he will never think in precisely the same way when he is thinking as a member of the party as he will when he is thinking as a member of a particular trade or other interest. At the least, as a member of a party he will have to think about winning votes, and exclusive concern for the interests of his particular trade is not likely to be successful in that aim. No doubt in some countries at some times the political party may become little more than a company formed for the purpose of sharing out the spoils of office, though even there it may be concerned to prevent exploitation by rival interests. But where higher standards rule, the party and its interests always provide some sort of counterweight to the influence of other special interests.

Many other points of interest may arise in connection with political parties, and whole volumes have been written about them. Here it must suffice to say a word about one further question, and that is the effect of the number of parties that exist in any particular country.

The one-party system which exists in some countries is, strictly speaking, outside the purview of the present discussion. For we are considering the party system as part of the machinery of democracy, and the one-party system is obviously not democratic at all. It has all the oligarchic tendencies that are inherent in any party and none of the democratic correctives that the existence of more than one party provides. One of the great advantages of the party system as we know it from the democratic point of view is that it always provides a possible alternative government and gives the electorate a choice between them. Under the one-party system there is no alternative government and no genuine choice before the electors, so that the influence of the mass of the people on political decisions is reduced to a minimum. The system is, in fact, one way of establishing an oligarchy.

But the difference between the countries where there are two main parties and those in which there is a number of parties is real and important. There are, of course, intermediate arrangements which approximate to one or the other. n Australia, for instance, there are three parties, but two of them, the Liberal and Country parties, are united in a more or less permanent coalition. For practical purposes that may be regarded as a two-party system. Or there may be two main parties, and one or two other parties which are so small as to make practically no difference, like the occasional Socialist congressmen who have sat from time to time in the American House of Representatives. But the broad difference between a two-party and the multi-party system is clear.

There is a close connection between this and the different systems of voting in force in different countries. Where one form or another of proportional representation is adopted there is a much stronger tendency towards the existence of many parties. There is no logical necessity about this. There have been countries where the single-member constituency and election by a majority vote, as we know it, was the rule and where none the less a number of parties existed. In one or two cases, under very exceptional conditions, the two-party system has remained in force in spite of the adoption of proportional representation. But, obviously, proportional representation is a great help and stimulus to the multiplication of parties, and in general its advocacy comes in the main from those concerned to establish the position of minority parties. The two, therefore, cannot be considered entirely separately.

Those who prefer the two-party system will find little to attract them in the idea of proportional representation. It is true that under an electoral system like our own the number of members of each party in the representative house will not always, or indeed generally, correspond exactly to the total number of votes cast. But there is not necessarily any disadvantage in that. For the elected house to play its part in the working of democracy, in the ways previously described, it is not in the least necessary that it should be an exact replica of the divisions of opinion in the country. It must be remembered that the first function of an elected house, in parliamentary democracies,[1] is to produce a government which can

[1] This part of the discussion applies only to parliamentary governments. I find it difficult to envisage how proportional representation would affect the working of a presidential government like the United States. But it would obviously make much less difference there.

govern. To do that it must command a majority in the elected house, but there is no necessity for that majority to be in exact numerical proportion to the majority in the country. It is, no doubt, theoretically possible for a majority in the representative body to be elected by a minority in the country, but in practice it very rarely happens. In the sort of circumstances in which it could happen it might not necessarily be altogether undesirable. For instance one party might pile up huge majorities in one or two populous districts, while the other commanded small or moderate majorities over the greater part of the country. It is at least arguable that excessive domination by one or two districts is undesirable and that the wide spread of the support for a party should be taken into account as well as the aggregate number of votes.

At the risk of being open to misconstruction, it ought to be said that it is possible to exaggerate the importance of numerical majorities. Decision by a majority vote is not a divine ordinance, but a practical device for reaching a decision when people disagree. And, as a general rule, it is impossible to suggest a better one. Obviously if one party so manipulated the arrangement of constituencies as to make it difficult or impossible for the other party ever to win a majority of seats, whatever its vote in the country, that would be the negation of democracy. But if, under a system generally accepted, as a result of the kind of circumstances which might, on another occasion, tell in favour of the other party, a party gains a majority of seats without obtaining a majority of votes, there is nothing there for tears. The important thing is that the system should be generally approved and its results loyally accepted.

In considering the relative merits of the different systems it is important to remember the point made in a previous chapter, that in voting at an election the voters are not merely deciding which particular members are to be elected but also deciding, directly or indirectly, what sort of government is going to emerge as a result of their votes. Under a system of proportional representation and many parties the elector votes for his ideal party, knowing, as a general rule, that it will not be able by itself to provide a government. The parties in the elected house will then negotiate among themselves to see what sort of government they can produce between them. But the government so produced is not submitted to the judgement of the electorate. Under a two-party system, on the other hand, most of the negotiating has been already done before the election. Sometimes a good deal of it is necessary, for under this system each party is to some degree a coalition, as far as opinions are concerned. The difference is that, being organised as a single body, it commands a degree of group loyalty and a consequent cohesion that an avowed coalition cannot ordinarily attain. In any case the result of this system is that the elector knows in general what sort of government he is voting for with a much greater degree of certainty than is possible under a multi-party system. And there is little doubt that in countries with long experience of the two-party system the ordinary elector prefers it that way. For it certainly gives him a much more direct say in the choice of a government than he gets under the other system. There is no doubt much more to be said for or against proportional representation, but from the point of view of the working of democracy that seems to be the most important consideration.

Chapter XII

THE STATE AND OTHER SOCIETIES

FROM the consideration of one particular society or association or organised group within the state, namely the
political party, we pass on to a more general consideration of
the relations of the state to the other societies of which its
citizens are members. Probably every individual in a modern
state is a member of one or more societies besides the state.
At the least, he will belong to some local group organised as
one society such as a city or a county. In addition he may
very likely be a member of a business concern, a university
or other educational institution, a trade union or professional
association, a Friendly Society, a church, a political party,
and so on, down to a social or recreational club. The position
of such societies in relation to the state has at various times
been the subject of considerable controversy. As it happens,
at the present time there seems to be a comparative lack of
interest in the question, at least in this country. But in the
years before the First World War and for some time after it,
it was the subject of lively discussion, and might at any
moment become so again.

These societies differ widely in character, and from the
point of view of their relation to the state these differences
may be important. Many of them, of course, are politically
insignificant and raise no problem in this connection. No
one, for instance, is likely to be worried about the relations
between his local cricket club and the state. But even among
the most important ones the differences are considerable.
The political party, for instance, is obviously in a special
position. In a representative government such as ours the

party is hardly a society distinct from the state. It could be more profitably regarded as itself an organ of the state or as a part of the machinery of its government, and the conflict between parties as a stage in the normal process of deciding which group of people is to have the chief influence in directing the policy of the state.

Another kind of society which has a special position of its own is the local society, the city or county or province, which in most modern countries is a recognised legal unit with a government of its own. This is, in some ways, a sort of microcosm of the state. Like the state its qualification for membership is territorial, and just as everyone must normally belong to some state so, within the state, everyone must normally belong to some local government unit. Further, the local body will be concerned with much the same kind of function as the state, though on a smaller scale. Opinion and practice may vary widely between one state and another, or in the same state at different times, on the question which matters should be decided by the government of the state and which had better be left to the decision of the local authority. In any case they are recognised as matters which are the proper concern of a territorially based society, and the only question is whether they are more appropriately dealt with by a larger or a smaller group. In unitary states, such as our own, the final decision on such a question is recognised as belonging to the government of the state, and the local bodies exercise such powers as are delegated to them by the central government. In federal states, such as the United States, the division of powers is laid down by a written Constitution and the effect of such a Constitution is generally that any alteration in this respect has to be accepted by both sets of authorities. Any alteration of the American Constitution, for instance, has to be approved both by a large majority of the Congress and a large majority of the individual states. Of course, there are also smaller local government units within the individual federated states or cantons or provinces, whose powers are not generally a matter of constitutional right. But the upshot of this seems to be that these local bodies would be most reasonably regarded, not as societies separate from the state but as subdivisions of the state. Such conflicts as can arise should be thought of as conflicts between different organs of government, similar to disputes between two government departments or between President and Congress in the United States.

There is another class of societies which are, in general terms, constituted by the voluntary action of individuals uniting for the pursuit of a common purpose. This class includes a wide variety of different groups. By comparison with the state they may be described as voluntary societies, but, just as we saw earlier that there is a small degree of voluntariness about membership of a state, so there may be an element of compulsion in these other societies. In this country, for instance, no one is under any obligation to become a barrister, but if he wishes to do so he must join one of the Inns of Court. In other professions or trades there may be a professional association, but the individual members of the profession may be entirely free to join it or not. Sometimes, as in the case of the trade unions, there is a constant attempt to make membership compulsory for all people in a particular trade, but the attempt is only partially successful, and has no legal basis. Another important class is that of the churches or organised religious bodies. Here it is the general rule in modern states that membership is entirely voluntary. The same applies, of course, to most of the other associations or societies of which mention has already been made.

From the point of view of the lawyer these societies or associations can be classified under several different heads. In our own country, for instance, they may be corporations, quasi-corporations, trusts, partnerships, and so on. These distinctions may be important in determining matters of legal procedure. But from the political point of view, which is concerned with their relations to the state and the general part they play in the public life of the country, the distinctions are only of minor importance. Something more will be said of this later. But the fundamental fact is that they are organised societies; that is to say bodies of people associated together, with a defined procedure for arriving at decisions which are accepted as binding on the whole society. In this respect they are just like the state, and in fact, though we should not ordinarily use the term, they each have a sovereign in the same sense as the state.

The first and most important question for consideration is whether any of these societies have any inherent rights or claims over their members as against the state. To translate that into the terms that we have been using, we should ask whether there are any matters in which individuals should develop the habit of obeying the commands of some other society instead of, and if necessary in contradiction to, those of the state. This, be it noted, is a question of what ought to be rather than of what is. For in fact there can be no doubt that at the present time in most, if not all countries, the habitual way of thinking is that in the final resort it is the state that should be obeyed whatever the question at issue. Certainly those responsible for the decisions of the state would never recognise the claims of any other organised society as against their own. If a man breaks the law of the land he will be proceeded against and it will be no defence to say that he was obeying the orders of some other society. On the other hand, there is not, as has at certain times been suggested, anything in the very nature of things which makes this absolutely necessary. As we saw earlier, there is no physical impossibility about the habit of obedience being distributed between different authorities for different purposes. But it is a perfectly reasonable matter for argument whether it would be convenient or desirable to develop such a habit. That is the most intelligible meaning that we can give to assertions about the 'rights' of other societies as against the state, namely that we ought, for one reason or another, to develop the habit of obeying these societies rather than the state in certain matters.

This question of the right or duty of an individual to refuse obedience to the state because he thinks that the commands of some other society have a superior claim must be distinguished from the question of the individual's right or duty to disobey the state because his own conscience tells him that what the state commands is morally wrong. Of course, the two overlap and cannot always be clearly distinguished: it may have been, for instance, the individual's private conscience that led him to join the particular society and accept its obligations of membership in the first place. None the less the distinction is a real one. An individual or a number of individuals may disobey or resist the government of the state without thinking of any other society at all. As we have already seen, people will, in fact, refuse obedience to the government of the state if its commands become intolerable, and if enough people do so the government loses its authority, at least as far as the particular measure is concerned and possibly altogether. But in such cases the people concerned are really thinking and acting as members of the state, with the aim of making the state's policy better in some respect and with no idea of advancing the claims or interests of any other society.

On the other hand, there may be cases where people refuse to obey or to co-operate with the state because they are so directed by some other society to which they belong, though left to themselves they would not have chosen to do so. Thus in 1930 the bishops of Malta and Gozo forbade their flock, under threat of ecclesiastical penalties, to vote for the Constitutional Party, which at that time commanded a majority in the elected house and would certainly have received a large body of support at the forthcoming elections if it had not been for that interference. Though not strictly illegal this action was clearly contrary to the spirit and intention of the constitution, and the British Government responded to it by

suspending the constitution altogether. The case, inciden·
tally, is a good illustration of the kind of conflict that might
arise between the state and another body, in this case the
Roman Catholic Church, even when the vast majority of the
citizens of the state were also members of that other body.
The particular occasion of the conflict was the action of the
ecclesiastical authorities in imposing disciplinary measures
on certain clerics, which, as the head of the government
maintained, infringed the civil rights that were guaranteed
to them by the state.

This case further illustrates the kind of society which might
possibly come into conflict with the state, for, naturally, with
the vast majority of societies to which people belong no question of such a conflict can arise. There seem to be two groups
in particular in which the potentiality of conflict exists. One
is that constituted by the churches or religious bodies: disputes between church and state have been endemic throughout the history of the Western world. In modern times the
most frequent and most serious difficulties have arisen in
connection with the claims of the Roman Catholic Church,
which presents the added complication of being an international body whose membership cuts across state boundaries. But on a small scale even more exacerbated conflicts
have occasionally arisen with some minor sects, as with the
Mormons in the United States in the days when they practised polygamy or the Doukhobors in Canada who refused to
wear clothes or to send their children to school. In general,
it is easy to see how any body which claims to have special
access to an infallible source of knowledge about right and
wrong might come into conflict with the state, which, without
claiming infallibility, demands obedience to its orders about
what is and what is not to be done.

The other direction in which we might look for possibilities
of conflict would be to the trade unions. But here it would be
a matter of aspiration rather than of achievement. For, in
fact, in most countries the trade unions, generally speaking,

recognise the authority of the state and are as law-abiding as anyone else. There have been, however, from time to time those who wanted to bring about, by peaceable or violent means, a drastic reconstruction of society and who hoped to find in the trade unions a firm foundation for their move- ment. The most obvious instance is to be found in the Syndicalist movement which flourished in France, with some reverberations in other countries, in the early years of the present century. A little later the Guild Socialists in England put forward similar ideas in a somewhat milder and more reasoned form. Without going into the details of their theories, we can say that the general feature of these move- ments is the demand that the various industries should be taken over and controlled by those engaged in them, particu- larly, of course, the members of the trade unions, and that they should have the absolute right to run them as they think fit. The state in most forms of the theory was envisaged as continuing to exist, but was to be confined to the exercise of its own proper functions, however they were conceived, and had no right of control over or interference with the conduct of industry. It is worth remembering that, as a rule, these movements were as fiercely opposed to state Socialism as to Capitalism, and from the point of view of the present discus- sion their particular interest is as a protest against the idea of 'the omni-competent state', to use a favourite phrase of the period. In this protest they had the sympathy of others who did not share the rest of their views, and in particular they tended at one time to form a sort of holy, or unholy, alliance with some of the advocates of the rights of the churches as against the state.

The general feature of all these views is that the state, the territorial organisation, is regarded as just one society among others, very important, no doubt, but without any claim to absolute dominion over the rest. The state exists for certain limited purposes, and the authorities of the state can claim control over its members only within the scope of these purposes. Other societies exist for other purposes and where these are concerned they have equal and co-ordinate authority with the state. If the state tries to go beyond its functions the members of the other societies can and ought to resist and to obey the other societies rather than the state. What the proper functions of the state are was a question on which there were considerable differences of opinion. Professor G. D. H. Cole, for instance, in his Guild Socialist days, argued that the state, being a territorial organisation, was most properly concerned with those purposes that people had in common by reason of 'neighbourhood', or territorial contiguity. But it was very far from clear what these purposes were supposed to be. On the face of it, it would seem that few, if any, common purposes of any importance arise merely from the fact of living on the same tract of land. On the other hand, nearly all purposes are affected to a greater or lesser degree by this. It is obvious that the pursuit of any purpose in common is a very different thing for people living in the same area from what it would be for a group of people scattered throughout the world. In fact, the Guild Socialists seem to have envisaged their guilds as societies within the same territorial boundaries as the state, not as international bodies cutting across state boundaries. The only case of any importance in this connection of a society whose membership is not determined by geographical contiguity at all is the case, already quoted, of the Roman Catholic Church. And the claims of that body still represent the most serious possibilities of challenge to the final authority of the state, possibilities that have been realised from time to time in various countries.

As against all this, the argument of those who would defend the claim of the state to be accepted as the supreme authority would probably run on lines like this:

Every community of people living together, above the most primitive level, will almost inevitably develop a number of societies within itself to which its citizens can attach themselves. Each of these societies will be pursuing its own particular purpose or purposes, and the purposes of the different societies may often come into conflict or competition with each other at every level. A trade union may clash with the employers or with another union, and the organised medical profession with the Osteopaths or Christian Scientists. The Automobile Association and the Cyclists Touring Club will press their conflicting views on road safety. The archaeological societies may protest against quarrying on the Roman Wall, which the local quarrymen may support. An angling association may oppose a scheme of industrial or municipal development which seems likely to spoil the fishing on a particular stretch of river. These are but specimens of the innumerable possibilities of conflict. Probably in a community of perfectly wise and perfectly good beings these controversies would settle themselves. But with ordinary human beings that could not be relied on. It is a reasonable generalisation from experience that the most enthusiastic members of a society will always tend to regard the purposes of their particular society as more important than any others, and to be most uncompromising in the pursuit of them. And these are the people who, as a rule, have most influence on the policy of the society.

It seems reasonable, then, to suppose that there should be some authority standing above all these particular societies and acting on behalf of the community including them all, which can decide between them, keep each one in its place, and generally co-ordinate their varying purposes. And such an authority must necessarily be supreme as against any other society. The only alternatives would seem to be, on the one hand, to let the conflicting societies fight it out between them and the strongest win. Even then there would, presumably, have to be some rules of combat and an authority to lay them down and enforce them. Otherwise it presents us with the prospect of a series of faction fights which would end in anarchy. On the other hand, there might conceivably be a rigid constitution, written or customary, which would define precisely the limits of authority of all the different societies, the state included. There is nothing in the nature of things which would make this impossible: in fact, something rather like it has often been the case in communities at certain stages of political and social development. But in an advanced modern state it would need a constitution of almost impossible complexity. In any case such a state of things would be suitable only to a static society, and would make difficult or impossible the developments that would be constantly needed to meet changing conditions. One can think of many reforms which would have been most unlikely to take place if the rights of existing organisations had been entrenched in an inviolable constitution.

The conclusion would seem to follow that in the modern world there is everything to be said for recognising some authority whose decisions will, in the final resort, be accepted as against those of any other organised society. And if there is to be a supreme authority it can surely be looked for only in the territorial state. It would be difficult or impossible to imagine a society whose membership cut across territorial boundaries exercising effectively the supreme authority in every country in which it had members. But it is not merely a matter of practical convenience, for the territorial community has a great deal more in common than the mere fact of geographical neighbourhood. It may be that there ought not to be any territorial boundaries and that the ideal to look forward to is a world state. But there is a long way to go before that is a matter of practical politics. And in the meantime the territorial community is much more nearly a microcosm of humanity than any society devoted to the pursuit of some particular purpose can be. For it contains within itself groups pursuing a variety of different purposes, people with different interests, different trades or professions, and, usually, different beliefs and opinions. It is a condition of a satisfactory society that these groups should be able to live together with a reasonable degree of harmony, and for that purpose the recognition of an authority superior to them all seems neces-

sary or at the least highly desirable. That is what the state
is, and, from this point of view, its function can be described
as the co-ordination of purposes. No doubt any existing state
will often fall short of the ideal. It may become too much influenced or dominated by a particular group inside it with
particular interests of its own. It will certainly be accused of
that by groups which want to dominate it themselves, though
the accusations will not necessarily be true. But in any case
that is the ideal to work to, and there is generally some recognition of this, however fitful and uncertain it may be. No
institution is perfect, and even if the state does not fulfil its
function as we should like, there is no other society which can
take its place.

Supposing, then, that we admit, for the sake of argument,
that the state should be recognised as having a claim on our
obedience superior to that of any other society, we are still
only at the beginning of our problems. To say that the state
must have the last word tells us nothing about what that last
word ought to be. In other words, what policy ought the state
to adopt towards the other societies within it? There are
many different possibilities here, and it is for the state to
decide between them. That means in a democratic community that we can all of us have our say in the matter, and
that we all of us have some share, however small, in the task
of making the decision.

The position of the societies or associations within the state
has long been a matter of argument among legal theorists.
Some of the varying views put forward have had practical
consequences of importance. But to the layman it may well
seem that these discussions, in the past at any rate, have too
often tended to present as necessary deductions from the very
nature of things what were really matters for the free choice,
on grounds of general policy or legal convenience, of those
responsible for the decisions of the state. This impression is
particularly strong when we examine some of the discussions
that have taken place on the question of corporate personality.

The question was asked whether an association was a person in anything like the same sense as an individual human being. And various answers were given, that its personality was merely a fiction, that its personality was conferred on it by the state, that its personality was really inherent in it, and so on. The matter was further complicated by those who asserted or implied that the state had a personality in a sense that no other association had.

There is a great danger in these discussions of becoming bogged down in disputes about verbal definitions, particularly in dealing with that elusive term 'personality'. The fundamental facts are that a number of individuals can associate together for the pursuit of some purpose and that they can organise themselves, that is to say that they can establish some defined method by which decisions can be taken that are accepted as binding on the whole body. There is no fiction about this, nor is the possibility created by the state, though, of course, the state can forbid people to associate for any particular purpose. Once formed, the association can take decisions as a body, and in that respect it is like an individual. It is unlike an individual in that there are some kinds of decision which are outside the bounds of physical possibility for anything except an individual. An association cannot, to borrow Maitland's illustration, marry or be given in marriage. But it can exercise control over property, it can give instructions to its members and apply sanctions if they are disregarded, it can employ servants, it can make contracts, it can sue or be sued in the courts. The *possibility* of its doing these and similar things lies in the very nature of the facts. Whether in any particular case it is *allowed* to do any or all of them and what procedure it is to follow in doing them is a matter for decision by the state. That is not because the state has personality in some different sense from any other association, but because the state is recognised as the association which has the final claim on our obedience.

The conditions under which associations are allowed to act,

within the limits of physical possibility, as individuals vary in different countries and under different systems of law. In England, and elsewhere where the legal system is based on the English Common Law, the time-honoured method by which an association can receive recognition by the state as an individual has been through incorporation. That is to say, by an explicit declaration it becomes 'one body corporate and politic', to quote the words of a university charter, with power to sue or be sued, to hold or dispose of property, and so on. This may be done either by a particular act of government, as when a charter is granted to an institution, or, in modern times, under a general law, as when a limited company is formed in accordance with the provisions of the Companies Acts. In earlier days this was regarded as a special privilege, to be carefully guarded, and in the seventeenth and eighteenth centuries threats of punishment were made, judicially or legislatively, against any body which presumed to act as a corporation without a proper grant. But in the meantime various legal devices were being developed, partly by judicial decisions and partly by legislative acts, which enabled unincorporated associations to behave, for all practical purposes, as if they were corporations. In particular, there was the device of the trust, by which the property of the association was vested in certain particular individuals as trustees. They became the legal owners, but could only make any use of the property in the interests of or as directed by the association. The association, thus, while not legally capable of owning property, could, within the terms of the trust, exercise complete control over the way in which it was used, and this, for practical purposes, was what really mattered. In modern times other legal rights and responsibilities have been laid on unincorporated associations, and the whole tendency has been for the legal distinction between corporate and unincorporated bodies to be reduced almost to vanishing point.

From the political or social point of view the distinction had long ceased to be of any great significance. If we considered what the association meant to its members and what part it played in the life of the country we should see immediatcly that its importancc in that rcspcct had little relation to its exact legal status. Maitland said fifty years ago, 'It has often struck me that morally there is most personality where legally there is none'.[1] He would hardly have intended this dictum to be taken as a universal rule, but there are plenty of instances that would seem to bear him out. Thus, practically all churches or religious bodies in this country are unincorporated. So are the Inns of Court and the Stock Exchange. Some colleges at Oxford and Cambridge are corporations possessing charters, and some are not. But it may be doubted whether most of their members arc ever conscious of thc difference. In general, we may note that it is nowadays extremely easy for any group of people to become incorporated. Yet many associations prefer not to be, simply on grounds of procedural convenience, and their importance and efficiency are in no wise affected.

There are various general questions which the state may have to determine with regard to the position of the various societies and associations within its boundaries, apart from the matter of their precise legal status. How far, for instance, is a society free to grow and develop and add to or modify its original purpose? An individual, of course, can normally change his purpose in life or his opinions or his profession without forfeiting his property or being subjected to any kind of legal inconvenience, as long as he keeps within the bounds of the criminal law. But in this respect a society, at any rate of the kind with which we have been mainly concerned, can hardly be thought of in quite the same way as an individual. For the purpose seems to be an essential condition of the life of a society in a way which it is not for an individual. An individual is born and grows up and gradually finds out or decides what his purpose in life is to be. But a society does not normally form itself first and then look about for a pur-

[1] F. W. Maitland, *Selected Essays*, p. 201.

pose: the purpose is formed in the minds of individuals and the formation of the society follows from this. To some degree, then, the purpose seems an essential part of the individuality and identity of the society, which may need to be established for certain legal purposes, particularly when any question of ownership of or control over property arises. But there is also the question of continuity of membership and of constitution to be taken into account, and the relative importance of these different factors is a matter in which differences of opinion and practice may well arise.

According to our ordinary ways of thinking at the present time, the state is in a different position from other societies in that in its case membership and government are all-important. A state is as free to decide what purposes it should follow as an individual would be. But that is not because it has 'personality' in any sense that other societies have not. It is simply because we do not recognise any authority above the state which could limit or define its purpose for it. As we have seen, it is quite conceivable that a situation might be established in which the state's purposes were strictly defined and any action that went beyond these limits was declared *ultra vires*. It is true that the state is not the kind of society which is consciously formed at a particular time for a particular purpose: no one now thinks in terms of the Social Contract theory. But it is not unique in that respect. The same would be true of the family, which at certain stages of civilisation is a definite society with powers and responsibilities of its own. We are, however, mainly concerned here with the kind of society which is definitely formed for a particular purpose by the wills of a number of individuals. It is here that the question arises how far such societies can change or modify their original purpose without losing their identity in the eyes of the law. In no country and under no system of law, as far as I know, is the right of such a society to change its purpose absolutely unlimited. But there appear to be considerable differences in the strictness of the limitations, particularly where it is a question of adding to or modifying the original purposes in a way which might be interpreted as a natural development of them. Under English law the tendency seems to be towards interpreting the original purposes most strictly and insisting that no deviation from them can be allowed without the express consent of the state, to be given either by special legislation or by some organ of government authorised to act for the state for that purpose. At the beginning of the present century there were one or two well-known legal cases which appeared to establish this in cases where it might have been thought doubtful.

Thus, by the Osborne Judgement in 1909 the courts decided that the practice, which had long been followed by some trade unions, of subsidising parliamentary candidates and members was illegal, as the acts legalising trade unions did not expressly give them this right. Legislation was necessary to restore to them a right which they had previously assumed that they had. Probably more interest was aroused among political and legal theorists at the time by the Scottish Church case. Here, it may be recalled, the Free Church of Scotland decided by a large majority to amalgamate with the United Presbyterian Church. But a small minority, which became known as 'the Wee Frees', objected, on the grounds that certain doctrines which the Free Church had maintained at the time of its foundation sixty years before were incompatible with the doctrines of the United Presbyterians. This minority brought an action and the House of Lords, overruling the decisions of the lower courts, decided in their favour, with the result that all the property and endowments of the Free Church became legally the property of the small body of the 'Wee Frees'. This decision aroused great excitement. It was condemned by some of the leading academic lawyers of the time, such as Maitland and Geldart, and created grave misgivings in the minds of many churchmen, even outside the ranks of the Free Church. The main line of criticism was that it refused to recognise a Church as a living body with any possibility of growth and denied it any right to develop or modify or even to interpret its own doctrinal formulae. In a well-known phrase of Maitland's, 'The dead hand of the law fell with a resounding slap on the living body of the church'. Speedy legislation was necessary to remedy the impossible situation, and the property was divided between the contending parties in the Free Church in proportion to their numbers.

It is probably true that English law is stricter in this respect than some other systems. But at the present time the excitement over cases such as these seems to have largely died down. The churches, as far as one can judge, have not in fact found themselves intolerably cramped or frustrated by their legal position. There does not, indeed, seem to be any lively demand from any society or association for a fundamental alteration of the law. There generally seems to be some way round to be discovered in any awkward situation. And on the other side there is another consideration which is worth bearing in mind. And that is the position of minorities in the various societies. For problems of the kind that we have been discussing do not commonly arise in practice unless some minority in a particular society feels aggrieved by the decision of the majority or of the recognised authority within the society. And when the problem has been finally settled it has generally been agreed that some consideration should be given to the minority. So it was, for instance, in the case of the Scottish Free Church. In a standard legal work written some years ago the author used language which seemed to suggest that in correcting by legislation the situation that arose in that case Parliament was somehow expressing disapproval of the legal decision.[1] It seems a doubtful inference in any case. But the important point to notice is that the action of Parliament did not simply restore the situation to what it was supposed to be before: for that would have left the whole property in the hands of the majority of the Free Church, and the

[1] F. Hallis, *Corporate Personality*, p. lvii.

minority out in the cold. But, as it was, the 'Wee Frees' were secured a proportionate share, which, on the face of it, seems a fairer arrangement. Similarly, when by the Act of 1913 the trade unions were given the right to impose a political levy it was not granted to them unconditionally, but with provision for the right of the objecting minority to contract out of it. Obviously, no society could function at all if there were too many possibilities for a minority to thwart the will of the majority. But it might well seem justifiable for the state to be able to intervene in order to secure some degree of consideration for minorities.

There remains one further question for consideration in connection with the attitude of the state to other societies, and that is the question whether the state should favour or discourage the establishment of such societies. It is important to distinguish this from the question just discussed, though they are often confused. It would be perfectly possible for a state to insist that the aims of any society should be clearly stated and strictly interpreted and observed, while at the same time making it easy for societies to come into existence and allowing them a wide range of functions. That, on the whole, is the attitude adopted in this country. As a rule, the state and the judicial authorities take little notice of any association formed for a purpose not itself illegal, except when the question of the ownership of or control over property arises. There are many societies which, strictly speaking, have no legal status at all. But if a society does seek legal status it is very easy to become a corporation or a quasi-corporation, such as a trade union or a friendly society or a trust, by going through a few simple formalities. If the original conditions are carefully drawn it can have a very wide latitude in what it does, and official sanction for any alteration in these conditions is, within certain limits, easy to obtain, unless there is a strong objection from a minority.

Further, there has been a tendency in recent times for the government itself to set up semi-independent bodies, such as the British Broadcasting Corporation, to control certain services in preference to bringing them directly under the state. The position of the universities is a typical illustration of the British attitude. Most European universities are definitely state institutions, under a ministry. Their professors are state officials, appointed and paid by the state, and their budget passes through the legislative body just like that of any other government department. It should in fairness be stated that in the more liberally-minded countries this is compatible with a high degree of academic freedom. But in this country, though they now receive the bulk of their income from the state, the universities remain independent corporations, receiving subsidies for services rendered. It is unnecessary to go into the peculiar procedure by which the value of these services is decided. But everything is done to secure the independence of the universities in the ordinary conduct of their affairs. This is generally accepted as desirable. Even those who, from time to time, suggest that Parliament ought to be able to scrutinise more in detail the way in which the money voted is spent invariably disclaim any intention of encroaching on the independence of the universities. Again, certain organised professions here are allowed a degree of control over the admission and professional conduct of their members which is very rare elsewhere.

This general tendency, which is, on the whole, characteristic of this country, can easily be developed into an explicit point of view. It would maintain that it was desirable to have a number of centres of corporate life and authority in the community, and would welcome the flexibility and variety that this would produce. It would not challenge the position of the state and its government as the final and supreme authority. But it would argue that as a matter of policy the state would be wise not to attempt direct administration, through the regular machinery of government, of too many activities. The function it can most profitably exercise is that of supervision and co-ordination. This, it should be said, is not incompatible with some, at any rate, of the elements that went to make up the Socialist movement in the country. There is nothing in it which is contrary to the demand for greater equality, which has always been one of these elements. Another element is distrust of the profit motive and fear of the exploitation that that might produce. But this would not apply so far as the other societies were non-profit making concerns. Even those for whom the main attraction of Socialism lay in the vision of a perfectly planned and organised society could, I think, make considerable concessions to this point of view without sacrificing the essentials of their ideal.

In other countries and at other times the attitude has been very different. The French Revolutionary assembly in 1792 declared that 'a state that is truly free ought not to suffer within its bosom any corporation', adding that this applied even to those which were doing valuable service. This goes back to Rousseau, with his avowed distrust of any subordinate organisation that might break up the unity of the General Will, though it was forgotten that Rousseau expressed doubts whether his views could really be applied except in small communities like Geneva or the early city-states. And it was carried forward throughout the nineteenth century. Up to 1901 it was a criminal offence in France for more than twenty people to form an association, for any purpose except one, without the express permission of the state as represented by the Prefect. The one exception was a society with a *but lucratif*, a business concern, for which things were made much easier. The French authorities evidently shared Dr Johnson's view that a man is seldom more innocently occupied than in getting money. In 1901 religious organisations were dealt with very unfavourably, as part of the anti-clerical campaign of the time, but for any other kind of association the restrictions were largely relaxed.

These instances serve to illustrate the varying possibilities in the treatment of other societies by the state. It does not seem possible to lay down any general rules on the matter though certain tentative conclusions may suggest themselves. To join together with other people in pursuit of a common purpose seems a natural human tendency, and, so far, restrictions of it seem a denial of individual freedom which needs justification in any particular case. On the other hand, some societies may themselves have potentialities of coercion against individuals which may need to be watched. And, in some cases, there is no body capable of doing this except the state. But of this more hereafter. On the other hand, no society of any importance could function properly without some degree of control over its members. If, for instance, a member does not obey the rules which the society has decided on it seems reasonable, as a general rule, that the society should have the power of expulsion or suspension from membership. The more completely voluntary membership of the society is, the more would this power be justified.

Difficulties arise when a particular society seems to be trying in some way or to some degree to dominate the state, of which it is only a part and perhaps a comparatively small part. There are various ways in which this can be attempted either openly or surreptitiously, and it is rightly resented by those who are trying to think as members of the state. One particular instance of this, more noticeable in some other countries than in our own, may be found in certain actions of the churches, particularly the Roman Catholic Church. The anticlerical legislation in France at the beginning of the present century was often denounced as amounting to religious persecution, and there was some justification for this. But it can only be fairly judged as a reaction against the long-continued attempt of the church to dominate the state to the detriment of the interests and points of view of non-Catholics. Even at the present time difficulties occasionally arise in various countries, particularly in matters of marriage and divorce and related questions. Few people nowadays would deny the right of a church to lay down rules for the conduct of its own members in such matters, to forbid divorce or the practice of birth-control, for instance. But that is a very different thing from attempting by pressure or by any other means than normal political persuasion to enforce such views on the state as a whole. It is not always easy to decide how far this is being done, but the possibility of it is undeniable.

Other societies, also, such as big financial concerns, have at some times and in some places attempted to attain some sort of control over the state. But in all such cases, when people begin to be conscious of themselves as members of the state, they will react against such attempts, and the societies in question will have only themselves to thank if the state begins to control them to an extent which might not otherwise have been necessary. In any case, we can recognise that participation in the work of a society is a natural and healthy form of human activity, and that in the modern world the need for it cannot be met by the state alone. A vigorous growth of societies and associations is therefore to be welcomed. But at the same time the members of the various societies have to realise that they are also members of the larger community which contains them all and to learn to look beyond the aims and interests of their particular societies to this larger community as their supreme interest. That, at any rate, is the ideal of democracy.

Chapter XIII

THE STATE AND THE INDIVIDUAL—
INDIVIDUAL LIBERTY

THE relation between the state and its individual members
has been the subject of lively discussion for many years,
not only for political theorists but also as a question of practical politics which affects the lives of numerous people. There
are many different aspects of the question, and some of them
have been more to the forefront at some periods, others at
others. Here it will be possible only to indicate some of the
more general considerations which may serve as a basis for
an attempt to clarify the various points that can be and have
been raised in this connection. Some of them, it may be
noted, are not peculiar to the state but arise in connection
with any organised society in relation to its individual members.

It may be as well to begin with the simple and obvious
point that the state is a community or association of individuals. There is no entity which we can call 'the state' apart
from the individuals which compose it.[1] It would seem to
follow, then, that there is no necessary or essential opposition
or conflict between the state and its individual members. Few
people, perhaps, would maintain in so many words that there
was. But undoubtedly ways of speaking which imply, or at
least suggest it, can be met with from time to time. The very

[1] Of course, for some legal purposes the action of the state, or of any
association, can be distinguished from the actions of its individual members.
But that is rather a matter of certain individuals acting in a particular capacity. An essential part of the process of bringing associations within the
scope of legal procedure has consisted in deciding which concrete individuals could be held responsible for the acts of the association. There are no
actions, in the final analysis, other than those of individuals.

title of Herbert Spencer's well-known pamphlet, *Man versus the State*, has a strong suggestion of such a view. But, on the whole, when people speak of conflict between the state and the individual, though they may speak of it in general terms, it will be found that they are in fact thinking of a particular state in particular circumstances. And there is no doubt that conditions can arise in which talk about the opposition between the state and the individual has a real meaning.

As has already been argued at length, though the state includes all its individual members, the amount of influence that the different individuals can exercise on the decisions of the state varies enormously from one state to another. Thus, there may be a state in which a small, well-organised group of people has managed to secure an overwhelmingly predominant influence over the decisions of government, so that for practical purposes its actions may be regarded as the actions of the state. Such a group may be intent on pursuing its own material interests, or on enforcing its own beliefs and doctrines on the rest of the state. And it may be in a position to pursue such a policy, within very wide limits, without regard to the interests or opinions of all the other individuals. Here it does make sense to speak of an opposition, potential at any rate, between the state and a large number of its individual members, and to assert the claims of the individuals to have their interests regarded and to form their own opinions as against the state. Broadly speaking, the more democratic a state is, that is to say, the more opportunity there is for the great body of citizens to exercise an effective influence on the decisions of governments, the less likely is such a situation to arise. But even here individuals who are out of sympathy with the majority may come to think of the state as an alien body in opposition to themselves. It would probably be agreed by most people, except the adherents of certain revolutionary doctrines, that this is, in principle, undesirable, and that ideally it should be the aim of those responsible for the decisions of the state to prevent any individuals from feeling that their interests or points of view are so ignored or neglected that they can no longer feel themselves as members of the state. But in practice this aim, admirable though it is in general, requires to be pursued with discrimination. For the kinds of people who might come to feel like that vary very greatly over a range which would stretch from high-minded conscientious objectors at the one end to habitual criminals at the other. Concessions that might be desirable in one case would hardly be appropriate in the other. In between there is the considerable number of people who see their own interests so clearly and other people's so dimly that they are apt to feel grossly oppressed at any infringement of their interests even if it is clearly to the benefit of a much greater number. No doubt it was a consideration of such cases which led a cynical observer to remark, 'Scratch a freedom and you find a vested interest'.

It is obvious that a great variety of practical problems may arise in the application of these general considerations. How far, for instance, should the state recognise the right of conscientious objection by individuals to obligations imposed on its members? Again there have been in recent times, in this country and elsewhere, many occasions on which the question has been raised how far the state should exercise its powers of requisitioning private property in the interests of the community. It must be noted, however, that in many of these cases, where assertions have been made about the need for protecting the rights of the individual against the state, it is not strictly speaking the powers of the state as such which are in question, but the powers of some particular organ of government which, in the special circumstances of the time, has obtained the authority to make decisions on behalf of the state. In particular, protests have often been made against the leaving of decisions affecting individuals to the discretion of government departments and civil servants. It has been argued that such decisions should be made only in accordance with legislation passed by Parliament, and that the interpretation of such legislation in individual cases should always be a matter for the courts of law. Naturally enough, this point of view has been urged with particular force by various eminent lawyers: it is not, perhaps, self-evident to the ordinary individual that he could invariably expect a better deal from the courts than from a departmental decision. But be that as it may, the essential point here is that in either case it is a matter of action by the state. The question at issue is through which of the organs of government the state, in such cases, should act.

To return to the main question, it is always a problem for the citizens of a democracy, where everyone can have some say in the decisions of the state, to decide how far an individual or a small group of individuals should be sacrificed to what is or is believed to be the interests of the great majority. But it is no use attempting here to lay down any absolute and clear-cut rules for the solution of this problem. There are, no doubt, extremists who would say that a particular individual would have no claim to any consideration if the interests of the majority were at stake, and there are, or at any rate were, others who would say that individuals were endowed with a number of absolute rights which should not be infringed whatever advantages might accrue to the rest of the community. But it will probably be clear that from the point of view adopted in this book neither of these extreme points of view could be accepted. It is rather a matter of two opposing principles both containing something of value, and the practical question is how far we shall carry either of them. We might express them by saying that, on the one hand, no individual is so unimportant that his interests or his point of view could be ignored as entirely negligible. On the other hand, no individual is so important that his rights could be asserted to the complete thwarting of the pursuit of the interests or the carrying out of the views of the majority. Where the line between the two should be drawn cannot be stated in a general formula, for the possible cases where the problem might arise vary so widely. On the other hand, it is clearly desirable to establish, as far as possible, some general working rules, which we expect to be followed in normal cases. We might hope to arrive at something between a single general law from which all particular applications of it could be logically deduced, and a separate consideration of each particular case.

The kind of thing here suggested can be illustrated by the ways in which certain recurrent situations are dealt with in different countries. For instance, when compulsory military service is established in a country there is nearly always a certain number of individuals who object as a matter of conscience on religious or moral grounds to taking part in it. Some countries refuse to recognise the right of such individuals to any consideration and treat them, if they persist, as ordinary law-breakers. Others grant exemption from military service only to members of certain recognised religious sects. Great Britain has gone further than any other country in granting exemption to all genuine conscientious objectors, while coupling it in most cases with the requirement that they should undertake some alternative form of service. Again, there is the question of the rights of private property. In this country, it is generally accepted nowadays that the state should be prepared to acquire, by compulsion if necessary, any form of private property that is needed for the public benefit, but only on condition that fair monetary compensation is paid. Some people in some countries, on the other hand, would maintain that the state should feel free to confiscate any form of property without any compensation at all, while at the other extreme there might be those who would maintain that the state should never take property from an unwilling owner, whatever compensation it was prepared to pay. Again it is a generally accepted rule of political behaviour in the Western democracies that an individual should not be subjected to legal punishment, fines, imprisonment, or death, except for a specific offence against the law after a fair trial for that particular offence in the courts. We should not recognise the right of the state authorities to execute or imprison a man just because they thought that, in the public interest, he was better out of the way. A partial exception has been admitted in time of war when individuals have been incarcerated without trial because there was reason to think that they might be a danger to national security. We should however draw the line at putting them to death, and we should generally hold that the incarceration was justifiable only as long as the danger lasted. But it must be noted that even in this country there were left-wing enthusiasts who protested against the release of Sir Oswald Mosley at the end of the war, apparently on the grounds that he was a bad man and ought to be kept shut up. And, more generally, it does not appear that these principles would be accepted or acted on in all countries.

These, then, are some of the problems that arise in connection with the relations of the state to its individual members. But, probably, the aspect which would first spring to people's minds in this connection would be the use of the coercive power of the state. That would arise when or in so far as the state decides how individuals should behave, instead of leaving the choice to them, and enforces its decisions when necessary by the infliction of punishment. It is in this connection that talk about individual liberty most commonly arises. And the word 'liberty' occupies such an important place in political discussion that it is worth while devoting a little time to attempting some sort of analysis of the idea or ideas suggested by the use of the term. We must not expect to get a clear-cut definition which would stand up to cross-examination in a court of law or a Socratic dialogue. Political and moral ideas in general are not susceptible of that. But it would be very foolish to dismiss any of them as unimportant because we cannot find a neat formula for it.

Few political ideas have, in fact, been so liable to the confusions that can be caused by sophistical puzzles as the notion of liberty. It is obviously very liable to attack from the only-a-difference-of-degree argument, the fallacies of which have already been noted. Other sophisms, too, are possible. It might, for instance, be said that liberty consists in the ability to get what we desire. Among the things that most people desire are freedom from want or the assurance of adequate food, clothing, and other material necessities, freedom from fear of outside aggression, freedom from fear of unemployment, and other similar things. But many of these could be most certainly assured to us in a well-run prison humanely administered. So liberty might mean being shut up in prison. This is, of course, a caricature, and no one, in fact, would argue exactly in these terms. But anyone who at certain periods has engaged in argument on the subject of liberty with advocates of various totalitarian systems of government will see that the caricature has a recognisable likeness to the original.

In some recent writing an attempt has been made to clarify the idea by making a distinction between 'freedom from' and 'freedom to', and suggesting that both are equally legitimate senses of 'freedom'. But in fact this distinction seems more likely to add to the confusion. In its commonest use the phrase 'freedom from' simply means not having something undesirable, as when we speak of being free from disease or pain. In that sense the term becomes so wide as to be of little value. As our prison illustration shows, 'freedom from' various things can be quite compatible with a complete lack of liberty in any ordinary sense. In a slightly different use one form of 'freedom from' is simply a correlative of 'freedom to': to be free *to* do something implies being free *from* interference in doing it. It is, perhaps, best to stick to the word 'liberty' which has not, in ordinary use, the same possibilities of ambiguity as 'freedom'. It normally has some reference to possibilities of action and could hardly be used in the purely negative sense that 'freedom from' could bear.

If we examine the ways in which people talk and have talked

about liberty as something desirable we shall probably find that, though they may not be able to give a watertight general definition of what liberty is, they are usually pretty clearly conscious of when they are being deprived of it. And it may be as well to approach the matter from that end and try to get at an idea of what liberty is by first examining its opposite. It is clear, then, that we are first conscious of the absence of liberty when we are prevented from doing something that we want to do or forced to do something that we do not want. On further inspection, however, we find that we do not normally talk about liberty in all such cases. For instance, we might, after reading some of the popular space-travel fiction, want to go to Mars or the moon. But we should not naturally speak of our inability to do so as an infringement of our liberty. We should probably not even talk in such terms if we were prevented from going to some place by an earthquake or a flood. In all normal uses of the term we talk of being deprived of our liberty only when we are prevented from doing what we want by the action of other human beings, more particularly when that action is deliberate and intentional. It should be noted, as was pointed out in a previous chapter, that when we speak of an infringement of liberty in this sense we do not necessarily confine it to actual physical obstruction. Probably in the majority of cases when we speak of being prevented we mean, not that we are being physically hindered, but that we are threatened by certain unpleasant consequences or penalties, deliberately imposed by other human beings, if we act in a certain way. Of course, in most of our actions we are influenced by the thought of their probable consequences. But we do not naturally think of these consequences as infringing our liberty unless they are imposed by other people.

This is an important distinction. It may be argued that it is not altogether logical as it may be just as unpleasant for us to be prevented from doing what we want by natural conditions as by the action of other human beings. But in fact we do not feel the same about it in the two cases. And to understand that and to get a clearer conception of the idea of liberty in general we must not keep our eyes exclusively fixed on the patient, that is to say the person who is going to be hindered or left unhindered in doing what he wants. We must also think of the agent, the person who is going to do or not to do the restricting. Liberty or the lack of it is, in this sense, a relation between human individuals, and, if we think of it as a general ideal to be aimed at, not merely as something which each person wants for himself, we have to think of both sides of the relation. It was suggested earlier, in the special case of political liberty, that to the idea of liberty, in the negative sense of absence of restraint, we must add the correlative idea of tolerance. When a dislike of being thwarted and frustrated in the activities that we care about is supplemented by an equally strong dislike of thwarting other people we have the beginnings of a real belief in liberty. It means, in a well-worn phrase, a respect for the personalities of other people and a belief that this is a necessary basis for a satisfactory relation between the members of any society. Of course, other considerations may come in as well. For instance, freedom of discussion may be valued because in many subjects it may be a necessary condition of getting at the truth. But this is not the fundamental element in the general belief in liberty.

This attitude of mind will not necessarily prevent anyone who holds it from imposing some restrictions on other people if he is in a position to do so. The strongest believer in liberty will recognise the necessity for this in some circumstances. And he must be prepared to find himself accused of being illogical if he is unable to lay down beforehand precise rules which will decide exactly when restrictions are necessary. In fact, the most that we could hope to do in this way would be to put forward some general suggestions, while remembering that they could apply only for the most part and could not be turned into rigid universal rules. John

Stuart Mill attempted this in his well-known distinction between actions which affected other people and actions which affected only the agent himself. It is only in the former case, he maintained, that restriction would be justified. He has been much criticised on this point, but the criticisms have not always been quite fair. For the distinction is a real one, but is a matter of more or less, not of two sharply defined classes. And in any case it is certainly not a sufficient test by itself but would require supplementing by other considerations.

The important thing, however, is the attitude of mind, the general bias against compulsion and in favour of liberty. There is no infallible way of deciding when this is present and active in any particular person. But we know what it means, and we also know what the opposite of it means. For there are strong tendencies in human nature, which most of us can probably verify in our own experience, making for compulsion and against liberty. There is the impulse to dominate, and the satisfaction that the exercise of power over other people brings. This tendency, no doubt, varies in strength as between individuals, but it is a reasonable supposition that we are particularly likely to find it in those who have in fact reached a position of authority. There is the natural tendency to anger at being thwarted or opposed, which may easily extend itself to opposition in matters of opinion or belief. We can see here how the same impulse which in the beginning drives a man to demand liberty for himself may easily develop into the impulse to deny it to other people. There is the feeling for the group which tends to make its members intolerant of any divergence from established standards of behaviour or even of opinion on the part of individuals or minorities. These and other connected tendencies, singly or in combination, are present to a greater or lesser degree in most people, and provide a constant drive in the direction of the suppression of liberty. They are often not clearly recognised or admitted even by those who are under their influence. That is why we not uncommonly find extremely authoritarian individuals or governments proclaiming their attachment to liberty as a general principle while denying it in practice in most particular cases. In any case the general distinction between the two opposing attitudes ought to be sufficiently clear.

What is the special position of the state in all this? It has already been pointed out in a previous chapter that the state is by no means the only agency by which liberty can be restricted. In reality possibilities of coercion are omnipresent in any society, wherever, in fact, a group or an individual has the power of inflicting penalties, official or unofficial, on other individuals. No doubt the state through its recognised government has special opportunities for making itself unpleasant to individuals. It is more difficult to escape from it and there is no effective protection against it. Further, other individuals or organisations depend for some, though by no means for all, of their opportunities of repression on the position and powers given to them by the state or the laws. On the other hand, there are other relations which are closer and more continuous than the relation between the government and the governed in a state. But, on the whole, the powers of the state in this direction are the greatest, and therefore the problem of liberty is of special importance for anyone concerned with state policy from the Prime Minister down to the ordinary voter. But their problem can comparatively rarely be stated in the form of a simple antithesis: Shall we restrict or shall we leave free? Much more often it takes the form of asking how far we shall restrict the liberty of some individuals in order to prevent their restricting the liberty of others. And that in practice will present us with a complex interweaving of possible restrictions and liberties which may be very difficult to disentangle.

There is another distinction which ought to be made when we are considering the question of control over the actions of individuals. And that is the distinction between the state and the community. The state is the community considered as an organised body. This qualification means that we speak of the state acting only when it is a matter of explicit decisions consciously taken on behalf of the community by a recognised and accepted procedure, as when laws are passed, executive actions taken, and so on. But besides these there grow up in any community all sorts of habits, customs, fashions, and conventions which have never been definitely decided on or laid down by anyone, but yet exercise a considerable degree of control over the actions of individuals. They may range from fashions in dress or manners to accepted ideas about moral right and wrong. We do not nowadays think or speak of these as acts of the state though in the earlier stages of social development they are not clearly distinguished from the laws. Even at the present time there may be occasional borderline cases as when a custom acquires some sort of legal status, but the general distinction is clear. Further, the two act and react on each other. The explicit decisions taken by the authorities in the state will often be influenced to some degree by the conventional codes of conduct of the particular community. And conversely the actions of the state, such as legislation, may in the course of time come to have an effect on the accepted ideas of right and wrong. For the purposes of the present discussion the important point is that these customs and conventions may have a coercive effect on the behaviour of individuals just as much as the laws enacted by the state. They are as a rule rather more flexible and less precise, except perhaps in some details of behaviour, but none the less as far as they go their control is something very real. They have their own sanctions, the fear of unpopularity, of disapproval, of derision, or just of 'being different', and these can be pretty effective. The result is that we cannot measure the degree of individual liberty in a country merely by the presence or absence of restrictive laws. We could well imagine a country in which there was very little in the way of legal control over behaviour, but a very rigid control by means of these social conventions.

These, then, are some of the general conditions which may give rise to restrictions on liberty. And the same conditions may in their turn give rise to a reaction, against these restrictions, in the name of liberty. It remains to see whether we can get any more definite picture of the forms that these restrictions can take, and of the kinds of activity in which restrictions are or have been most keenly felt. Naturally it will be possible to touch only on the more important kinds: it would be impossible to enumerate all the countless minor frustrations which particular individuals feel or have felt at particular times.

With regard to the first point it seems possible to distinguish two main forms which such restrictions can take. They are not necessarily sharply distinct and one may pass into the other. They can also co-exist, though there is generally an emphasis on one side or another, but they can also on occasions come into conflict.

On the one side, the restrictions most felt may be those imposed by an established set of institutions, a system of generally accepted laws or rules, which assign definite rights and duties and powers to different individuals, the limits of which must not be infringed. We can easily see how individuals may come to feel that their activities are being cramped and frustrated by such institutions, and how in consequence a movement may spring up to get rid of them. For an instance of this in history we might look to the period of the Tudors in our own country, when the restrictions of the medieval system with its feudal rights, its craft guilds, its privileged corporations and the like began to seem intolerable both to strong rulers at the centre and enterprising merchants throughout the country. On a smaller scale, one can see the same thing in many societies or organisations, where a network of detailed regulations may completely cramp the initiative of individuals.

On the other hand, there may be circumstances in which people feel that the chief threat to their free activity comes from the arbitrary actions of those who have power. Then they will begin to feel the need for established institutions and rules to determine individual rights and powers, in order to protect them against this danger. It is easy to see how these two tendencies may come into conflict. Thus, when there is a revolt against established institutions, the enterprising and energetic people who take the lead may often be anxious to push on with their work without being hampered by consideration for the rights of particular individuals and groups, if these get in their way. And this may go on till more and more people come to feel that they need to be protected against their liberators, and long to get back to a system of established laws and rules, which will be valid even when inconvenient to those in power.

It is a risky thing to attempt historical generalisations, without numerous qualifications, but it does seem that something of this kind could be observed in the French Revolution. Though in its early stages appeals were made to supposed traditional rights, and in spite of the Declaration of the Rights of Man, it seems to have been on the whole a revolutionary movement, mainly concerned to break the bonds of an outworn system and sweep away existing rights and privileges. There is no doubt that it did release a great deal of frustrated energy. In spite of the arbitrary behaviour of the revolutionary governments, and even to some degree under the early dictatorship of Napoleon, the Revolution still seemed to countless people, both in France and abroad, a movement of liberation. But as Napoleon's rule became at the same time more arbitrary and more systematised the revolutionary fervour largely faded away. After the restoration of the monarchy the Liberal movement in France, which provided the main opposition, disavowed a good deal of the work of the Revolution, particularly its methods, and pinned its faith to the construction of institutions and laws which would secure individual rights and limit arbitrary power. At other periods we can see the two forms of the demand for liberty being put forward at the same time by different groups, sometimes in opposition to each other. Thus, in nineteenth-century England the business men were putting forward demands for the most complete freedom from restrictions in the conduct of their own businesses, while the wage-earners were demanding restrictive laws and trade union rules to protect their liberty from arbitrary action by their employers.

We may next consider the kinds of activity in which the question at issue between liberty and compulsion seems to be of particular importance. It is certainly necessary to make some distinction here and not to regard all restrictions on liberty as equally serious. There are occasional individuals to be met with who have what would seem to most of us an almost pathological revulsion against any kind of control, to the extent, for instance, of saying that a course of action good and right in itself becomes positively wrong if it is ordered by a superior authority.[1] But I think that the common sense of mankind would reject this view. Even if it were true that there was always something undesirable about ordering and being ordered, the undesirability might be so slight that it could be endured without any serious hardship if other advantages resulted therefrom. If we were looking for a test of importance we might, perhaps, find a point in the suggestion made earlier that the main idea underlying the demand for liberty was a respect for individual personality. This is, of course, a vague phrase, though not necessarily meaningless because of that. But without my attempting a detailed definition here, most people would probably agree that it had something to do with people's characters. And, looked at from that point of view, the relative importance of different kinds of activity would depend on the extent to which they influenced the formation of character and expressed the character when formed. No doubt, this would leave many opportunities for differences of opinion in its detailed application. But it would

[1] For some illustrations and discussion of this see my *Pacifism Conscientious Objection*, pp. 99–102.

at least give us a starting-point for the examination of any particular case.

Starting from that, then, it is surely clear that there are some cases in which the decision between two alternative courses of action has no bearing on character at all. An obvious instance could be found in the rule of the road. Whether we drive on the left or on the right is of no importance from that point of view. What is of importance is that there should be a general rule and that it should be observed. And this is an obvious instance where the decision has to be taken by a superior authority and not left to individual initiative. That is an extreme case, but there are others which approximate to it. After the last War a certain individual refused to carry an identity card and subsequently established his right to do so in the courts. In some quarters this was hailed as a great blow for liberty. Yet it is hard to see what difference it makes to one's character or personality whether one carries an identity card or not. The danger of making so much fuss over trivialities of this kind is that it may divert energies and distract attention from really serious threats to liberty.

What, then, are the elements which are of prime importance in what we mean by character and personality? Without attempting an exhaustive examination, it ought to be possible to indicate one or two of obvious importance. One is clearly to be found in our emotional attitudes and relations to other people, our likes, dislikes, hopes, fears, ambitions, and the rest. A great deal of this is fortunately beyond the reach of external control: it would certainly be a grave infringement of personal liberty if it were possible for a superior authority to dictate to us exactly how we should feel towards other people. What can be done, of course, is to control the overt expression of these feelings, and a certain amount of such control would be universally recognised as desirable. We cannot make it a criminal offence to feel angry, but we can punish people if their anger leads them to commit murder or violent assault. We cannot make parents love their children, but we can punish them for cruelty or neglect. Even here, however, the believer in liberty would hold that it would be easy to go too far. If every angry word, for instance, or every expression of dislike were made a criminal offence our daily lives would be lived in a constant state of apprehension which would be fatal to any genuine self-development.

The important point is that the restrictions on the expression of emotion which would be generally accepted as desirable are imposed primarily for the protection of other people, to save them from being murdered or cruelly treated or neglected, and not for the sake of making the offender feel differently. The only direct effect on him, if any, is to make him act differently from fear of punishment, and it is a truism to observe that that is of no value so far as the development of his character goes. Indeed, in so far as it develops a general habit of thinking in terms of fear of punishment as the only motive for acting properly to other people, its effects will be bad. This is not to deny that, incidentally and indirectly, the infliction of punishment for certain kinds of action may have, under certain conditions, a genuine reformative effect on the wrongdoers, actual or potential. It may, so to speak, put the idea into their heads that there is something wrong about certain kinds of action which they had taken as a matter of course before. And an idea, once implanted, will sometimes grow of its own force. It is, of course, very difficult to disentangle the different influences which may work in this direction in any particular case. But there does seem good reason to believe that, for instance, some of the legislation passed in modern times for the protection of children has, on the whole, had the effect of increasing, where it was needed, people's awareness of children as important beings who deserve consideration for their own sakes. A similar impression will probably be made on anyone who studies the history of the movements for the prevention of cruelty to animals.

No doubt, this general line of argument is dangerous, in

that it may easily be misused by those whose real motives in advocating repression are very different. But that is no reason for ignoring the possibility altogether. In any case, however, it is only of very limited application. And the general principle stands that, with these slight exceptions, emotional attitudes neither can nor ought to be controlled from outside by superior authority.

Another element of the greatest importance in an individual's personality is that of his opinions and beliefs. And that is one reason why in discussions about liberty the matter of freedom of thought and freedom of speech or discussion has always taken such a prominent place. These two, it must be emphasised, cannot really be kept separate as some people have supposed. Dr Johnson, for instance, argued that it was an error to 'confound liberty of thinking with liberty of talking', for no authority could prevent our thinking as we pleased. But this is a fallacy, or at any rate true only to a very limited degree. Of course, if we have once formed an opinion we cannot be forced to change it, though we can be forced to say that we have done so. But in the formation of opinion, if it is to be real opinion and not just a repetition of phrases, freedom of discussion is essential. Thinking does not take place in a vacuum, and anyone who wants to think seriously about anything must be free to seek for information where he can and to hear and consider other opinions. So far as he is prevented from doing this his thinking will be controlled almost as much as his talking. It is important to remember that our freedom of thought is being infringed by not being allowed to hear other opinions as well as by not being allowed to express our own.

This has already been discussed in a previous chapter with reference to the special case of political thought and discussion; and some of the possible threats to liberty and the possible safeguards for it have been suggested. But, of course, the general principle extends much more widely. It extends, for instance, to religious liberty, the battle for which has not yet been entirely won. And it extends more widely still to any questions on which difference of opinion is possible. Many of them may touch our daily lives at some point, and in any case a general atmosphere of repression can permeate the whole social life of a community.

This is in part the answer to the view that we used to hear put forward in certain quarters, to the effect that an exaggerated importance was being attached to liberty of opinion, which was really only a matter of interest to a few intellectuals, and that all attention ought to be concentrated on the much more urgent needs of society, such as raising the standard of living. No doubt it would be as well to be reminded, if there were the slightest danger of our forgetting, that there were other good things besides liberty of opinion which we ought to aim at. But no evidence has ever been adduced that liberty of opinion and speech was in the slightest degree incompatible with the pursuit of these other ends. Further, it would be very hard to defend the suppression of free discussion on the grounds that we were thereby securing greater liberty in some other direction. The free expression of opinion by one person could never be said in any normal sense to be a direct infringement of the liberty of anyone else. So altogether there seem to be good reasons why liberty of opinion should be taken as the test case in any discussions of liberty in general.

There remains the much-discussed question of liberty in our economic activities. This is an ambiguous phrase. It might quite logically be extended to all the activities by which people earn their livings. But almost any activity can become a way of earning one's living. The priest or minister, for instance, earns his living by preaching the Gospel and administering the sacraments, but it would sound very unnatural to speak of these as economic activities. The tendency of ordinary speech, on the whole, is to restrict the term to the production and distribution of material goods. Yet from the point of view of a discussion about liberty the fundamental considerations are very much the same for all kinds of professional activity. The work we do to earn our livings is obviously a very important factor in the development and expression of character and personality, and in any form of it there can be a greater or lesser degree of liberty to carry on our own work in our own way, subject only to such limitations as the nature of the job itself imposes. But it is true that difficulties arise in connection with work in commerce and industry more obviously than in most other activities, so that it is worth while to give a special degree of consideration to that.

The whole question of liberty in the conduct of industry is full of complications and it would need a separate volume to disentangle them all. What is most commonly suggested by the phrase is the freedom of industrialists and financiers from interference by the state in the conduct of their businesses. But that may involve the possibility of considerable restriction of the liberty of other people. It is important to remember, once more, that the state is not the only possible enemy of liberty. Then again in considering problems about the organisation and conduct of industry so many factors come in besides the matter of individual liberty. There is, for instance, the question of efficiency of production, which may make the difference between a high and low standard of living, and in extreme cases between life itself and starvation. It is perfectly possible that this can be attained only by the sacrifice of a good deal of liberty. Thus, it is clear that, as far as freedom from direct control by superior authority goes, the peasant farmer and the independent craftsman represent the ideal of liberty. Yet when these, particularly the latter, have disappeared from the scene it was because they could not make a living for themselves, still less produce enough to meet the needs of the community. They were replaced by large-scale industry, and in that there is obviously no question of complete liberty to do one's own work in one's own way for the great majority of those concerned. Then again there is the question of possible exploitation of the consumer, which may call for some restrictions on the liberty of action of those responsible for it, as by the old laws against regrating and forestalling or by modern legislation against monopolies. Altogether it is difficult or impossible to isolate the question of individual liberty from all the other considerations that have to be taken into account in deciding questions of economic policy.

What, then, is the position of the state in these matters? There are two main ways in which the state can interpose in economic activities. On the one hand, it can leave the owner-ship and control of industry in private hands while laying down a variety of laws and regulations which limit the free-dom of action of those in control. At all times industry has had to work within a framework of such rules, and in modern times there has been a continuous development of them, from the first Factory Acts at the beginning of the nineteenth cen-tury down to the exchange controls, export permits, and the like of the present day. At all times, too, they have been denounced by those who felt their restrictions as an infringe-ment of liberty, as, indeed, they were. But, on the whole, the tendency seems to be for the resentment to die down as people become used to them and habituated to working within their framework. The aim of such rules, it need hardly be said, is to canalise the energies generated in the conduct of industry in the directions in which they will be most beneficial to the community. Whether, or how far, they are successful in this aim could be decided only by a careful examination of particular cases.

But the state itself can also take over the ownership and con-trol of any industry. How far that will make for efficiency of production in any particular case is a question that does not call for discussion here. But as far as individual liberty is concerned there seems no reason in principle why it should be any less in a state-owned concern than in an industry in private ownership, at any rate for the great majority of those affected. Any large-scale industry means that all the people

in it, except the very few at the top, are working under orders
from someone else. Indeed all co-operative activity involves
in practice a large amount of subordinating one's own opinions
and one's own wishes to those of other people. This, however, is not to say that there may not be great differences of
degree within these limits. There may be more or less encouragement of individual initiative in subordinates and
readiness to delegate responsibility to them. There may be
more or less willingness to listen to new ideas and suggestions and more or less possibility of free discussion and
criticism of policy. There may also be a question of how far,
if at all, an organisation or an authority within an organisation
should attempt to control or influence the behaviour of its
members in their private lives or in any matters which are
not directly concerned with their duties in the organisation.
All these, and similar questions, can make a great difference
to the general atmosphere of liberty in any kind of organisation. Some suggestions have been made earlier of the sort of
institutions which might help to preserve this, among which
I should be inclined to put first in importance the existence
of strong trade unions and professional associations, separate
from the control and management of the industries or other
organisations. But it is easy to expect too much from institutions. There is, in the last resort, no substitute for the
maintenance of a general public opinion in favour of liberty,
for which each one of us has some responsibility.

There are, of course, many other problems which arise in
connection with the relations of the state to its individual
members. There is, for instance, the whole question of the
'Welfare State'. How far should the state organise and supply
services to its members, such as a health service, instead of
leaving them to personal effort and private charity? There is,
undoubtedly, in most modern states a strong movement in
that direction. But there have not been wanting critics of
this tendency, who argue that it is undermining the initiative

and sense of responsibility of individuals. We may find reason to suspect that some of these criticisms rest in part on a kind of nostalgia for an imaginary golden age in the past which never, in fact, existed. In any case, it is far too early to say what the effect is actually going to be. But perhaps by now enough has been said to illustrate the sort of problems which have to be faced by those with any degree of responsibility for the decisions of the state.

Chapter XIV

RELATIONS BETWEEN STATES—
NATIONALISM AND INTERNATIONALISM

IN no field are questions of what is and of what ought to be so closely intermingled as in the field of international relations. Indeed, 'facts' in this field very largely consist in the accepted ideas in the various communities of what ought or ought not to be done. No one, of course, would deny the importance of other influences. Obviously, for instance, every state would be influenced in its external policy by its geographical position, its size, its natural resources and similar factors. But it is difficult to make any generalisations about the effect of these things, and in any case the way in which the state reacts to them will be greatly influenced throughout by the accepted ideas of what is and what is not legitimate behaviour for statesmen. This may sound like saying that the determining factor in the foreign policy of a state was to be looked for in its accepted standards of right and wrong, and such a statement would certainly seem odd to many people. For it is very commonly asserted that moral considerations play less part in the relations between states than almost anywhere else, if, indeed, they play any part at all. There are possibilities of confusion here which are worth a moment's attention.

When people speak of morality in the relations between states they are very often thinking more or less vaguely of the states as a number of individuals, and are considering whether in their relations to each other they are observing the same sort of moral principles as we expect the actual individuals within the state to observe in their behaviour towards each other. But states are not individuals in any exact sense, and the actions of states are, in fact, the results of the decisions taken by some particular individuals and influenced to some degree by many others. In the relations between states, more obviously perhaps than in any other field, the operative decisions are necessarily, under modern conditions, taken by a small group of people, the rulers or the government. But they will be influenced in their decisions by the accepted ideas in their community of the general aims that statesmen ought to set before themselves and the general principles on which they should act, both in their relations to other states and in their actions within their own state. It should be added that, being themselves members of the community, they will probably share these accepted ideas to a great extent, and they will certainly, in their turn, have a special degree of influence on the form they take. These accepted ideas and standards of conduct are properly spoken of as moral ideas, because they claim to be of general application and to be binding on individuals irrespective of private and personal likes and dislikes, interests, pleasure, or convenience: they may, indeed, on occasions demand a considerable sacrifice of these things.

These accepted moral ideas, of course, differ considerably from one country or from one time to another. And when they are in sharp contradiction to our own we are apt, at times, to speak of them as immoral. For instance, in ancient Sparta, in its best days, there were very rigid standards of conduct which often called for a good deal of suppression of natural impulses and desires. We should naturally speak of these as moral standards, and there were things in them which we should admire today. But in many other respects they seem to us positively repellent. That is to say, we disagree strongly with their moral ideas and think their moral judgements wrong. In that sense we can speak of them as immoral. But it is in a different sense from that in which we should use the term when we wanted to suggest that moral considerations did not come in at all. If, for instance, we could imagine a society in which it was generally accepted that everyone would pursue his personal interests and desires without the slightest regard for anyone else, we should in the full sense speak of that as an entirely immoral state of things.

We can apply this argument particularly to the code of conduct which we expect to be observed by our statesmen. In most countries at the present time, as indeed in many other ages, statesmen and rulers are not expected to use their power purely to advance their own private interests without thought of what is to the benefit of their country. No doubt some of them do to a greater or lesser degree, but they so far recognise the code that they would not venture to admit this openly and publicly, and if they were known to be acting in that way they would be generally discredited. This will at least do something to restrict the possible range of such behaviour and to make it easier for those actuated by mere public-spirited motives to rise to the top. As usual, there are various intermediate possibilities here. A statesman may, for instance, follow in general the course he thinks best for his country but at the same time may not be above making something out of it for himself 'on the side': such conduct would be regarded with varying degrees of tolerance in different countries and at different times. But in general the accepted ideal is that the statesman should do what seems to him best for his country, and regard his private interests as irrelevant.

But, to return to the special subject of this chapter, the most austere and self-denying devotion to this ideal may be compatible with very varying views about the duty of a statesman when his decisions affect other countries besides his own. At the one extreme it might be held that he should regard the interests or rights of other countries as just as irrelevant as his own private interests, and the advancement of the interests of his own country as overriding any other possible principle of action. This is itself a moral principle, and when people say that moral considerations do not enter into the relations between states, what they really mean is that statesmen act on this moral principle and regard it as their duty to think only of the interests of their own country and to ignore everything else. Whether, in fact, statesmen are so single-minded as this is a debatable question. Certainly many people would maintain that it is by no means necessary or inevitable that they should be so. And they would argue, further, that it was desirable to get the view accepted that, while the interests of his own country must always be the first consideration in the mind of a statesman, it is not the only consideration that he ought to take into account. What does seem to be clear is that whatever view we adopt it must become part of the generally accepted assumptions of the community if it is to be effective. Statesmen cannot, in the long run, rise very much above or sink very much below the standards of conduct that are generally expected of them. This is the more obviously true the more democratic a community is, but the rule always holds to some extent.

This matter of special duties owed to particular groups or communities has often been something of a problem to the moralist. The great moral and religious systems that have most influenced human conduct, Christianity, Stoicism, Buddhism, and others, have always taught that morality is not a matter of frontiers, but that in some sense benevolence and other duties are owed equally to all human beings just because they are human. But humanity is, in fact, divided up into a number of different groups, and we find it difficult or impossible, in all normal circumstances, to adopt the same attitude to members of other groups as to those of our own. Up to a point this can be reconciled with the idea of a universal morality. We can say that it is not practically possible for most people to extend the range of their activities to the whole of humanity, and therefore they must restrict themselves to their own particular community, whatever it is, and concentrate on doing their duty within its limits. In fact, they will, as was suggested earlier, regard their community as a microcosm of humanity. This is, no doubt, what the Roman

Catholic thinkers have in mind when they justify patriotism as a special expression of love of one's neighbour. This attitude will work all right within certain limits, but the difficulty arises when the action of one community affects others, and when there is a clear conflict of interest between them. Can we expect one community to sacrifice its interests to those of another?

We should, perhaps, make a distinction here, which would be particularly clear in democratic states, between the attitude to be adopted by statesmen in power and that of the community as a whole. The statesmen are elected for the purpose of doing the best they can for their own country. They are there as trustees for the whole body, and a trustee for other people has not the same discretion in his actions as an individual responsible to himself alone. It could reasonably be argued, then, that the statesman has no right to take any action involving a clear sacrifice of the interests of his community, unless he is assured of widespread popular approval. How far, if at all, he could expect this approval is another matter. There is a possibility, which has occasionally become a reality, that a country as a whole might be ready to make temporary sacrifices of some good things, in order to help other countries, provided the sacrifices were not too great. But, as long as separate national communities exist, it would be idle to expect one community to accept voluntarily a permanent or considerable sacrifice of its interests for the sake of other communities. What we can expect, and to some extent get, is the acceptance by a community of certain general rules limiting the methods which it could legitimately adopt in the pursuit of its own interests. It should be possible for a strong public opinion to be developed to the effect that it was absolutely wrong to start an unprovoked war whatever advantages might be gained by it, that disputes wherever possible should be submitted to arbitration, that treaties should be kept, and the like. It might be argued that it would, in the long run, be to the interest of the community itself to observe these rules. But it is very doubtful if it could be shown that this would invariably be so. In any case, there might be occasions when the immediate gains from breaking the rules were so obvious and the future advantages of keeping them so vague and remote that it would be impossible to rely on a calculation of hypothetical interests to secure that the rules were kept. It would at least need to be reinforced by some sort of conviction that keeping the rules was good and right in itself.

It would seem desirable at this stage of the argument to consider somewhat more in detail what we mean by the 'interests' of a state or community. What do we include under the term, and how does this bear on the relations between states? Without attempting an exhaustive enumeration, we should probably recognise two or three things which seem to stand out most obviously, as being commonly indicated by the term and as being proper aims for the statesmen, who represent the community, to pursue. They are not entirely disconnected, for they act and react on each other. But they are distinguishable, and in some circumstances they can appear as rival claimants.

(1) The most obvious 'interest' is the material welfare, the standard of living, of the members of the community. This is very widely accepted as one of the most important aims of a state's policy, and the success of that policy is often judged by the degree to which the standard of living of the particular state in question rises above that of other states. Of course, this depends on many other factors, the possession of natural resources, for instance. But states differ widely in the use they make of such resources as they have got: we may even find states, such as Denmark, with little or nothing in the way of natural resources attaining a standard of living considerably higher than that of most other countries. Again, it depends not only on the collective decisions of the state, acting through its recognised government, but also on the actions of its individual members of every kind. But, once more, the policy of

the state can make an enormous difference in encouraging or
frustrating this, in knowing when to act and when to refrain
from action, in co-operating with and guiding the actions of
individuals into the most useful channels. But all this is in
the main a matter of internal policy, and we want to consider
here the ways in which the actions of the state in pursuing
the welfare of its members may impinge upon the material
interests of other states.

It is sometimes said that we are all members of one world,
mutually dependent on one another, and that it is not really
possible for one country to benefit itself by impoverishing
another or for one country to become richer without benefiting
the rest. There is, no doubt, an element of truth in this: one
country may benefit from the enrichment of another and may
suffer from the other's impoverishment. But as a universal
rule it is clearly untenable. For its logical conclusion would
be that no one can ever be better off than anyone else. Yet
obviously some countries, just like some individuals, are better
off than others, that is to say have a greater proportionate
share of the total wealth produced. And there could be no
warrant for supposing that the actions of the states themselves
could not make any difference in this respect. At any rate it
would take a lot to convince them that it was not worth trying.

The most obvious and direct way, more popular in earlier
ages than the present, is by war. In the last fifty years we have
become familiar with the argument that war cannot possibly
pay. And, whatever we may think of the argument in its
original form, it is obvious nowadays with the latest developments of weapons of destruction that an all-out war between
great Powers would be destructive of material prosperity for
all alike. On the other hand, a quick and easy war by a great
Power against a small one, unequipped with nuclear weapons,
might in certain circumstances be very profitable. It might,
for instance, secure for the great Power control over some
scarce and valuable raw material, at its own price and on
its own terms. Short of this, there are various ways in

which one country might try to profit at the expense of another, by the imposition of tariffs, by bargaining over the prices of certain products, by the increase or reduction or abolition of profit from foreign investments, and by various other means. It must be recognised that very often when a country tries to do this it injures itself as much as or more than its intended victim. But there is no necessity about this, and when it does happen it is often because other motives have come in besides the pursuit of material welfare.

(2) Another 'interest' which it is generally recognised that statesmen would properly pursue on behalf of their countries is independence, the freedom from control or domination by other countries. It is the assumption at the back of a good deal of our thinking that the natural and proper order of things is the existence of a number of independent sovereign states, and that it is wrong for states to attempt to encroach on each other's independence. It might be quite possible to recognise that, in practice, few if any states can be completely independent and at the same time to maintain that complete independence represents the ideal and that the nearer we can get to it the better. That is, in fact, the kind of assumption on which statesmen usually work. It is, for instance, what, in the main, is in their minds when they talk of national safety or security, meaning by that the need for a state to be in a position, through the strength of its own armed forces or by other means, that would secure that no other state should be able to establish control over it by force.

The relation of this demand for independence to the demand for material welfare is complicated. Sometimes when a community demands independence from the domination of another Power, it claims that it is being exploited to its own disadvantage by the dominating Power and that it needs independence in order to pursue its own material welfare. But it cannot be doubted that, in some circumstances, it may be economically worse off by becoming independent. The situation is complicated when the threat to independence comes, or is thought to come, from economic relations, when, for instance, one country becomes dependent upon another for essential goods or services. It is this supposed danger which has led so many countries to try to become as self-sufficient as possible and to produce everything for themselves. In theory, no doubt, it would be a considerable step towards the ideal of complete independence if every country could be completely isolated economically and take nothing from any other country. But, even if it were possible, it is certain that most countries would be a great deal poorer. Up to a point they might accept a certain amount of that as the price of greater independence, and various slogans have been coined to express such an attitude, like List's 'Defence is better than opulence'.

(3) This leads on to the third 'interest' which we need consider here, namely power, which means, in the main, military power, or, more widely, the ability and resources to wage a war successfully against other countries. This is obviously closely connected with the last, as one of the chief reasons why power is desired is as a guarantee of independence and security. But it is very easy to go beyond that, so that power becomes something desired for its own sake, not only the potentiality of power but the actual exercise of it by way of domination over other countries and peoples. We all know how the love of power and domination can develop in individuals, and, broadly speaking, an individual, when he begins to think in terms of his country and its interests, is likely to want for his country the same kind of thing as he wants for himself. People can often get a vicarious satisfaction of their own desires by transmuting them into similar desires for their country or other groups to which they belong. It is not so long ago that this was regarded as a perfectly normal ambition for any country that was in a position to pursue it. But nowadays it is less respectable, and even countries which still in fact entertain it hesitate to express it openly. It may still survive in literary form:

> *Wider still and wider may thy bounds be set.*
> *God who made thee mighty make thee mightier yet.*

But even here it seems rather out of date. None the less, there is no guarantee that under favourable conditions it might not revive. The impulse to dominate is undoubtedly an element in human nature, and may be the real driving force behind actions taken ostensibly for some other purpose, such as national security, or the pursuit of wealth, or even the propagation of some doctrine believed to be true.

It would be possible to think of other kinds of interest that might be pursued. There is, for instance, the desire for prestige or admiration, which is not necessarily the same as the desire for power. But these are the ones that most obviously affect the relations between states. It is time now to consider a further complication. We have been talking hitherto in terms of states, and the further complication arises when we begin to talk about 'nations', 'nationality', and 'nationalism'. What ideas do these words indicate?

The popular use of these terms is very far from being consistent or logical, though in practice this does not cause as much confusion as might be expected. Grammatically 'nation' ought to be used for a concrete group of people, and 'nationality' for the characteristic they have in common. Sometimes that seems to fit in with ordinary usage. Thus, 'nation' is very often used as the equivalent of 'state'. We speak, for instance, of an association of sovereign states as the United Nations. Similarly we speak of 'international relations' meaning by that the relations between states, and of the 'national debt' meaning the debt owed by the state. In that sense, we use 'nationality' to indicate the legal status of a member of a state, as when we speak of a naturalised foreigner acquiring British nationality. In other connections, however, we use 'national' and 'nationality' to indicate something different from membership of a state. We speak of national movements within a state, which assert the claims of nationality against the claims of the state. In that sense, we have come to use 'nationality' as indicating both the concrete group and the common characteristic of the members, doubtless because the word 'nation' has become too closely connected with the state. Thus we speak of the old Austro-Hungarian state as containing several different 'nationalities', not several different 'nations'. And the Irish proclaimed that they were 'a nation once again' when they became a separate state, having previously, presumably, been a 'nationality'. This seems to suggest that 'nationality' in the concrete sense indicates a group of people who aspire to become a separate state of their own. When they have achieved that they become a 'nation', and before they achieve it they are part of a state which is not a nation.

This rough preliminary definition needs certain qualification. The desire to form one state might arise from other motives than from a sense of nationality. It is quite conceivable, for instance, that two or more groups might decide to coalesce into a single state for the sake of self-defence against a powerful neighbour, or for the sake of the economic advantages that it might bring. They would not, in that case, form a single nationality, though they might grow into one eventually. Something of that kind seems to have happened in the case of Switzerland. Swiss nationality is really a development of the nineteenth century. Before that there was an alliance of several independent states, often hostile to each other, and divided by language and religion and differences of social structure, but held together by ties of common interests. Yet by now few countries have a stronger sense of nationality than Switzerland.

The feeling for a nationality is clearly a particular case of the group-loyalty about which something has already been said in the discussion of political parties, and it expresses itself in the same way as the other forms of this. But the special question here is what the group is. What do the individual members have in common which makes them say that they are of the same nationality and distinguishes them from other nationalities? The essential element, and the one that is practically of most importance, is the desire to form one state, but, as we have just seen, that by itself is not enough. It must be the desire to form one state, as it were, for its own sake and not for any extrinsic advantages that it might bring. If we attempt to analyse this further, we shall find that we can only take refuge in vague terms, because the facts themselves are not susceptible of precise formulation. We can say that the people who form one nationality feel that they are the same sort of people, that they have something in common with each other and different from others in their ways of thinking and looking at things, in their habits of behaviour and the like, to an extent that makes them think or feel that they will be happier and more comfortable working with each other in a single political unit than they would be if divided or united with people whom they feel to be different from themselves. Nationality, in fact, is something subjective existing in people's minds, and we cannot, in general, say much more than that people are of one nationality when they believe themselves to be so.

That is not to say that there are not more objective factors which are of great influence in forming that state of mind. But we cannot pick out any one of them as being sufficient or even essential for producing it. The simplest and most obvious case is where people who feel themselves of one nationality have been for a considerable time united in one state, as France or England: it might be debatable how far we ought to speak, without qualification, of Great Britain in this connection. In such cases, they will have acquired a long-standing habit of living and working together as a single political unit, they will have developed common institutions and ways of doing things, they will have common memories, history, and traditions. This applies also to nationalities which have once constituted separate states of their own and are striving to recover this status again. Polish nationalism during the period of partition undoubtedly rested very largely on the memory of the former kingdom of Poland, and Czech nationalism to some extent on that of the kingdom of Bohemia. On the whole, it seems to be rare for a body of people to develop a sense of nationality unless they have at some time been under one government or formed a political unit. There are, however, exceptions to this. Italy had not been under one government since the time of the Ostrogoths, but Italian nationalism in the nineteenth century was a strong emotional force, though there seems to be some doubt whether it was felt with equal intensity in all sections of the population.

In this latter case, the possession of a common language no doubt played a part along with other influences, and language is an important factor in national feeling. It is not an essential factor, as the examples of Switzerland and, with some qualifications, of Belgium show. Nor does it by itself produce a tendency towards national unity: otherwise Britain and the United States would still be conjoined, instead of becoming, in the well-known epigram, 'two nations divided by a common language'. But obviously it strengthens the sense of unity, if other influences favour it. Polish nationality, again, depended to a considerable degree on a common language: Germany, before 1914, attempted, without success, to force the German language on her Polish population, and we used to hear stories of Polish school children being whipped for saying their prayers in Polish. In other countries national movements have included an attempt to revive or impose a national language in order to secure unity and to emphasise the difference from other nationalities.

There are many other influences which may work in the same direction. There is geographical unity in the sense of residence within well-defined natural boundaries. Religion may sometimes strengthen the sense of nationality, as in the case of the Catholic Poles between Protestant Prussia and Orthodox Russia. In other circumstances it may cut across national divisions, and may even become a rival, though generally an unsuccessful one, for the loyalty of the people concerned. It is, perhaps, hardly necessary at this time of day to discuss the idea, once popular, that differences of nationality have a racial basis. It is now generally recognised that differences of race, whatever meaning we may attach to that somewhat elusive concept, are not in the least co-terminous with differences of nationality, and may have little or nothing to do with them. In any case, to enumerate all the possible influences which might contribute to the formation of a distinct nationality would involve a lengthy historical examination of a large number of particular cases, which would need a volume to itself. Here we must be content to accept national feelings and national aspirations as given facts, which have to be taken into account in any estimation of political possibilities.

One preliminary qualification would seem to be in place here. The kind of differences which distinguish one nationality from another and the consciousness of and feelings for them are clearly things which admit of differences of degree. In different degrees they can be present, not only in particular nations but in different parts of the same nation. The differences which distinguish, say, America from France are of the same kind, though much greater in degree, as the differences between the inhabitants of Brittany and Provence or New England and the Deep South. The consciousness of this may, though it does not necessarily do so, lead to a demand for some degree of local autonomy combined with a wish to remain part of the larger unit for more general purposes. This kind of nationalism within a nationalism expresses itself very naturally in the establishment of a federal organisation of the state. This may work satisfactorily, and, when it does, it will certainly not diminish the strength of national feeling *vis-à-vis* other nations or states.

Leaving aside this particular complication, we have to consider briefly the main effects of national feeling as a political force. We may begin here with an obvious distinction. On the one hand, we have the established nations, which have been political units, under one government or ruler, for a long period, going back, in some cases, to a time before people had begun to think in terms of nationality. On the other, we have the 'nationalities', the people who aspire to become a single political unit but have not yet achieved their aim. The former case has already been discussed. It is the latter which provided the really explosive element in Europe from the time of Napoleon up to the First World War. It was hoped then that the problems it raised could be solved by the principle of self-determination, that is by inviting the people concerned to decide for themselves which nationality they felt themselves to belong to, and consequently which state they wished to join. The complications that arose in the practical application of this from the mixture of populations and from rival national claims can be studied in the histories of the Treaty of Versailles and the political developments that followed from it. But, in spite of all the difficulties, the principle itself was logical and reasonable. More recently similar problems have arisen from the nationalist movements in Asia and Africa.

If we consider nationalism or national feeling as a political and social phenomenon, there are two or three things that cannot fail to strike us. Nationalism is often put forward as a great moral principle, but it seems, on balance, to be unfavourable to the observance of other moral principles. The cause of nationality, like all causes, is a stimulus to courage and self-sacrifice, which we should normally regard as good things. But there are other things which are generally considered good, and whole-hearted devotion to a cause may often demand that these should be ignored, or regarded as evils to be combated, if they hinder the pursuit of the cause. Thus, truth and fairness are generally regarded as good. But nationalist movements do not pay much respect to them, and they have on occasions been openly denounced as treachery when they were inconvenient to the nationalist cause. Again, friendliness and good will between men are commonly regarded as desirable.

But the ardent nationalist regards such feelings towards those whom he looks on as enemies as wholly undesirable, and he may on occasions stage acts of violence with the deliberate intention of producing or intensifying hatred.

One noticeable feature of nationalist sentiment is the extent to which it induces in those who feel it an attitude of intolerance towards similar feelings when directed against themselves. A century ago the Hungarian nationalists, under the leadership of Kossuth, included as an essential part of their claims the right of the Magyars to domination over the Slavs and Roumanians within the borders of the kingdom of Hungary, and they denied to these peoples any of the rights that they claimed for themselves. The Poles after 1919 repressed with considerable severity any nationalist movements among the Ruthenians and Ukrainians. The Irish refuse to recognise the right of Northern Ireland to vote itself out of the Irish Republic. Mr De Valera is reported as saying in that connection, 'self-determination only applies to nationalities'. He did not explain what practical criterion of nationality there can be except self-determination. It is easy to see what is meant by saying that people belong to a particular nationality because they think they do, but hard to understand how it can be maintained that they belong because someone else thinks they ought to. Yet such a view seems not uncommon among ardent nationalists. During the negotiations that led to the Versailles Treaty, an English journalist reported a conversation with a Polish propagandist. The Pole urged the claims of Poland to the Masurian districts in the south of East Prussia. But when the Englishman suggested a plebiscite, he was told that that must at all costs be avoided. For though these people were undoubtedly Polish they might not be as fully conscious of the fact as they ought to be, and needed a period of Polish rule to make them realise where they really belonged.

Another doubt that suggests itself is about the kind of policy that nationalist feelings will tend to produce after their primary aim of political independence has been attained. What other good things might be expected to follow from the attainment of this aim? To the whole-hearted nationalist such questions might seem largely irrelevant, as national independence is to be regarded as good in itself, whatever the results. Consider, for instance, the question of material welfare. Of course, any state must have some care for that. But it is one of the things that nationalist movements seem most ready to sacrifice, if necessary. No doubt, for purposes of propaganda they may hold out hopes of a great increase of prosperity to their adherents. But it would be difficult to find many cases where this has in fact resulted. More often than not the success of nationalist movements has resulted in a worsening of the economic situation. Again, the demand for national liberty is not necessarily favourable to other kinds of liberty. It used sometimes to be thought that there was some special connection between nationalism and democracy. But the facts seem to suggest that, while they may sometimes be conjoined, there is no necessary connection between them. German nationalism, for instance, has generally been authoritarian rather than democratic, and when the Saarlanders voted to rejoin Germany in 1935 they were deliberately putting themselves under dictatorial rule in obedience to their national feelings.

There seem to be two main sorts of aim which national feeling would tend to pursue, once the main object of separation and independence had been attained. On the one hand, an obvious expression of national feeling would be the pursuit of power and domination, about which something has already been said. On the other, as a supplement or alternative to this, there is the idea of developing a national character and a national culture which would mark off the particular nation from other nations. Max Weber, the German sociologist, said in his Inaugural Lecture in 1895, 'What we have to bequeath to our descendants is not peace and human happiness, but the eternal struggle to preserve and build up our national character.'[1] But it is far from clear what this involves. Obviously, our way of looking at things, our attitudes, our approach to problems, all our activities in fact, will inevitably be influenced by our national environment. It hardly needs an 'eternal struggle' to secure that. But something more than that seems to be demanded here, something which seems to take the form of a conscious effort on the part of a nation to be different just for the sake of being different. This may easily develop into a kind of spiritual isolationism or even xenophobia, and it is doubtful whether much of any value has ever emerged from such an attitude. The advocates of cultural nationalism sometimes talk as if the only alternative was a dead level of uniformity everywhere. But this is a fallacy. There are always great possibilities of variety between individuals or between smaller groups, and, on the whole, a strong national feeling is likely to be unfavourable to such variety within its own borders.

However, when all is said and done, national feeling is a very strong force, and there is always a *prima facie* case against attempting to hold down a strong force. In particular, when it is a case of people choosing under what government they want to be and to which group they want to belong, it would seem that it is always, in itself, desirable that they should have a free choice. Self-determination, whatever practical difficulties may arise in its application, is in itself a sound principle and ideal to aim at. That is not to say that it is an absolutely sacrosanct and inviolable principle that must never be infringed whatever the circumstances. But a very heavy burden of proof rests on anyone who would infringe it in any particular case.

A special difficulty arises when there is no very deep or widespread national feeling, but a small group of enthusiasts is trying to arouse it. They may sometimes claim that they are the true nation and that their claims should be met, irrespective of the wishes of the mass of the people concerned.

[1] M. Weber, *Gesammelte politische Schriften*, p. 20.

Sometimes, even, they may hold, as did the notorious Macedonian terrorists, that they are justified in using violence to enforce national feelings and national claims on an indifferent or hostile population. But there are many stages short of that. In general, the attempt to create a feeling of nationality where it does not exist to any great extent before can be justified only on the view that such a thing is good in itself irrespective of other results it may produce. Certainly, tried by any extrinsic standard of values, material welfare, human happiness, moral improvement, cultural achievement, it could hardly be approved. But in such matters we may often find ourselves faced by an almost religious faith which is beyond the reach of argument.

Are there any prospects that national feeling and national divisions might diminish or be replaced by something else in the foreseeable future? Here we can only indicate possibilities, and the chance of their realisation is a matter of pure conjecture. It has often been pointed out that nationalism, as we know it, is a comparatively recent growth, and some have even gone as far as to say that the very idea of nationality is a product of the nineteenth century. This, however, would be an exaggeration. From the earliest ages mankind has been divided into different groups, whose members developed a common consciousness of themselves as different kinds of people from the others. But these differences, except in a few cases, were not regarded as politically relevant. It would not have occurred to most people that they could override loyalty to one's king or lord, or to the Church, or even at some periods to one's order or social class. Earlier still other loyalties came in. It is interesting to speculate what would have been the result if the principle of nationality and self-determination had been generally accepted at some earlier period. There would, for instance, have been no Roman Empire, no common Western civilisation, and, in all probability, no Christianity as we know it. Whether that would have been an advantage or not each man must judge for himself.

In any case, what all this suggests is that it is natural and probably inevitable that some sense of nationality should exist, but not inevitable that it should occupy the overriding place that it does at the present time. Yet it has become deeply ingrained in our habits of thought, and, when a nationality has existed for some time as a distinct state, it has become ingrained in habits of political action, in government, law, and institutions. It would obviously need some very powerful counter-influence if it was to be overridden or relegated to a subordinate place.

The general notion of Internationalism, in spite of occasional and momentary outbursts of enthusiasm, has little emotional appeal. We can say that we are all parts of one world, but we do not really feel it, in the sense in which we can feel that we are parts of a national or other group. A well-known writer once said that we have got to learn to expand our feelings of national patriotism into a world patriotism. But the two would not be the same sort of thing. The group-loyalty, of which patriotism is a special case, depends upon consciousness of the group as distinct from other groups. If that were overcome it would mean, not the development of another group-feeling, but rather the development of a feeling for all the individuals that constitute humanity, and a sense that they are all equally important just as human beings. Many of us are capable of feeling a certain degree of that: if we saw an injured man by the roadside a feeling of common humanity might lead us to go to his help without asking of what country or creed he was. But for most of us the possible occasions for the exercise of such feelings are rare. And, in any case, to forget altogether the separate groups to which one belongs and to think only of human beings is possible only for very exceptional characters. Most of us, if we could get rid of all feeling for the groups to which we belonged, would probably end by thinking only of ourselves.

There are influences which may transcend national boundaries, such as religion. But here the fact that there are many different religions makes it a dividing as much as a uniting force. It is true that the division between religions often cuts across the division between nations. But, even when it does, religion has not in practice shown itself a very effective force in reducing tension between nations. There have been times, indeed, in which religion has been brought into the service of national or political ends. Three or four centuries ago there were periods in which it seemed that Catholicism was becoming an instrument for the furtherance of the ambitions of the Spanish monarchy, just as nowadays the quasi-religion of international Communism has become an instrument of the national aims of Russia.

Another thing which can transcend national divisions is the pursuit of knowledge and learning, though in some branches this, too, can be distorted to serve nationalist aims. We all know, for instance, how history can be re-written for that purpose. It is much harder to do that in the case of the natural sciences, though there have been occasional attempts at it even there. Still, taking it by and large, the pursuit of knowledge does represent the recognition of certain values to which national differences are irrelevant. Unfortunately its influence does not penetrate very deeply in any country.

Perhaps more could be hoped for from the realisation that, in some circumstances, national self-interest itself might demand some sacrifice of national separateness. Certainly, nothing does more to bring nations into closer unity than the fear of a common danger from a potential enemy. But if this succeeded in overcoming certain national divisions it would only be to intensify others. Perhaps we might try to persuade people that the whole world would be better off if we all co-operated together to raise living standards, and that this would involve some degree of international control and direction and sacrifice of national independence. But, as has already been suggested, though this might be true on the average in the long run, there would be every reason to believe that for some time to come it would demand a considerable sacrifice of the standards of the more fortunate nations. And, from all the indications that we have, that is a sacrifice that few, if any, nations would willingly make. Some people have thought that the most we could hope for would be the gradual growth of a number of different international organisations to carry out particular services where the need for them was most obvious: the original pattern of such things was set by the International Postal Union, and others have developed since. These might as they increased develop more and more the habit of international co-operation, until it gradually became part of our established ways of thinking. But all this is a matter of speculation about the future. In the meantime those who are interested in transcending national differences will press their governments to make the greatest use that they can of the existing organs of international co-operation, such as the United Nations Organisation and its subsidiary bodies. It is, perhaps, as well that the start of the United Nations was not attended with the same exaggerated hopes as were entertained for the old League of Nations.

Chapter XV

CONCLUSION—POLITICS, ECONOMICS, AND ETHICS

THERE can be, properly speaking, no conclusion to a book on Political Theory. There is an indefinite number of particular political questions that can arise, and many of them have their theoretical side. There is, therefore, no end to the possible additions that could be made to a treatise such as this. All that can be done here is to clear up one or two loose ends that seem to have been left untied. One of them, that may well occur to possible critics, is the position of economic considerations in relation to the matters previously discussed. It is often asserted, though perhaps less stridently than it was twenty years or so ago, that Economics provides the real key to the understanding of all public affairs, that economic motives are the primary or fundamental moving forces, that the economic structure of society is the determining factor in political, or indeed most other activities, and more to the like effect. So, though economic considerations have been mentioned from time to time in the preceding pages, some people will certainly feel that not nearly enough attention has been paid to them.

Now, it is obviously true that questions which, on any definition of the term, would be called economic occupy a large part of the attention of statesmen and governments. That has always been so, and is not a special discovery of the present age. But it does not follow that they necessarily raise questions of political theory. The same would be true of questions about the organisation of defence and the armed forces. We may ask what sort of wars we are likely to be engaged in, and what sort of army would be most suited for that purpose. Or we may ask more detailed questions, such as whether battleships are obsolete, or which pattern of rifle is the most efficient. There are many other similar questions on which the government would have to come to a decision. But no one would suggest that any general political theory was directly involved in these decisions, whichever way they went. A great many economic questions seem to be essentially in the same position, questions, for instance, about the raising of the bank rate or the imposition of exchange controls. These are strictly technical questions and the specialists in the subject can tell us what results, given certain conditions, are likely to follow a particular course of action. Indirectly, any of these questions may get mixed up with questions of general political principle. But strictly the political theorist has no more obligation to deal with the technical knowledge of the economist than with that of the military expert. No doubt, it will be an advantage to him to know something about either of these specialisms. But that would be rather in the nature of what journalists call 'background information', and its chief value would be as a help to knowing when the specialist is speaking with authority and when he is not.

But 'economic considerations' means something wider than the special studies of professional economists, and there is room for a brief examination of some of the things that the phrase may suggest. What, for instance, could be meant by saying that the 'economic motive' is the primary motive in human activity? Probably, to the ordinary man the first thing that the phrase 'economic motive' would suggest would be the desire to get money. But it is a commonplace that the desire for money is not a simple motive in itself, except in certain abnormal states of mind, but is the result of other desires for the variety of things that money can bring. These include not only the things that we can purchase directly with money, but the incidental results that in some conditions the possession of money can produce, such as power, prestige, the outward signs of success and the like. For the moment we can leave these out of consideration, merely asking in passing whether the desire for prestige, even when it leads to the pursuit of money, would naturally be described as an economic motive. But even when it is a matter of the things we definitely pay for there are difficulties in defining with any precision the denotation of the term.

Thus, we should normally think, in the first place, of the concrete material objects that we can see and touch. The desire to possess and to use or enjoy these things is probably the first form of the economic motive that would occur to us. But even among these things we shall find different kinds which are desired for different reasons. The most obvious and elementary kind is that of the objects that are needed to satisfy our basic physical needs, food, drink, clothing, shelter, and the like. These are the things that are needed to keep us alive and in reasonable health and strength. The desire for such things might properly be described as basic or fundamental, in that normally they are the necessary pre-condition for the satisfaction of any other desires. As a rule people think about keeping alive before anything else. But when these basic needs are satisfied, other desires, independent of them, come into play. In fact at a comparatively low level of satisfaction of their physical needs people begin to want other things as well: the Roman mob demanded their games as well as their bread. But these other things may appeal to quite different elements in human nature. A man may want to buy pictures because he enjoys looking at beautiful objects. If he tries to make enough money to do this, is his motive economic or aesthetic?

The point can be made even more strongly if we consider not only the tangible goods but also the various kinds of services for which we pay. These have to be included in the scope of economics just as much as the material goods. Some of them, indeed, are closely connected with the production and distribution of these goods. But others are not. People may, for instance, feel the need of the services of ministers of religion, and may be ready to pay for them. There may also be a good deal of organisation involved in meeting people's religious needs. In fact, from the point of view of the economist, it may look very like any other business concern which exists to supply some need of the public, and the same problems of efficiency of organisation, of the amount of the national wealth to be devoted to the purpose, and the like, may arise here as well as anywhere else. We do not, in fact, naturally speak of the need for religious services as an economic need or motive, nor do we speak of the organisation of the church as part of the economic machine. But there really seems no logical reason why we should not.

The fact is that the phrase 'economic motive' does not stand for any clear and distinct idea at all, and it is not commonly used by economists, who, from the nature of their profession, have to think clearly about their subject. As the instances given above suggest, it is hard to draw any line between the economic motive and other possible kinds of motive. In the end we seem reduced to saying that the economic motive is the desire to get what we want. And as we all naturally desire to get what we want or what we desire, statements about the importance of the economic motive become empty tautologies. Thus, when a modern writer describes the chief characteristic of the post-Reformation world as the fact that 'the pursuit of wealth for its own sake became the chief motive of human activity',[1] it seems difficult to attach much more meaning to that than that the desire to get what we want or to satisfy our needs is the chief motive of all human activity. And we may well ask when it was anything else. Of course, ideas of what constitutes wealth may change, and people may want some things more in some periods or some societies, and others in others. But that is another matter.

There is, however, one possible distinction which may be

[1] H. J. Laski, *The Rise of European Liberalism*, p. 20.

suggested here. The language that has been used hitherto rather suggests that the desire for wealth is to be understood primarily as the desire of each individual to secure what he wants for himself. But in fact a great many people are not all the time thinking of themselves alone, but have others for whose welfare they are concerned. Thus, parents may sacrifice themselves in the hope that their children may be better off. Such conduct is generally respected and we should not naturally say that the parents were actuated by an economic motive, but rather by a moral motive. The same would apply, perhaps more strongly, if the interests of a wider group than the family were concerned. Perhaps, then, the only way in which we could attach some precision to these terms would be by saying that an individual is actuated by economic motives when he is thinking of his own wants without regard to anyone else and by moral motives when he is thinking of other people's wants without regard to his own. When he is concerned to satisfy the wants of a number of people who incidentally include himself he is actuated by a mixture of both kinds of motive. And that is, in fact, the situation of most people who are concerned with public or political affairs.

There is another view which deserves more serious attention. This is the theory, put forward in an extreme form by Marx and his followers and in various modified forms by other writers, that the economic structure of society is the basic factor that determines the form of the political structure, and, indeed, of most other activities, such as religion, art, or morality, as well. 'Economic structure' is usually taken to mean the way in which the production and distribution of material goods is organised. This, in turn, is largely determined by the technical processes of production which are available at any particular time.

The advocates of this view have not, as a rule, much to say about motives. Human behaviour is treated as, in the main, determined by institutions and the structure of society. This avoids some of the possibilities of confusion noticed in the preceding paragraphs. On the other hand, it will seem to many people to be one of the weaknesses of the Marxist case, as usually presented, that it pays such slight and superficial attention to psychological analysis. This sometimes seems to be claimed as a virtue, and it is argued that the so-called 'objective' factors are of more importance than what is going on in individual human minds. But, in fact, institutions and the like are just as much psychological facts as are impulses and desires. They are really, if fully analysed, just sets of acquired habits, and habits have no existence outside human beings. Further, habits have to be formed, and, even when they are formed, they can be altered or broken. The mere fact of the habit cannot in itself be an explanation of why it is formed, and why it is kept or modified or abandoned altogether. Even if we looked for the cause of this in strictly 'objective' factors, such as occurrences in physical nature, they could still produce these effects only by working on and in the minds of individual human beings. And if that side of the process is neglected we can get only a very one-sided and inadequate picture of the whole.

This is not, however, the main point, and, quite apart from this, we have to recognise the basis of truth that there is in the theory. The political structure of a society, by which we mean, in general terms, the machinery by which decisions are reached that are accepted as binding on the whole society, is obviously the result of many influences. Among these the economic structure, that is, as defined above, the machinery by which the material goods required for the satisfaction of man's needs are produced and distributed, is likely to play a very important part. It is not the only possible influence. In some countries at some periods, for instance, it seems pretty clear that the military structure, the organisation needed for defence or conquest, has been a decisive factor in determining the form of the political structure, and in many other cases it has played some part. But probably in most cases it would be subordinate to the economic factor. There are other influences, also, which may play a part.

What this means is that if we are examining historically the development of the political structure of any particular state, it is always worth while looking for features of the economic situation which may have influenced the development. But it does not mean that we can lay down beforehand any absolute rule that this must have been the sole, or even the main factor in every particular case. We can, perhaps, say that it is a kind of limiting factor. That is to say, for any political system to function at all it must not be incompatible with the economic system functioning; people must be provided with the necessities of life if government is to go on. But there are wide possibilities of variation within these bounds, and we cannot say except by trial and experiment how wide those limits are. Further, the 'economic structure' of any society is not something fixed and unalterable, nor is it something which we simply have to accept as a given fact. Except in entirely custom-ridden societies, it is something which is fluid and changeable into a protean variety of forms. And this change and variety itself needs an explanation which cannot always be found in the nature of the economic structure itself. The political structure may and often does influence the development of the economic system, and we cannot set any *a priori* limits to the extent to which it can do that. The only necessary condition, as we have seen, is that the economic machine must keep moving, in other words that the work of production and distribution of material necessities must go on. But to argue from that, as Marxist writers seem to do, that those chiefly responsible for the decisions of the state must necessarily aim at maintaining and protecting the existing economic system, just as it is, is a complete *non sequitur*. It is true that there are always strong influences at work favouring the maintenance of any existing system, economic or otherwise. Those who benefit most from it will, on the whole, tend to support it, though there are many striking exceptions to such a rule.

But not the least of the influences in that direction is the natural conservatism of mankind, based on the fact that we are by nature habit-forming animals. That is, in part, the reason why the 'revolutionary situation' which Marxism postulated as an inevitable development is in fact a rare and exceptional phenomenon which arises only in very special circumstances.

The further Marxist deductions are equally lacking in cogency. They seem to consist in taking certain influences or tendencies which are observable at certain times and showing what would happen if they were developed to their logical extremes and no counter-influences arose to check or modify them. Thus it is true that those who control private industry will exercise influence on the public policy of a country, though it is, incidentally, no longer true that those who control are necessarily those who own. If all industry were private, if there were no nationalised industries and services and no co-operative societies, if there were no trade unions and no Civil Service, this influence might become predominant. As it is, it is only one among many influences, and the extent of it varies enormously from country to country and from time to time.

It is the same with the alleged inevitability of an ever-intensifying class struggle. The prophecy that the division into two classes will become harder and sharper and that the differences in wealth and status will continually increase has been falsified by events. But that is not to say that there is no truth in the idea of a class struggle. The fundamental fact is that, as long as the supply of good things in the world is limited, there will always be the possibility of a conflict over the division of the wealth available at any one time. There is, also, the possibility that any particular group may combine to advance its interests against those of some other group: in doing that it will doubtless develop some degree of group loyalty, a sentiment that does not always tend to make the members of the group more clear-sighted in seeing where their individual interests really lie. In all the circumstances in which modern industry grew up it was natural that many of those concerned should be most conscious of the conflict between the employer and the wage-earner. But that is not the only possible form of conflict. When people are thinking of increasing their share of the available wealth the conflict can just as well be horizontal as vertical, between different industries as much as between different ranks in the same industry. Something of the kind may, indeed, be happening at the present time, even though old loyalties may obscure it from the eyes of those most concerned. Conflicts between the agricultural interest and the manufacturing interest have long been familiar in many countries. But when we really come down to it, so far as it is merely a question of the division of existing wealth, everyone's interests are opposed to those of everyone else.

One element in the original Marxist doctrine would be of great importance for political theory, if there were any reason to suppose it true. That is the theory of the eventual disappearance of the state. The argument here really boils down to this: the fact that the state must keep the economic machine going somehow is interpreted as meaning that it must preserve 'the existing system of productive relationships' exactly as it is. That means, in turn, that it must necessarily do everything to maintain the unfettered control of capitalist employers over the conduct of industry. As the only threat to that comes from the discontent of the dispossessed masses, these have to be kept down, and this work of repression is the main, if not the sole, function of the state. When the social revolution has swept away capitalist domination and thereby removed the causes of discontent the state is left with no work to do and will gradually 'wither away'. It is doubtful whether this view needs to be taken very seriously nowadays. It has in effect been abandoned even by the Marxists themselves, though they still seem to pay lip-service to it as a kind of millennial aspiration. Every step in the argument is, to put it mildly, highly debatable, and certainly does not follow logically from the preceding one. As for the final conclusion, it is difficult to attach any precise meaning to it. The state cannot be defined by mentioning one possible function that it may perform under certain conditions. The state is simply the territorial community organised, in one way or another, so that decisions may be reached which will be valid for the whole community. And it is hard to see in what conceivable circumstances it would be unnecessary or impossible for a territorial community to arrive at any decisions of general application.

It need hardly be said that the above does not pretend to be anything in the nature of an adequate treatment of Marxism. For that would necessitate a close examination of a large field of political and social phenomena in the present and the past, in order to see how far the Marxist analysis does or does not apply. There is no dearth of literature at the present time which attempts that. My intention here is simply to indicate briefly why more attention has not been paid in this book to economic factors. These factors, of course, have an important influence on political decisions, and some of the ways in which this influence may work have been indicated from time to time in the preceding pages. But they are never the sole influences and there is no reason to give them a general priority. There are no necessary laws by which political phenomena can be deduced from economic phenomena, and political theory is an independent study, so far as any study concerned with human life can be independent from the rest.

Though it is not essential to the argument it seems desirable to reassert here the conviction that any satisfying explanation of political or social occurrences must be given in psychological terms, or, to put it in more popular language, in terms of what is going on in the minds of individual human beings. That does not mean, as it is sometimes taken to mean, that by examining individuals in the clinic or the laboratory we can reach general conclusions about the ways in which their minds work and then apply these, without more ado, to explain the political or social behaviour of large groups of people. Such an examination might give us valuable hints or suggestions, but it will not take us very far until it is combined with the scrutiny of the actual public behaviour of masses of people in a society. This is an essential part of the material from which any conclusions could be drawn, and without an extensive knowledge of it clinical examination of individuals would be just as likely to mislead as to help in the explanation of political behaviour.

For an explanation, as thus envisaged, it would be necessary to attempt to analyse the main needs or 'drives', which appear, in varying degrees, to be innate in all or most human beings. It would also be necessary to get some idea of the way in which habits are formed, and, when formed, are transmitted from one person or one generation to another. We should also have to consider the kinds of motive which might lead to habits being challenged or broken. Other factors, too, such as the effect of physical conditions, would have to be taken into account. When we had distinguished and set out these possible motives and influences we might be able to give an account of particular political or social developments in terms of them. And that is the nearest thing to an explanation that we could hope to get.

Even so, such explanations would, in general, prove to be possible only *ex post facto*. When something had happened, and to some degree while it was happening, we could make it intelligible by setting out the different influences of this kind which had worked or were working to produce that result. But we could never expect to arrive at necessary laws which would enable us to prophesy beforehand with scientific certainty what is going to happen. And that is not merely due to the *de facto* limitations in our knowledge of the numerous and complicated factors involved, but depends on the very nature of the phenomena with which we are dealing. Speaking in very general terms, scientific forecasts are reliable because, or in so far as, the factors involved are measurable and calculable. Astronomers can foretell eclipses because the position, direction, and velocity of movement of the bodies concerned are known and can be measured, so that it can be calculated accurately when they will reach the relative positions that will produce an eclipse. But political and social movements or developments are not like that. Of course, the variety and complications of the factors involved are so great that it is physically impossible for human beings to know them all. But the difficulty goes further than that. For the factors involved are not, except perhaps in a very limited degree in a few cases, measurable at all, and, what is of greater importance, the different factors are not commensurable with one another. Thus, suppose that in a particular group or society there is a widespread emotional excitement which would, by itself, lead people to act against some deep-rooted and long-established habits and customs. Which influence will prove the stronger? There is no conceivable standard of measurement by which we could compare the relative strengths of the emotion and of the force of habit. If we said that one was stronger than the other, that could not mean anything except that the one did in the event prevail over the other. In other words, the measurement of the strength of the different forces tending to produce a certain result can take place, so far as it can take place at all, only after the result has already occurred. It can provide no basis for anything like a scientific law.

We do, of course, make forecasts, and they sometimes turn out right, particularly the short-range ones. But when they are successful, it is because they are based on a careful empirical study of the circumstances of the particular case, not because they are deductions from a more general law. By an analysis on the lines suggested above, it might be possible to get a general idea of the main influences that will in all probability be at work in determining the actions of human beings. But the only general assertion that we can make about these influences is that they can vary in strength relatively to each other, and which is likely to prove the stronger in any particular case can be decided only by an examination of the particular circumstances, and even that gives us nothing approaching certainty. The chief way in which this general analysis may affect our attempts at forecasting is negatively as a warning. It tells us the main factors that we have to take into account, and it warns us that if we make a forecast or propose a policy which ignores some of these factors altogether it is extremely likely to turn out wrong. And that is a valuable service.

There is one other factor which is quite incalculable. That is the effect that our consciousness of these various influences will have on the way in which they work in us. In so far as we become aware of the motives and tendencies working in us their influence on our behaviour will be modified, to a greater or lesser degree: it will rarely be removed altogether, but it will rarely remain just the same. If we realise that our objection to some suggestion arises entirely from a dislike of changing certain habits that we have formed, our opposition is likely to be weakened to some degree. If we realise the tendency to suggestibility in human beings, it may dawn in us that we have accepted certain views simply because they have been put to us loudly and confidently, and we are then likely to become a little more critical of them. We cannot, of course, get rid of our natural tendencies, and only a rare ascetic would wish to do so. But the more we become conscious of them, the more likely we are to find ourselves considering them in relation to each other as part of a whole life, and judging and evaluating them as such. That is a part of the beginnings of the development of a moral consciousness.

But, it hardly needs saying, the individual is not left to do this all by himself. To a large extent it is done for him by the society or societies to which he belongs. He finds himself in a society which has already developed an accepted code of conduct, which includes some kind of evaluation of these natural tendencies. Thus, in some societies the natural tendency to self-assertion and self-glorification is discouraged, whereas in some it is given full play. In some the man who easily loses his temper is frowned upon whereas in others he seems to be taken for granted. In all, or nearly all, societies there is some kind of accepted regulation and direction of the working of the sexual impulses, though the form this takes will differ widely. And there are more specific approvals and disapprovals of particular kinds of action. In general, the individual begins by taking over these attitudes or points of view from the society in which he finds himself.

This is the truth in the well-worn saying that morality is a social product. But though true, this statement is much less significant than has sometimes been supposed. For one thing, there is no sharp antithesis between a social and an individual product. Society is not an external force standing over against the individuals in it. It is made up of individuals, and there are no 'social products' which are not the work of individuals. Further, the statement that morality is a social product comes very near to being a tautology. Morality is mainly, if not entirely, concerned with the relations between individuals and their behaviour towards each other. And they cannot behave in any way towards each other unless they are living together in some form of society. It is equally obvious that each individual's behaviour towards others will be greatly influenced, if not determined, by their behaviour towards him. If they are to continue to live together, and still more if they are to co-operate for any purpose, there must be some kind of mutual adjustment between them, which involves some degree, however slight, of recognition of each other's rights or claims. Thus, the very fact of living in a society involves some kind of morality, that is to say the development of some system of behaviour capable of overruling the individual's immediate personal desires and passions. And the accepted code or standards of conduct in any society represent the rules or precepts or general indications of the conduct supposed to be most conducive to the development of satisfactory relations within the society.

A great deal of unnecessary trouble has been made over the fact that these accepted moral standards differ so widely from one society to another. The extent of these differences has often been greatly exaggerated, but no one could deny that they exist. But these different moral standards have at least this in common that they are all *moral* standards, that is to say, that they are regarded as having an authority superior to that of one's personal tastes and desires, that they demand some degree of consideration for others besides oneself, and that they are regarded as valid for others besides oneself. However, even if they allow so much, there are those who would say that the actual content of any moral code is entirely the product of the particular society in which it is developed. There can be no real right or wrong about it, and, though we can judge of an individual how far he lives up to the moral code of his own society, we can have no standard by which we can judge that the moral code of one society is better or worse than that of another. The difficulty is, as the ancient Greek thinkers saw, that once this point of view is accepted there seems no reason why an individual should observe the moral code of his own society if he can get any advantage for himself by breaking it.

Of course, these difficulties arise only when we have become fully aware of the nature of moral codes and their differences from one another. We then begin to criticise and ask questions about them. We may then find ourselves criticising the particular code of our own society, not with a view to undermining its authority but with a view to making it better. In fact, that sort of process is going on all the time to some degree, and the accepted moral standards of particular communities are constantly changing in one respect or another: things that once seemed tolerable or even praiseworthy come to be regarded as intolerable, and *vice versa*. The possibility of this seems sufficient proof that we do, in fact, assume that there are real standards of good and bad or right and wrong over and above the standards of any particular society at any particular time. Whether we have any right to assume this is another matter. It is the task of the moral philosopher to deal with such a question, and to consider whether any answer to it is necessary and, if it is, what sort of answer is possible. We can at least say that the mere fact that people can differ in their moral judgements is no proof at all that there is no real right or wrong about them. If it were, a great many other kinds of judgement would have to be dismissed as well. With regard to the special case of the differences between the standards of different communities, we can, if we like, regard these as representing various attempts to establish principles of behaviour which will produce the most satisfactory relations between individuals and the most satisfactory pattern of life for them all. Even if—or perhaps all the more if—we believe that there is a real standard of satisfactoriness here, which we have to discover and cannot make up just as we like, we should find nothing surprising in the fact that some communities had made a much better shot at it than others. But, as already suggested, the existence of these varying codes or standards shows a general recognition, however obscured by other influences, that some sort of standard of morality is necessary. For that reason they all deserve some degree of respect. That is why there is always a good case for the individual's conforming to the code of his particular community, unless he is quite clear after careful thought that he ought to depart from it. What a Catholic writer said about the special case of conscientious objection to military service can be applied more generally, 'If you are in any doubt give your country the benefit of the doubt'.

For the rest, each individual, once he becomes conscious of the problem, has to make up his own mind whether he is going to proceed on the assumption that there is a real right and wrong or better and worse in these matters. He might, for instance, ask himself whether he really believes that the German Nazis' approval of the persecution and massacre of Jews as compared with our disapproval of it is merely a difference of personal taste or local fashion. Most of those who have not given too much thought to the matter would probably have little doubt of the answer. In any case we have to adopt one point of view or the other as a working assumption.

We may note, in passing, that this does not mean that we can take one whole system of moral beliefs and say that that is right and all the rest are wrong. All systems are open to improvement to an indefinite extent, and some will fall short of the ideal in some directions, others in others. We can also make allowance for differences in the conditions of different communities, and recognise that some kinds of behaviour may quite reasonably be valued more highly or condemned more strongly in some conditions than in others. We may also come to realise that some points included in the conventional code of conduct are really morally indifferent. But, when all allowance is made for this, there will always come some point at which we have to make the decision in our own mind that some thing really is better or worse than another.

What, then, is the conclusion from all this about the application of moral considerations to politics? It has already been argued that, just because it is concerned with decisions which apply to a whole community of people, politics is inescapably subject, in the last resort, to moral considerations. But there are great possibilities of confusion in the application of this. Some political differences of opinion clearly rest solely on differences about the facts in the case. And there is no moral obligation to arrive at one conclusion about the facts rather than another, though there is a moral obligation to consider them as fairly and thoroughly as we can. A distinction is often made in this connection between ends and means, and it is said that our ends are a matter of moral decision but that the choice of means to them is simply a matter of practical expediency. In certain connections and within certain limits this may work satisfactorily, but if pressed too far it breaks down. For if we take any particular end which we regard as good, we shall often find that the actions that seem likely to attain it will often have other results or accompaniments as well which we should regard as evil. And we cannot leave those out of account in deciding whether we should take the action or not. Of course, there is such a thing as a choice of evils, and we may be justified in doing something which, taken by itself, would be regarded as undesirable, if it were the only means of avoiding a much greater evil. What does not seem justifiable is to take some particular end or state of things to be produced, and to say that, because it is good, therefore any action that will lead to it is right, regardless of any other results or accompaniments that might go with it.

We can often find some degree of this attitude in the advocates of great causes. By 'cause' in this connection I mean a relatively specific and definable state of things which can be brought about, if not at one particular moment, at least within a definite space of time. And it becomes a cause, in this sense, when it is adopted as the one overriding end by which all particular actions are to be judged. One instance of this kind of thing has already been mentioned, namely the cause of national independence from foreign rule. But there are others which have appealed to different people at different times as ends absolutely good in themselves which justified any means. We can think of causes such as the extirpation of heresy and the establishment of the true religion, the setting of the rightful king on the throne, the destruction of the capitalist system and its replacement by Socialism or even by anarchism, the winning of the suffrage for women, and many other movements of greater or lesser importance. The pursuit of such causes or crusades has often been the occasion for much self-sacrifice, devotion, and heroism. But it has also been at times the occasion of great suffering and of the complete abandonment of other moral restraints or standards. In fact one sometimes feels inclined to assert that the surest way of becoming thoroughly cruel, violent, untruthful, and unscrupulous is through unselfish devotion to a great cause.[1]

There is, of course, much more to be said on all this, and there are doubtless occasions on which we could do with much more of the crusading spirit. But it has to be asserted that if these other things, truthfulness, humanity and the like, are of value in themselves, we can never be justified in treating them as entirely of no account in the attainment of some particular end. And yet, on the other hand, few would deny that the duty, for instance, of truthfulness was not so absolute that there might not be occasions on which it was justifiable to tell a lie. What seems to be needed is a kind of scheme or point of view which will recognise, on the one hand, that some actions at least have a moral quality of their own and cannot be judged entirely by their relation to an end or result beyond themselves. And, on the other, it must recognise that no action can ever be judged entirely in isolation apart from its accompaniments or results or relations to anything outside itself.

Perhaps we could get something of the kind by developing the Greek notion of the 'good life' as the ultimate criterion of political, or, indeed, any other action. That would mean that the one thing good in itself was the attainment of certain states or attitudes of mind on the part of individuals, particularly in their relations to each other, and the possibility of expressing these states of mind in their actions. The passing of particular measures or the setting up of particular institutions would be considered as means to this, possibly important or even essential means, but of no value in themselves. But to a large extent the sharp distinction between ends and means would, from this point of view, cease to apply. At any rate, the 'end', as so conceived, is not a particular state of things to be realised once and for all at a definite period but

---

[1] I have developed this more at length in a lecture on *Principles and Ideals in Politics* published in the latest volume of the Hobhouse Lectures. A few passages from this lecture have been incorporated in this chapter.

something which is being realised, to a greater or lesser degree, all the time. Particular actions may be themselves expressions of these states of mind, and so far they can be considered as parts of the end, not merely as means to it. That does not mean that such actions are necessarily right, but it does mean that they have some value as part of a wider good. But as they are only parts they may, in particular circumstances, have to be given up in order to secure some other part. But there is always a real sacrifice of good in doing that. It is not merely a question of adjusting means, in themselves indifferent, to an end which gives them all the value they have.

There is a further consequence of this which is worth noting. If we think of an end as something attainable at a particular period, the actions taken to bring it about have no present value, but are judged purely by their relation to future results. But if we think of it as something continually attainable the future has no special prerogative over the present, or the remote future over the near future. We cannot, therefore, say that a present evil or sacrifice of good is always and necessarily justifiable if it produces good results at some future period, though no doubt it may be, if the one clearly outweighs the other in quantity and duration. It is a danger for some Utopian idealists that they fix their eyes so intently on a possible future that they tend to ignore the present as of no account at all.

It would be the subject of a further treatise to attempt to work out in detail a positive content for the idea of the 'good life'. We should probably feel inclined to disclaim the capacity for doing what the Greek thinkers attempted to do, that is to say drawing up a systematic and comprehensive sketch of the ideal. We might, as was suggested earlier, prefer to approach it from the other end. That is to say we should start from the consideration of particular political institutions, measures, or proposals, and examine them from the point of view of the kinds of effect they might have on the minds and characters of the individual citizens. Then we could ask ourselves whether we thought of that effect as desirable or not, and so our picture of the good life would gradually develop as we went along. Something of that kind has been attempted in the preceding pages, but, of course, the main task remains to be done.

It does, however, seem that one element in the 'good life' emerges as implied in the very conception of it. That is the attitude of mutual consideration and recognition of the needs and claims of other people besides ourselves. In Kant's famous phrase, every human being is to be thought of as an end and never merely as a means. Attempts have been made to depreciate the value of this principle on the ground that we cannot deduce from it any specific instructions as to how we are to act in particular cases. But such criticism really misses the point. The principle should be taken as the inculcation of a certain attitude from which we should approach the consideration of particular problems. As such, if it does not provide ready-made answers, it certainly makes a great difference to the answers that we discover for ourselves. Most of us, if we examine our consciences, would probably recognise occasions on which we had thought of other human beings merely as means to our own satisfaction. And it would certainly make a great difference to our behaviour if we consistently adopted Kant's maxim, even if it did not tell us exactly what we ought to do in every case. And if we look, not at particular actions but at more general institutions, it would seem very difficult to reconcile some of them, such as slavery, with this maxim.

This, then, must suffice as an indication of what can be meant by speaking of the moral basis of politics. But that is not to say that morality and politics are identical. A good deal of what we include in the 'good life' is not a matter of public or collective decision at all and there is plenty of room for differences of opinion as to the extent of this. From the other side a great many political decisions are not directly concerned with moral issues. But there is always the possibility that they may, even at a long remove, have some effect one way or the other on the attainment of the 'good life'. The working politician cannot be expected to be thinking about that all the time. For the most part he takes for granted the current ideas of his community about the moral limits within which he works. But these ideas are always liable to change and modification. And among the possible influences making for such development are the discussions that are going on all the time on political problems.

DEMOCRACY, ANCIENT AND MODERN

[Reprinted from the *Cambridge Journal* for November 1949]

IN the discussions that have been going on in recent years about the proper meaning of the term 'democracy', appeal has been made from time to time to the use of the corresponding term in ancient Greece. It seems, indeed, only reasonable that the Greeks, as the original inventors of the word, should be consulted about the proper use of it. On the other hand, there is no reason why we should always use a term taken from the Greek in its precise original sense. In general, however, it seems desirable on all grounds that there should be continuity, if not uniformity, in the use of the term, and that sudden reversals of its meaning should be avoided as far as possible.

It does not, of course, admit of doubt that the word 'democracy' comes into the English language from the Greek authors. We find it first in the sixteenth century when knowledge of these authors and of the facts of Greek history was growing. The first recorded use of it, in Elyot's *The Governour*, refers to it as the constitution in force among the Athenians, and the picture that the word conveyed to the English reader would, broadly speaking, be determined by what he knew of Greek writers and Greek history. In an age of monarchies and aristocratically ordered societies it was not usually regarded as a very desirable form of government. Indeed, it had little application to most societies of the time, except a few of the smaller Swiss cantons, and the word itself in the early stages seems to be of rare occurrence and mainly of

historical reference. In the seventeenth century when democratic ideas began to develop in this country, the word, too,
seemed to become more familiar and to be regarded as applicable to existing conditions.   Thus Baxter describes the
speakers in the Puritan army as calling 'sometimes for
church-democracy and sometimes for state-democracy'. The
reference to 'church-democracy' is of special interest, because
the congregational government of a church was something
much more like the government of a Greek city by the popular
assembly than anything that was practically possible in a
seventeenth-century state. This illustrates, incidentally, how
much the whole democratic idea in this country has been
influenced in its development by the religious interest and the
application to church government. At any rate, from this
period onwards the development of the use of the term has
been continuous up to the present time. And if we think it
desirable to preserve this continuity, there seems a certain
interest in recalling the original Greek usage for purpose of
comparison with the present day. This is all the more necessary because of recent years there have been some highly
debatable statements made about the meaning of democracy
in ancient Greece, from which some very misleading inferences
have been drawn about its contemporary application.

Let us consider first the view that the Greek use of democracy has no application to present circumstances, because to
the Greek it implied slavery and was, indeed, based on that,
and was therefore entirely unlike anything to which the term
would be applied now. Thus, Professor E. H. Carr in the
Cust Lecture, delivered in 1945, said, 'Not much will be
gained by carrying back the inquiry to the ancient world
where the term was first invented: for the Greek democracies
were openly based on the rule of a privileged class and would
hardly qualify under any modern definition of the term,
Western or Russian.' There was an amusing illustration, at
about the same time, of the way in which this idea has filtered
down to a more popular level. A Conservative statesman had

referred, in a speech, to ancient Greek democracy as the inspiration of modern democratic movements. This was quoted by a well-known left-wing columnist, who then pointed out that ancient Greek democracy was based on slavery and drew the conclusion, half-humorously no doubt, that the Tories must be wanting to reintroduce slavery.

This is a fallacy which has often been refuted and as often reappears. It is, of course, true that most Greek city-states, whatever their form of government, were economically dependent on slave labour, in the sense that, things being as they were, there would not have been enough man-power to carry on the essential work of production without the slaves. That, however, is not what is meant here. What is implied in remarks such as those quoted is that Greek democracy, in particular, was only possible because the citizens had slaves to do the work of production for them, thus leaving them free to attend to politics. And this is entirely untrue. In general, in democracies such as Athens, the majority of the citizens worked with their hands and a great many of them did not own slaves at all. Nor, with one or two exceptions, which do not affect the general picture, was there, in democratic cities, any special kind of work reserved either for slaves or for free men. Slaves could be found in the skilled professions, and citizens among the unskilled manual labourers. But all citizens in a democracy whatever their wealth, profession, or social position, had exactly the same political rights and privileges.

That is, perhaps, sufficient answer to this particular objection. But it is worth while spending a few moments in trying to see why a Greek would not have admitted that the existence of slavery was relevant to the question at issue between democracy and other forms of government. This question concerned the organization and government of a particular society, the πόλις or city. Now, we assume that the political society must normally include all those living in the same territory. But that was not at all the view held in Greece or

the ancient world in general. To them membership of the
citizen body was a matter of being born into it, or occasionally
being admitted by a special act of those already in it. The
fact of living, voluntarily or involuntarily, in the same territory was quite irrelevant. The question, therefore, of the
proper government of a particular society was quite distinct
from the question of its relations to those outside it. We
might recognise the same thing, if 'those outside it' meant
those living in a different territory. We might quite naturally
speak of a particular state as being itself democratically
governed even though it exercised despotic rule over territories outside. In some periods in the history of the Swiss
Confederation, for instance, some of the smaller cantons could
hardly be called anything but democracies, yet that did not
prevent them from taking their share in the rule of conquered
territories, whose inhabitants had no political rights at all.

We should perhaps find it easier to put ourselves at the
Greek point of view if we thought in terms, not of a territorial
state, but of one of the smaller societies within it, a club, for
instance, or a university. The question of the best form of
government for such a society might raise very real issues, and
we could perfectly reasonably advocate one form of government as being more democratic than another. But the distinction between the two would not be made any the less real
and important by the fact that, under either form of government, the society had employees, porters and charwomen for
instance, who were not members of it and had no share in its
government. All this should make it clear that the existence
of slavery in ancient Greece, important though it is for our
general estimate of its civilisation, does not destroy the relevance of Greek democratic ideas and experience to our own
time.

This being understood, what did democracy, as a form of
government, mean to a Greek? There is really no doubt about
that at all; and, if it were not for the confusion that has been
introduced into the matter by contemporary controversies, i

would hardly be worth while setting down the familiar facts once more. In the first place, the ordinary Greek normally thought and spoke of democracy as one of the three main forms of government which he recognized, the other two being monarchy and oligarchy or aristocracy. This was the normally accepted classification. Some serious thinkers criticised it as inadequate and tried to introduce various subdivisions or intermediate forms. But none of these suggestions became generally accepted, nor were they consistent among themselves. Plato, for instance, gives two quite different alternative classifications in the *Republic* and the *Politicus* respectively. In the latter he retains the threefold classification, but sub-divides each into a better or worse form, according to the degree to which they respect the law and act according to established rules. But, we may note, the law-abiding and the lawless democracy are both called democracies. Aristotle puts forward various suggestions, not always perfectly consistent with each other. But in one passage, to which we shall have to return later, he suggests the use of the term 'democracy' for what he regards as a perverted form of government in which the poor rule the state in their own exclusive interest. Polybius, on the other hand, who favours a classification rather like that in the *Politicus*, wants to keep the term 'democracy' for the good form of popular government and coins the word 'ochlocracy', government by the mob, for the perversion.

But for the ordinary Greek, throughout the whole period, the simple threefold division, monarchy, oligarchy, democracy sufficed. We find it taken for granted by Herodotus in his fictitious story of the debate between the Persian leaders after the downfall of the pseudo-Smerdis. And three hundred years later Polybius, in the passage just quoted, speaks of it as the ordinarily accepted classification, though he himself is not satisfied with it. All this shows how misleading it is to generalise about the meaning of the term to 'the Greeks' from the discussions of one or two thinkers. Mr Harold

Nicolson, for instance, in an essay in the *Spectator* a few years ago,[1] made the startling statement that 'to them [i.e. the Greeks] . . . it [democracy] was a term of abuse'. This is a generalisation from Aristotle which, as applied to 'the Greeks', is extremely wide of the mark. To the Greeks as a whole, democracy, like Socialism or Conservatism nowadays, was a term of abuse for those who disapproved of it, and a term of praise for the very large number who believed in it.

Apart from approval or disapproval, what the term 'democracy' would have conveyed to the ordinary Greek is quite clear. It would have conveyed to him, in the first place, a state in which supreme control was exercised by a general assembly of all the citizens. The general assembly, by the way, was not peculiar to the democracies but was found, in one form or another, in many non-democratic states, though in these its authority and function tended to be limited. What was peculiar to democracy was that the assembly was open to every citizen without distinction of wealth or birth or profession, and one man's vote counted just the same as another's.

Secondly, every citizen had an equal right to express an opinion or to make a proposal. Freedom of speech was generally regarded as one of the fundamental features of democracy. It was so regarded, for instance, by Plato, who thought that it was carried to lengths which were altogether unwholesome. It is true that, according to Isocrates, an unpopular speaker in moments of excitement sometimes ran a certain risk of being shouted down. But that was certainly not the usual thing. We have accounts of several occasions when decisions of importance were being discussed in the Athenian Assembly, and there is invariably reference to speeches on different sides. In fact one can say broadly that the Athenian democracy can very rarely, if ever, have taken an important decision without hearing arguments from all points of view.

In view of that, I find it very difficult to understand a state-

[1] *Spectator*, 31 August 1945, reprinted in *Comments*, 1944–8.

ment by Lord Lindsay in an article in the *Manchester Guardian* of 26 April 1946. He there says, 'Neither of the two parties which strove for power in Greek states had the smallest intention of tolerating the other. A recognised opposition was foreign to Greek democracy.' It is quite true, of course, that a Greek democracy would not have tolerated an attempt to overthrow the democratic constitution by force. In the less well-established democracies such attempts were all too frequent, and revolution and civil war were endemic in many Greek states. That was not so everywhere, however, and in any case is hardly in question here. Even the well-established democracies would probably not have tolerated a proposal to abolish democracy by legal procedure, though they seem to have been tolerant of a good deal of criticism of it in writing. There is, for instance, no hint that Plato ever got into trouble for writing the *Republic*. Within the limits of the democratic constitution, however, there was complete freedom of opposition and criticism on any particular question. It is true that, in a sense, there was no 'recognised Opposition'. But then there was no recognised Government, either. There was, however, often an observable tendency for those of like opinions to develop habits of working together politically, and modern historians often speak, without serious inaccuracy, of different parties in Athens. These were sometimes based on economic divisions, and Aristotle gives a list of the recognised leaders of the upper classes and the common people, respectively, over a considerable period of history. And in the age of Demosthenes there was clearly a relatively permanent division between the pro-Macedonian and the anti-Macedonian parties. We must, however, beware of thinking of these as in any sense permanent organisations, with a body of officials, like the parties we know. They were more akin to the rudimentary parties of the seventeenth and eighteenth centuries.

The third mark of democracy for the ordinary Greek would have been that all public offices were open equally to every citizen, irrespective of wealth, who was not disqualified by criminal conduct. This was made not merely a legal right but a practical possibility by other measures which were in fact characteristic of all democracies, whether or no we include them in the definition. In the first place, the offices were paid so that no one could be debarred by poverty from filling them. And secondly the great majority of offices, which in general took the form of boards or committees rather than of single posts, were filled by lot. This seems to us a curious method, but they dealt largely with routine matters, and the idea seems to have been that each board should represent, as it were, a fair sample of the whole citizen body. There were limitations on the possibility of being selected more than once, so that office must have come in turn to almost every citizen. There were, however, certain exceptions, for a few of the more important and responsible officers were elected by the whole body of citizens. And here the limitations on re-election did not necessarily apply, and there were well-known cases of the same man being elected to the same office year after year.

Even the most important officers, however, were not supposed to have any special responsibility for the framing of policy. That was a matter for the whole assembly, and in theory every citizen had an equal right to contribute to it. In practice, the chief influence was exercised by the leading orators, who might or might not themselves hold office at any particular time. Even in the carrying out of the policy the tendency of democracies was, on the whole, with occasional exceptions from time to time, to restrict the discretion of the officials and scrutinise their conduct very jealously. This was made easier by the rule, almost universal in the ancient world in all kinds of government, that appointment to any office was made annually. And in Athens, and probably in other democracies, there was a public examination at the end of the year of office of the conduct of every official.

In comparing ancient democracies with modern forms of government, it is of interest to remind ourselves what the responsibilities and activities were with which the popular organs of government most concerned themselves. Nowadays we should naturally think, before anything else, of legislation as being the primary function of the sovereign body. But, in fact, in Greek states legislation was not, as it is with us, a regular and continuous activity. The laws were regarded much more as a permanent framework, not to be lightly altered or added to. When genuine legislation did take place, it generally went through a complicated procedure which, while reserving the final decision to the popular assembly, entrusted the greater part of the work to a committee or sometimes to a single legislator. On the other hand, the Assembly was continually passing decrees dealing with particular cases. In extreme cases the line between a law and a decree might seem rather thin, but in general the distinction is clear, and more than one writer picks out the tendency to act by decrees instead of by fixed laws as a sign of degeneration in a democracy. But on the whole the Assembly seems to have been much more occupied with what we should think of as strictly executive discussions. The debates about which we have the fullest accounts are generally those on foreign relations, the making of treaties or alliances, and the declaration of war. And during a state of war, which for most Greek cities means for the greater part of their history, the Assembly would continually be taking decisions about the conduct of the war, the expeditions to be sent out, and the operations to be undertaken.

But besides all this there is an important function which, to our way of thinking, would be the most inappropriate for a popular body, and that is the judicial function. Yet it was characteristic of Greek democracies that the administrations of justice should more and more come to be considered an essential prerogative of the sovereign people. Some cases might actually be tried before the whole Assembly. More often, however, they came before a number of large popular juries of several hundred members each, empanelled by lot. It is clear that each of these was regarded as, in a sense, a microcosm of the whole people, and the whole lot together as the people acting in their judicial capacity. It must be remembered that these were completely lay bodies, and there were no professional lawyers and no professional judges to guide them. Plato is perhaps the only Greek writer to have developed the modern conception of the judge as a skilled professional with specialised knowledge of the law.[1]

For the purposes of comparison with modern times, it is of particular interest to consider the kinds of argument which were used for or against a democracy in Greece. Of the latter we can find systematic statements in Plato and in the late fifth-century pamphlet, commonly known as the Old Oligarch, which is preserved among the works of Xenophon. The arguments are largely directed against the special feature of ancient democracy, namely government by a mass meeting, with its emotional instability, its susceptibility to tricks of oratory, its lack of continuity of policy and its weakening of the sense of responsibility of the individual citizen. But there is a more fundamental criticism by Plato, who held that government was a most difficult and important function, which demanded a high degree of specialised ability and training, and should therefore be entrusted to the select few who possessed the special qualities necessary for it and could devote their whole time and their whole interest to it.

We have no such systematic statement of the case for democracy. But from remarks in the historians and other writers we can gather something of the sort of arguments that might be put forward. The earliest extant statement of the case that we have is to be found in the imaginary debate described by Herodotus in the passage already referred to. The emphasis here is laid on the security that democracy gives against the insolence of office, and oppression and misgovernment by those in authority. We also have an incidental remark by Herodotus himself about the greatly increased energy, enterprise, and self-confidence that the people of Athens showed once they had become free to govern them-

[1] *Politicus*, 305 b, c.

selves. In a debate at Syracuse, recorded or invented by Thucydides, the democratic spokesman claims superiority for democracy because, in the first place, it includes all the citizens, not merely a section. And he argues, further, that the judgements of a democracy are more likely to be sound just because they represent the collective wisdom of all the citizens to which everyone can contribute something. Aristotle also mentions this argument and admits that there is something in it. Plato, of course, would not have admitted its validity. But even he, in the second-best constitution described in the *Laws*, allows a certain element of democracy, his main reason being that the people will give much more willing obedience to the decisions of the government if they are given some share in it.

There are thus various practical advantages claimed for democracy. But the fundamental demand comes from the feeling that the city exists for the sake of all its citizens and that they therefore all have a claim to a share in the good things that it can give them. Participation in the work of government is one of these good things. It brings certain specific material advantages and prevents certain evils. But behind all this is the idea, which is hinted at in the famous Funeral Speech of Pericles, and emerges more or less clearly from the discussion in Aristotle, that a share in public life and activity is itself a good thing, part of the 'good life' for every man. A man is a better man for taking some part in government, and to make the citizens better men is the true aim of any measure and any institution. This was doubtless an ideal which was realized in practice very imperfectly or not at all. But as an ideal it is still capable of making its appeal.

In the light of all this, what bearing has the Greek use of the term on modern controversies about the meaning of democracy? What, for instance, would a Greek say about the rival claimants to the title among the states of the present day? Let us consider first the Parliamentary democracies of Western Europe. I think there can be little doubt that if an ordinary Greek, particularly a convinced democrat, were con-

fronted with these states his first reaction would be to deny
them the title of democracies at all. That would not be in
the least for the sort of reason that would be given by the
partisans of the so-called 'Eastern democracies' for a similar
denial. It would be simply and solely because the ordinary
citizens were not taking a continuous and active part in the
work of government. To call a state a democracy in which the
supreme power was in the hands of a small body, elected every
five years or so, and in which laws could be passed, judicial
decisions made, executive actions taken and even war or peace
declared without the people being directly consulted at all,
would seem to our Greek at first sight the wildest of paradoxes. His first inclination would probably be to deny that
democracy was to be found in the modern world at all.

On second thoughts, however, particularly if he was
acquainted with the more serious Greek writers, he might
begin to modify his opinion. He would recognise that democracy, as he knew it, was not possible at all in a state above a
certain size. And from that he might go on to ask himself
which of the forms of government that were possible in a large
country state inclined more in the direction of democracy and
which less. He would be encouraged in this by remembering
that, even in Greece, thinkers in the fourth century and later
were beginning to feel that the popular classification of states
into democracies and the rest was inadequate. Not only did
they try to introduce various intermediate grades, but they
also came to emphasise more and more the possibility of mix-
tures of these pure forms of government. At times, in fact,
they approached the idea of democracy, not so much as a class
into which any given state must either go completely or not
go at all, but rather as an element or ingredient which could
be found in a greater or lesser degree in a wide variety of
constitutions.

Looked at from that point of view, our Greek would probably concede that in a modern Parliamentary government
there was an element, possibly greater than he realised at

first, of democracy as he understood it, and that among modern constitutions there was no other direction in which he could look for it. The fact that at some point vital decisions were taken and, as a consequence, other decisions influenced, by the whole body of citizens, that everyone, rich or poor, had a vote and with trifling exceptions everyone's vote counted the same, that our leaders and ministers and members of Parliament could be turned out of office by a popular vote whenever an election came, that there were no legal restrictions on the right of any man to hold office or to sit in Parliament if elected thereto, that the practical obstacles were largely removed by measures such as payment of members, and above all that there was a great amount of freedom of discussion and criticism and expression of opinion—all these things would seem to him undeniable marks of democracy as far as they went, and he would regard them as going some way towards producing the results that the Greek democrat looked to democracy to produce. He would certainly not think that they went as far as he would like. He might suggest, for instance, that more countries should follow the example of Switzerland and introduce the Referendum and Initiative. He would look askance at our independent judiciary and our professional Civil Service, and would view with considerable suspicion our organised political parties. But, with all qualifications, he would probably admit a recognisable kinship between the democratic idea in his time and ours, and might agree that, on the whole, the best of us had advanced as far along the road to democracy as our unfortunate preference for large states made possible.

We may next ask what our Greek would say about the Soviet Union and the other countries whose forms of government approximate to that. There can really be no reasonable doubt about this. The governments of Eastern Europe possess none of the features, as set out above, which the Greek would regard as characteristic of democracy, and no Greek would have dreamed of applying the title to them. Indeed, he would find from his own experience a category into which they would readily fit. For Greek history provides many instances of what we should call 'left-wing dictatorships', from Pisistratus to Nabis. Indeed, this was one of the commonest ways in which the Greek 'tyrannies' or dictatorships arose, and some of them no doubt did, for a time at any rate, improve the position of the poorer classes. But the Greeks never fell into the confusion between government in the interests of the people and government by the people, and, as far as we know, they never even thought of applying the term 'democracy' to these popular dictatorships. They invariably spoke of them as what, by the Greek definition, they were, namely 'tyrannies'.

All this is really quite obvious. But an unfortunate confusion has been introduced by some recent writers, on the strength of some statements by Aristotle. Thus Professor Carr, in the lecture previously quoted, says, 'Aristotle defines democracy as "the Government where the supreme power in the polity is vested in those who possess no considerable property, i.e. the poor", and goes on to inquire if it is unjust if "the poor, being in a majority, distribute among themselves the property of the rich". . . . All this stands quite as close to the Russian as to the Western view of democracy.' And Mr Harold Nicolson, referring to the same passage in Aristotle, writes, 'If we use the word "Democracy" in its strictly Aristotelian sense as government by the proletariate in the interests of the proletariate to the exclusion of all other interests, then it applies more correctly to the Eastern or undiluted system of democracy than to the Western or diluted system'. Remarks such as these reveal such a serious misunderstanding that it seems desirable to give, in conclusion, a brief consideration to the significance of what Aristotle actually does say.

It is quite true that, in one or two passages, Aristotle speaks of democracy as the perverted form of constitution in which the poor, being a majority, have the power and exercise it exclusively in their own interests. But, even taking this description at its face value, it obviously refers to something entirely different from the Soviet or East European type of government. In the first place, in the sort of democracy of which Aristotle is speaking the poor majority really did rule, through the general Assembly with all its apparatus of public discussion and free voting. In a state such as Russia, on the other hand, whether or no we concede its claim to be ruled in the interests of the poor majority, no one could possibly contend that it was actually ruled *by* the poor majority. None of the procedure which any Greek, Aristotle included, would have regarded as an essential feature of democracy is present.

Secondly, the whole basis of the Eastern European governments is the claim that they are establishing a new order of society, in which the old distinction between rich and poor will cease to have any meaning. In particular, they are abolishing private ownership of the means of production and distribution, and establishing a state-controlled economy. There is no trace of any such programme among even the most extreme Greek democracies. In general, they took for granted private ownership of land and of such elementary forms of capital as there were, and did not prevent the owners from using these to enrich themselves. In the more extreme cases, they might from time to time attempt a forcible correction of disparities of wealth by measures such as the redistribution of land, among other private owners, and the cancellation of debts. But this could only be an occasional measure. For the rest, the tendency was to regard the rich as convenient sources from which money could be extracted for the benefit of the poor majority, by paying them for public services, relieving distress, subsidising food supplies and the like. In fact, it was a crude and clumsy form of the modern idea of the 'welfare-state', which is characteristic of most of the Western democracies, and which the so-called 'Eastern democracies' despise.

This tendency was undoubtedly present to some extent in all Greek democracies, but it was not that which made them democracies. It varied greatly in degree. In Athens, for instance, at many periods, the rich, though always subjected to heavy burdens, accepted them, at least as long as they were imposed by due process of law and not by spasmodic and arbitrary confiscation and spoliation, and as individuals took their full share in the democratic activities of the state, in which they often enjoyed considerable prestige and influence. Yet no one would ever have thought of Athens as anything but a democracy. In fact, she was generally regarded as the very pattern and type of all democracies.

Finally, it is necessary to insist that this selection of one or two passages gives an entirely one-sided and misleading picture of Aristotle's own contribution to the subject. The *Politics*, as is now generally recognised, is a patchwork compilation from different periods of Aristotle's activity as a teacher, and, as such, it is not always consistent with itself. There are these passages in which he suggests confining the term 'democracy' to the extreme and perverted form in which the poor majority rule exclusively in their own interests, and —a point on which he lays greater stress—carry out this policy in an arbitrary manner in particular cases, at the whim of a momentary majority, instead of by regular legal procedure. But these passages are very few. Much more often, he takes the general definition of democracy as consisting in the grant of political rights simply on the ground of free citizenship, with no special privileges for wealth. Within this general definition, he commonly recognises a number of different forms of democracy, some better and some worse, to all of which the term can properly be applied.

Consider this passage, for instance. In the city of Mantinea there appears to have been some kind of system of indirect election to office, about the details of which we know very little, but which certainly removed it some way from the extreme, or even the average, Greek democracy. Yet this is what Aristotle says of it. 'In some democracies, although they do not all share in the appointment of offices, except through representatives elected in turn out of the whole people, as at Mantinea, yet, if they have the power of deliberating, the many are contented. Even this form of government may be called democracy.' A number of other passages could be quoted to show that Aristotle habitually used the word 'democracy' in a much wider sense than the earlier quotations would suggest, and, we may add, in a sense much more consonant with its use in all other Greek writers and in ordinary speech and thought. But perhaps it will suffice to conclude with one more quotation from the *Politics*. 'Democracy and demos in their truest form are based upon the recognised principle of democratic justice, that all should count equally; for equality implies that the poor should have no more share in the government than the rich, but that all should rule equally according to their numbers. And in this way men think that they will secure equality and freedom in their state.'[1]

The conclusion of all this is obvious. The governments of Eastern Europe have no point of contact whatever with democracy as understood by the Greeks. A Greek, particularly if he were a critic of democracy, would only wonder why on earth they should want to saddle themselves with the name. The Parliamentary governments of Western Europe are certainly very unlike the Greek democracies, and a Greek democrat would hardly concede them the right to the name without very considerable qualifications. But he would be able to recognise certain elements which were common to both and to detect certain of the Greek democratic ideas working in these countries at the present time. This is not, perhaps, a very novel or exciting conclusion. But it is sometimes worth while spending a little time and trouble to discover that what we had always thought to be the case really was so, after all.

[1] *Politics*, 1318 a. The previous passage is in 1318 b. I have used the translation in the Oxford Aristotle.

INDEX

Proper names are given in italics

University Paperbacks

A COMPLETE LIST OF TITLES

Titles marked thus: * are to be published during 1965

ARCHAEOLOGY AND ANTHROPOLOGY

ART AND ARCHITECTURE

BIOGRAPHY

ECONOMICS

SCIENCE